AF599140

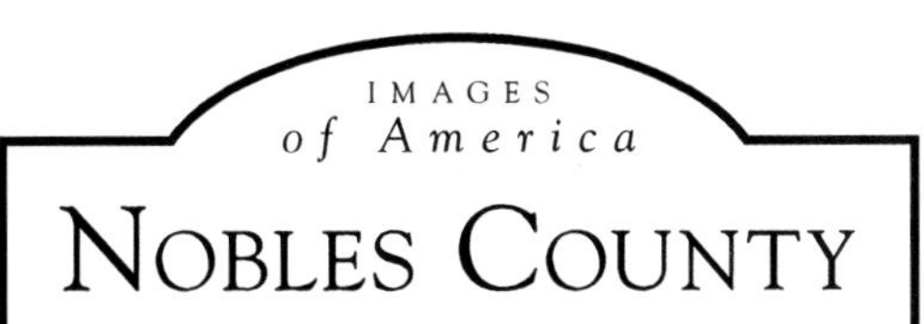
IMAGES
of America
NOBLES COUNTY

On the Cover: Not much can be said about the cover photograph because not much is known about it. It is believed to have been taken around 1900 by Worthington photographer E.F. Buchan. As an image, it is particularly appropriate for this book's cover, as it captures the central importance of agriculture to the growth and development of Nobles County. But as a photograph itself, this picture has its own unique history worth recording. Every year, Worthington holds a spring trash pickup where residents can place unwanted items on the boulevard, and they will be disposed of by city crews. A few years ago, a local woman stumbled across a curbside box that included several glass-plate photographic negatives she decided to rescue, even though she was not sure what she had found. Ultimately, the glass negatives were shared with Dr. Darlene Anderson, a retired physician, who used her computer equipment and personal expertise to digitally retrieve the images from these negatives that had essentially been lost for over 100 years. In addition to the cover picture, several other images in this book were shared by the owner of the glass-plate negatives, the Historic Dayton House. (Historic Dayton House.)

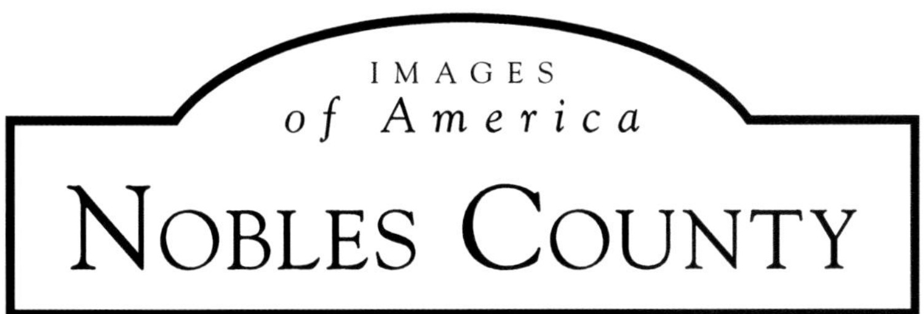

Nobles County Historical Society

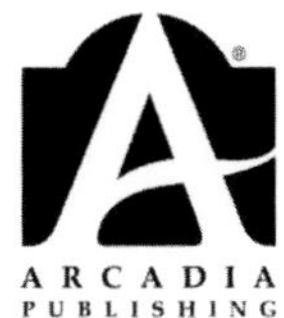

ISBN 978-1-4671-2488-1

Published by Arcadia Publishing
Charleston, South Carolina

Printed in the United States of America

Library of Congress Control Number: 2016949164

For all general information, please contact Arcadia Publishing:
Telephone 843-853-2070
Fax 843-853-0044
E-mail sales@arcadiapublishing.com
For customer service and orders:
Toll-Free 1-888-313-2665

Visit us on the Internet at www.arcadiapublishing.com

To Ray Crippen, who taught us the value and importance of recording local history.

Contents

ACKNOWLEDGMENTS

Writing a book and getting it published is not an inexpensive task, which is even more challenging for an organization like ours trying to manage on a tight budget. In the past, our limited resources dissuaded us from even considering such a project. This year, however, was different. The Nobles County Historical Society's publications fund was created through the generosity of the following local organizations—Worthington Windsurfing Regatta, the *Worthington Daily Globe*, and the Worthington Area United Way. Their cash donations helped to make this book idea a reality, and for this we are extremely grateful.

As a pictorial history, the success of this book will depend in large part on how well our selected photographs convey the essence of our county's story. Knowing this, we were determined to offer readers a visual perspective of the entire county, even the smallest villages. Likewise, we wanted to portray all aspects of community life as outlined in our chapters. Though most of the images presented in this book are taken from the society's collections, we felt there were some noticeable gaps. To fill these voids, we reached out to other residents who had some of the pictures we desired in their personal collections. They were gracious enough to loan them to us so we could include them in this book. We have identified these individuals by name and will credit them for the photographs they provided by putting their initials in parentheses after the captions: Audrey Brake (AB), Pat Demuth (PD), Jean Doeden (JD), LaVerna Feltman (LFe), Jerry Fiola (JF) LaVina Fiola (LFi), Bud and Sharon Fritz (BSF), Lois Graf (LG), Tim Graf (TG), Don Gregerson (DG), Historic Dayton House (HDH), Donna Lundgren (DL), Hans Peters (HP), and Bob Shore (BS).

Even though a picture is worth a thousand words, oftentimes background narrative of images can make them even more meaningful. To provide this context, we frequently researched the different communities' centennial books to more fully interpret these historical photographs. The townspeople who put these books together spent countless hours tracking down the photographs and personal stories that made these local histories come alive. We cannot thank them enough for the contributions their published histories made to this project and to the overall mission of the Nobles County Historical Society to collect, preserve, and interpret the history of Nobles County. We truly are kindred spirits.

—Nobles County Historical Society
Publications Committee

Introduction

In 1857, the territorial legislature created nine counties in Minnesota's southwestern corner, including Nobles. In the two years leading up to this time, the country had experienced a boom period that had generated considerable excitement about the potential for growth in previously unsettled territory. Unfortunately, people's enthusiasm was soon extinguished by three events that all took place within a five-year period. The cumulative effect of these developments would serve to discourage any serious attempts to settle Nobles County until the early 1870s.

The first barrier encountered was the Panic of 1857, which was caused by a collapse in the international economy and overexpansion in the United States. Due to resultant investor fears, grain prices declined, farmers defaulted, commercial credit dried up, and some railroad companies shut down or laid off many of their workers. Needless to say, these were not ideal conditions for building new communities.

Just as the economy was beginning to recover from this financial downturn, the country was thrust into the Civil War in April 1861. All discretionary resources were committed to support the war effort for the next four years.

On a more local level, on August 17, 1862, there was an uprising among the area's Sioux Indians, led by Chief Little Crow. Before the conflict was over some four months later, several hundred settlers had lost their lives. The risk of another such outburst subsequently deterred people from relocating to this section of the state.

By the 1870s, people's confidence had finally been restored, and they were now feeling secure enough to make a new life for themselves on the frontier prairies of Nobles County. Though a few isolated families had settled in the Graham Lakes and Indian Lake areas in the late 1860s, it took the convergence of three separate events to create the conditions that would lead to the county's first town being established in 1871.

The first factor contributing to Worthington's birth actually took place a few years earlier. Shortly after the Civil War, the federal government revised the Homestead Act to allow former Union soldiers to fulfill their residency requirements by substituting their years of military service. The allure of free land, up to 160 acres per claim, prompted many veterans to relocate to the prairies of Nobles County.

More specific to the timing of Worthington's founding was the decision by the Sioux City & St. Paul Railroad to locate a station in the vicinity for the trains it intended to bring to this section of the state. Ultimately, similar actions by different railroad companies led to the origins of almost all the towns in Nobles County—13 out of 15 to be precise. You've probably heard the term "railroad town;" Nobles County was a railroad county.

The third major element in Worthington's establishment was the influx of hundreds of settlers from Ohio, New York, Pennsylvania, and other states. They had been brought to the area under the guidance of the National Colony Company. Their leaders were seeking to create a townsite where people could succeed while abiding by their code of strict moral standards, particularly abstinence from alcohol.

In the case of Adrian and some of the other communities established in the county's western half, like Ellsworth and Lismore, another organization, the Catholic Colony Company, was instrumental in bringing hundreds of German and Irish Catholics to previously unsettled townships. These settlers came not only from other parts of Minnesota but also from Wisconsin and Michigan. According to county historian A.P. Rose, in his 1908 *An Illustrated History of Nobles County, Minnesota*, this development "was to the west end what the temperance National Colony had been to the east end five or six years earlier."

While Adrian was being formed in 1876, back on the county's east side, the towns of Brewster and Bigelow already had a four-year head start. Their origins were primarily related to the railroad's decision to place rail stops seven miles east and seven miles south of Worthington.

After these four towns were established, the next expansion did not take place until another train station was placed seven miles west of Worthington—Miller Station. As the townsite grew up around it, it was renamed Rushmore.

The next hub of rail activity was in the county's northeast corner, where two different railroad companies were in competition for the same market. The Sioux City & St. Paul Railroad was building its Heron Lake and Black Hills line, and Dundee was to be the eastern terminus. Meanwhile, just two miles away, the Southern Minnesota Railroad, looking to extend its rail lines, situated a train station in Kinbrae. In A.P. Rose's opinion, "the jealous rivalry of two railroad corporations was responsible for the founding of two towns so close together, and the towns have been the sufferers ever since."

Three years later, yet another railroad company, the Burlington, entered the Nobles County scene. It had been planning to extend its rail system from the south into Worthington, and it needed a train station in the Round Lake area. The townsite's first two buildings, constructed in 1882, were the depot and a section house to provide lodging for workers.

The Burlington Railroad was also expanding on the county's western side. In 1884, it laid track from Rock Rapids, Iowa, to the Ellsworth site, naming the town in honor of a stockholder, Eugene Ellsworth.

In 1886, the Worthington & Sioux Falls Railroad erected a depot approximately four miles southwest of Worthington. Initially known as Sioux Falls Junction, the village was later renamed Org.

The next two towns to be organized in the county share two unique distinctions: they were the only communities to be built around a church and the only two not to be located on a rail line. St. Kilian originated in 1887 with the construction of the St. Kilian Catholic Church, while Leota came into being when the first Bethel Reformed Church was erected in 1891.

For almost a decade, there were no additional townsites platted. However, the Burlington Railroad broke the silence when it decided to extend its line from Worthington to Reading (1899), approximately seven miles away, and then another seven miles to Wilmont (1899). The impact of the railroads on the communities' development cannot be overstated. A.P. Rose wrote, "The railroad was completed to the site [of Wilmont on] December 16, 1899, and, although it was in the middle of the winter, the building of the town commenced at once, and there was a rush of people to the site."

The county's last frontier to be settled was Lismore when the town was organized in 1900. The Burlington had originally intended to lay tracks straight west to connect with Hardwick, but challenges with the land's topography caused it to reroute the line south to the Lismore site.

With the passing of these 29 years, all of the county's 15 towns and villages had been established. The rest of their ensuing history, the details and the moments, are illustrated in the pictorial essay that follows. The selected images document life in Nobles County from 1870 to 1940.

One

Main Street

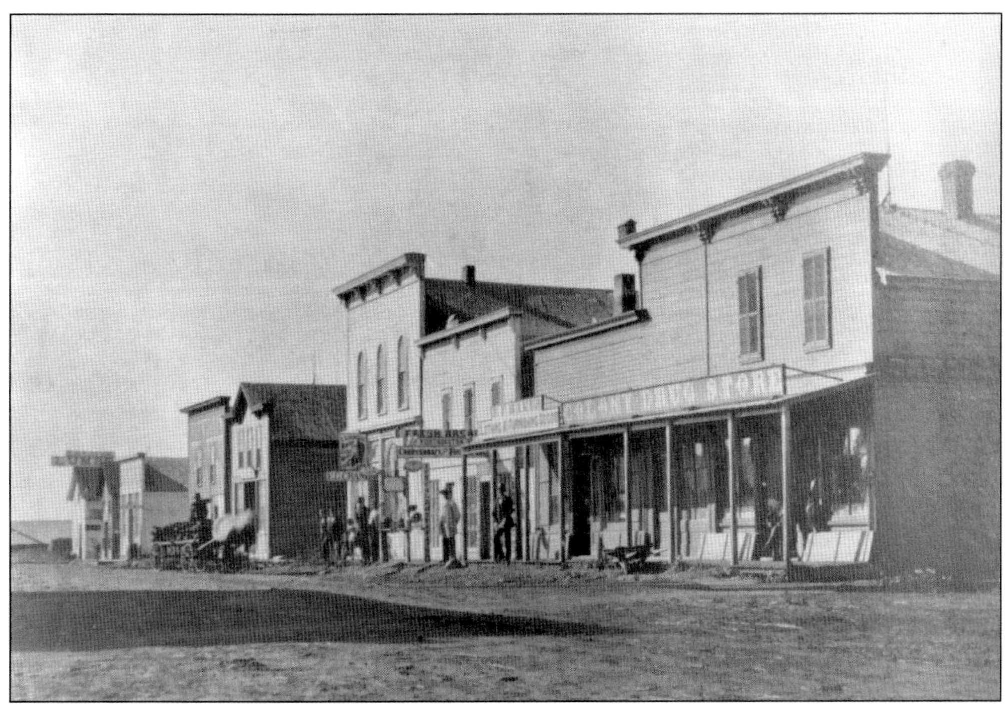

Nobles County's earliest known main street is shown in this 1874 photograph, taken just three years after Worthington was first settled. There are several businesses on the town's main street, now known as Tenth Street. The Colony Drug Store, on the southwest corner of Third Avenue, was one of the downtown's anchor stores. It offered dry goods, groceries, and hardware supplies.

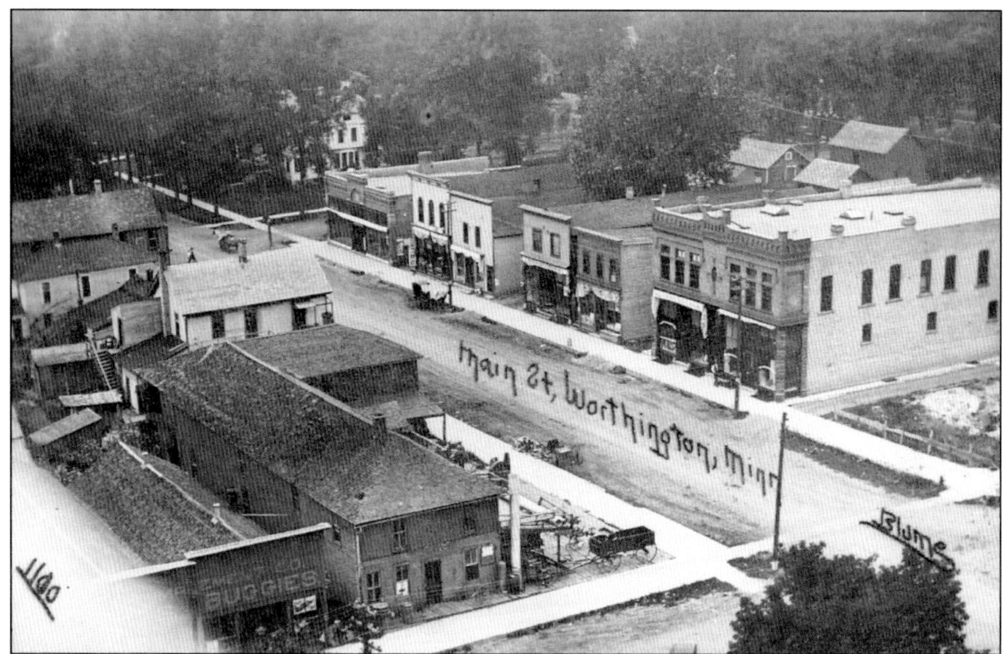

This view, most likely taken from the steeple of the courthouse, shows the shops located between Fourth and Fifth Avenues on Worthington's main street. The dirt and gravel streets were typical of Worthington's downtown between 1900 to 1910, before automobiles were common.

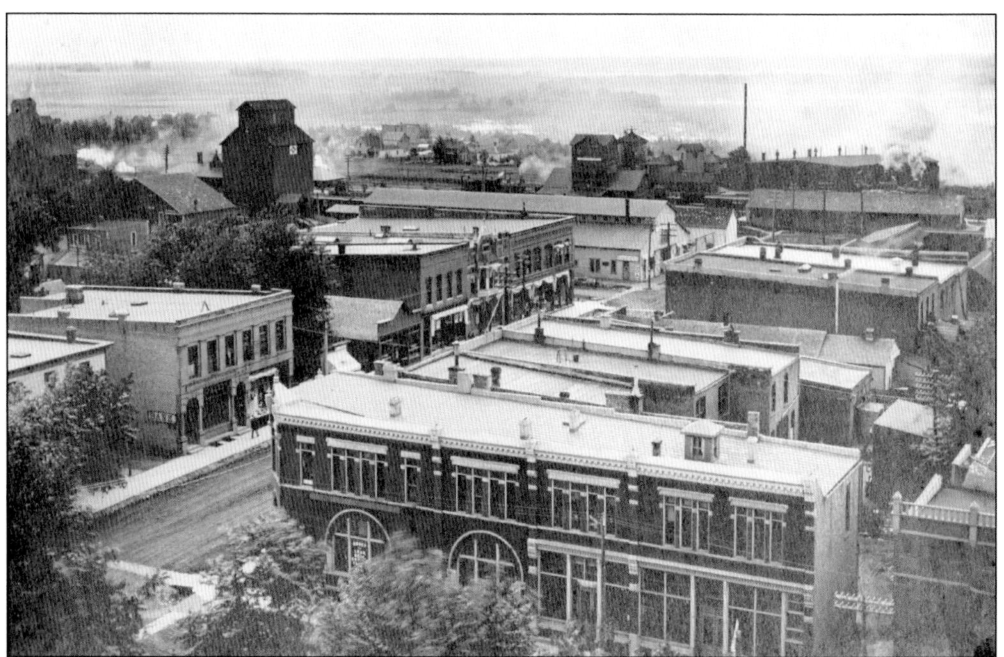
This photograph appears to have been taken from the courthouse steeple during the same period as the previous picture. The south end of the downtown, in the right background, features early business enterprises that were dependent on rail transportation services, including lumber yards and several grain elevators.

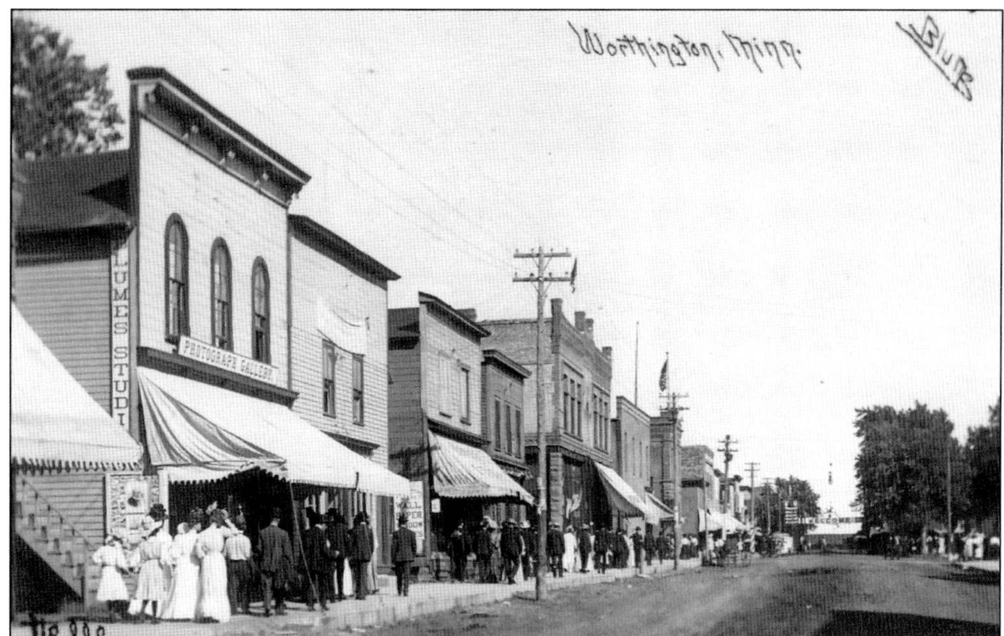

Though the date of this street scene is unknown, it appears to show some special community event. The storefronts are on the east side of Tenth Street, between Fifth and Fourth Avenues. The most visible structure is Blume Studio, the shop of the photographer who took this particular picture.

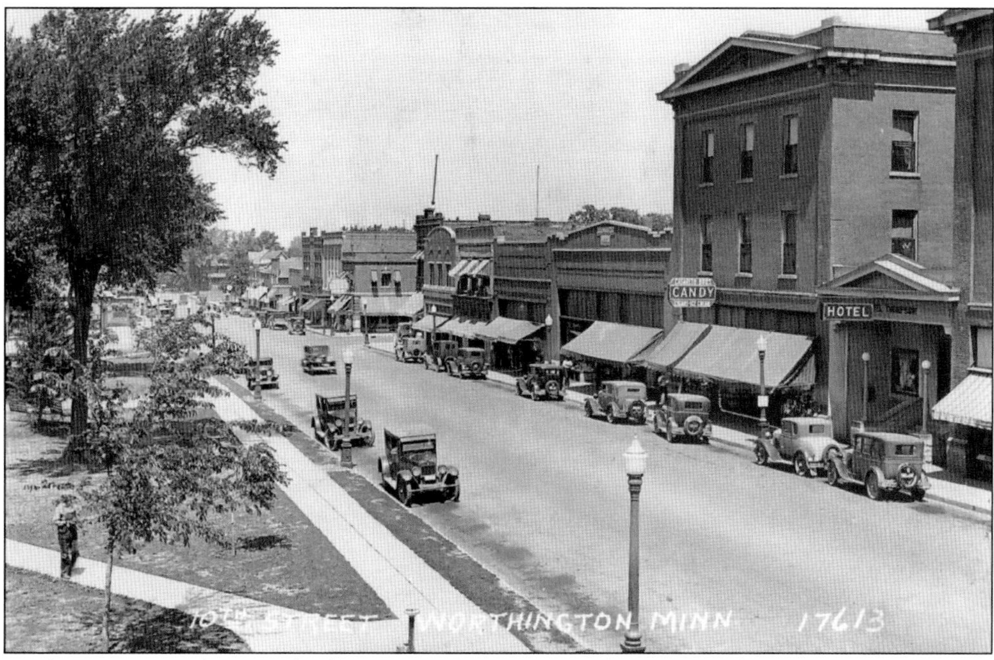

By the 1920s, Tenth Street had been paved to accommodate the steady traffic of automobiles. This photograph shows the main street businesses located between Fourth and Third Avenues, across the street from the courthouse square. The tall Hotel Thompson building dominates the east side of the street's skyline.

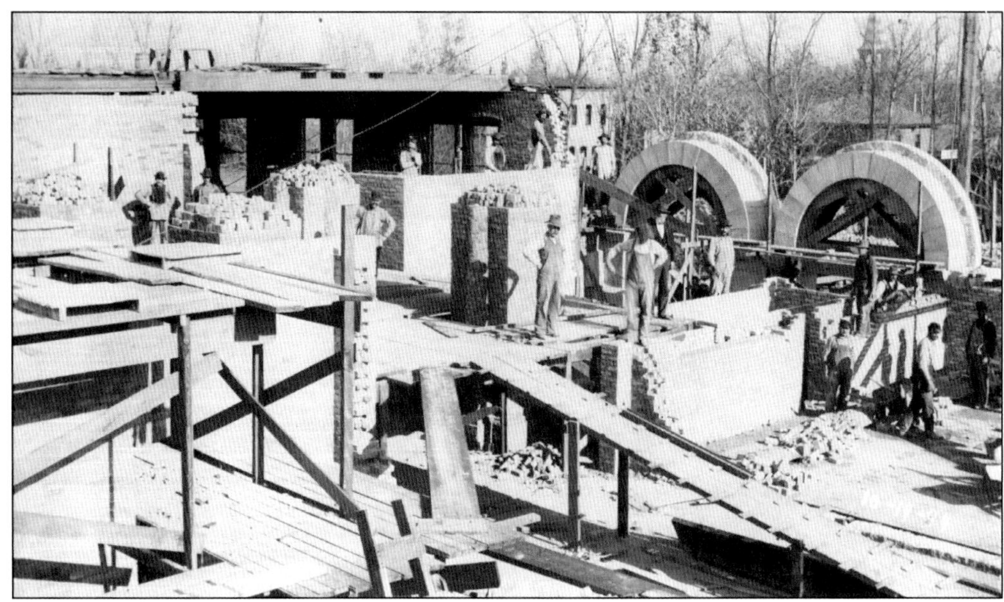

In 1894, on a split vote of three to two, the Nobles County commissioners authorized the construction of a new brick courthouse. D.J. Forbes of Adrian obtained a restraining order blocking the county's building plans. The case ended up being reviewed by the Minnesota Supreme Court, which ultimately ruled in favor of the county commissioners. The county proceeded with the building, offering the John D. Carrol Company of St. Paul Park $42,469 to complete the project.

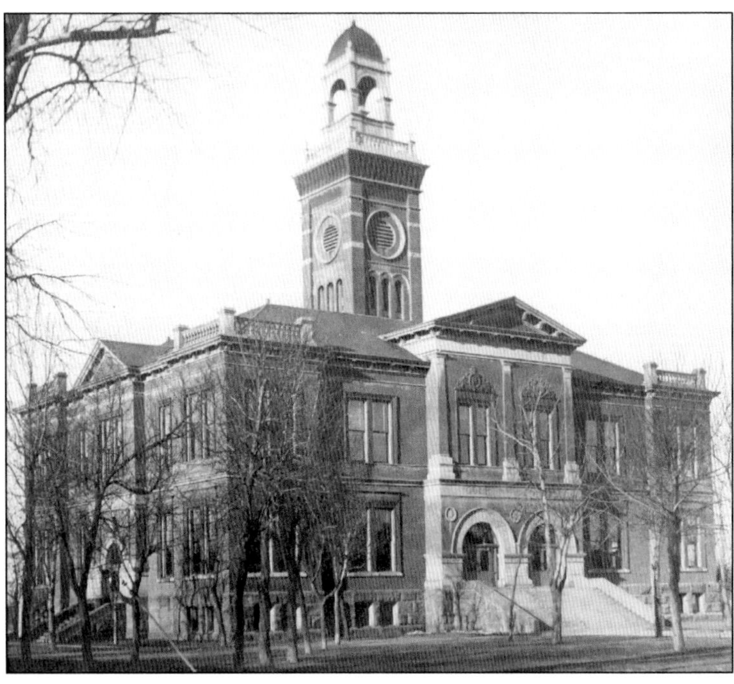

The Nobles County Courthouse was perhaps the county's most iconic and often-photographed building. Other than an accompanying jailhouse, it was the only building on a full city block in the middle of Worthington's downtown. Its tall tower was a popular observation point for photographers and citizens alike. For many years, a revolving beacon warned night-flying airplanes of the courthouse's location.

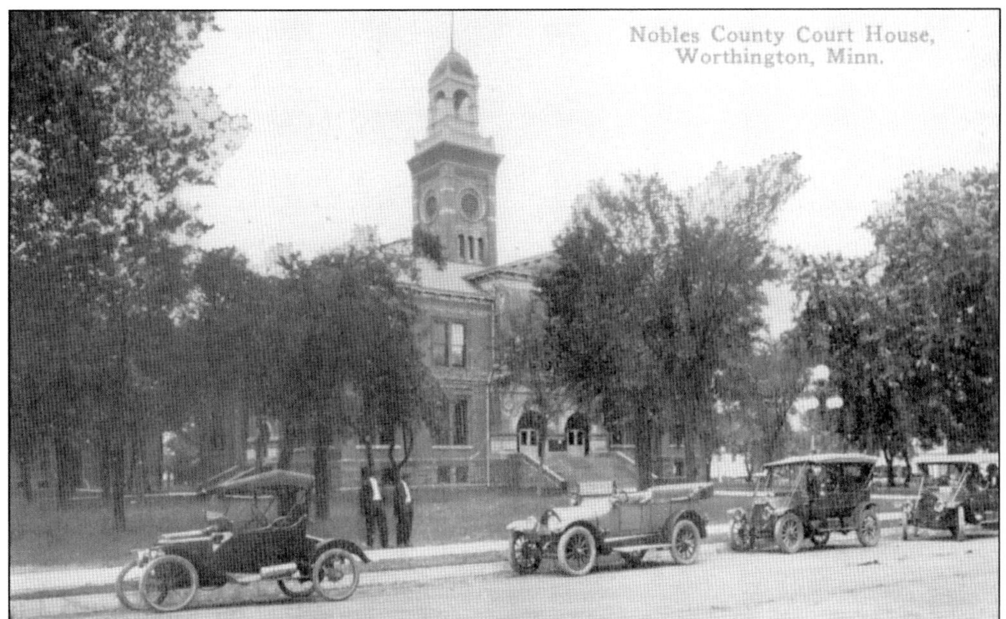

The land the courthouse was built on had been gifted to the county by the Sioux City & St. Paul Railroad Company when the townsite was first established. The condition of this land award was that it be used for courthouse purposes within three years. Unforeseen delays, including a grasshopper plague, prompted the railroad company to grant the county an extension. In 1877, a wooden courthouse was constructed, and it was used until this replacement was erected in 1894.

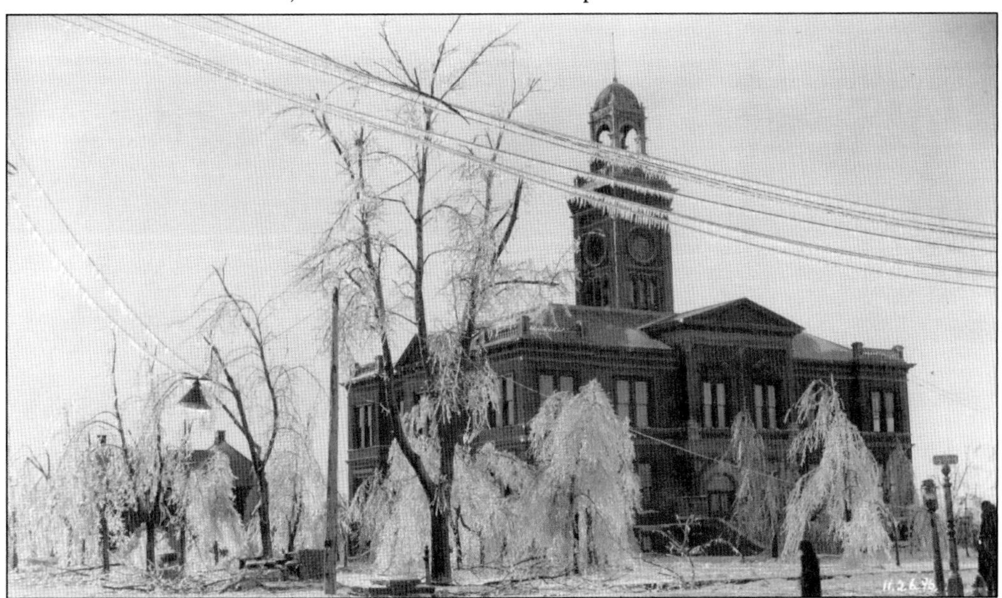

In August 1913, the Nobles County Courthouse tower was struck by lightning. When the resultant structural cracks were evaluated, one expert recommended replacing the tower. The commissioners decided only to repair it. The tower survived until 1948, when further deterioration necessitated its removal for safety reasons. Though less damaging than the 1913 lightning strike, the ice storm of November 26, 1896, seen here, shows how the courthouse grounds were significantly damaged by the inclement weather.

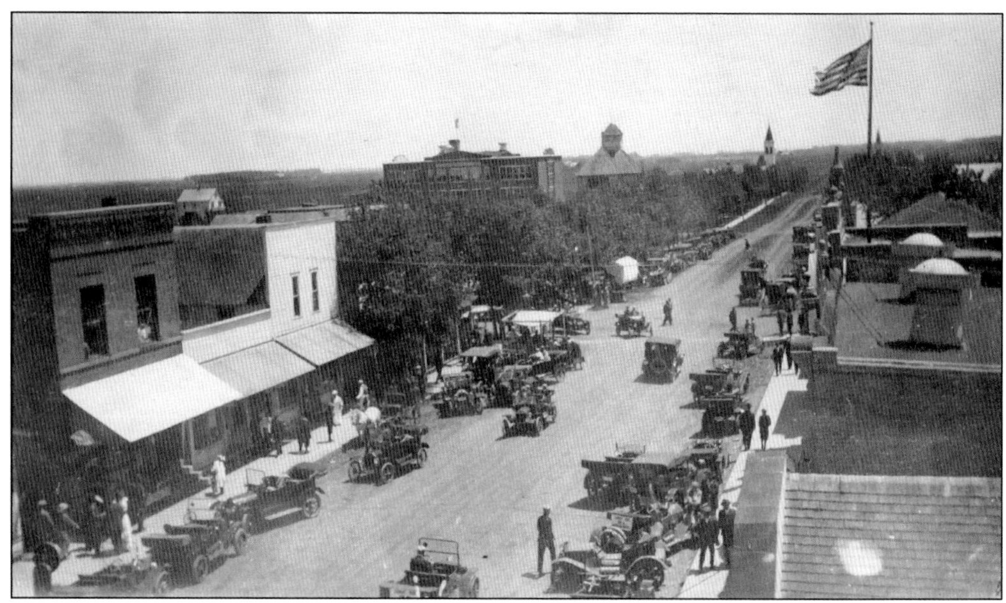

When the townsite eight miles northeast of Worthington was established as the county's second community in 1872, it was known as Hersey. A few years later, the railroad company changed the name of the town's railroad station from Hersey to Brewster, because there was already a Hersey railroad stop in Wisconsin. Shown here is Brewster's bustling downtown in the early 1900s.

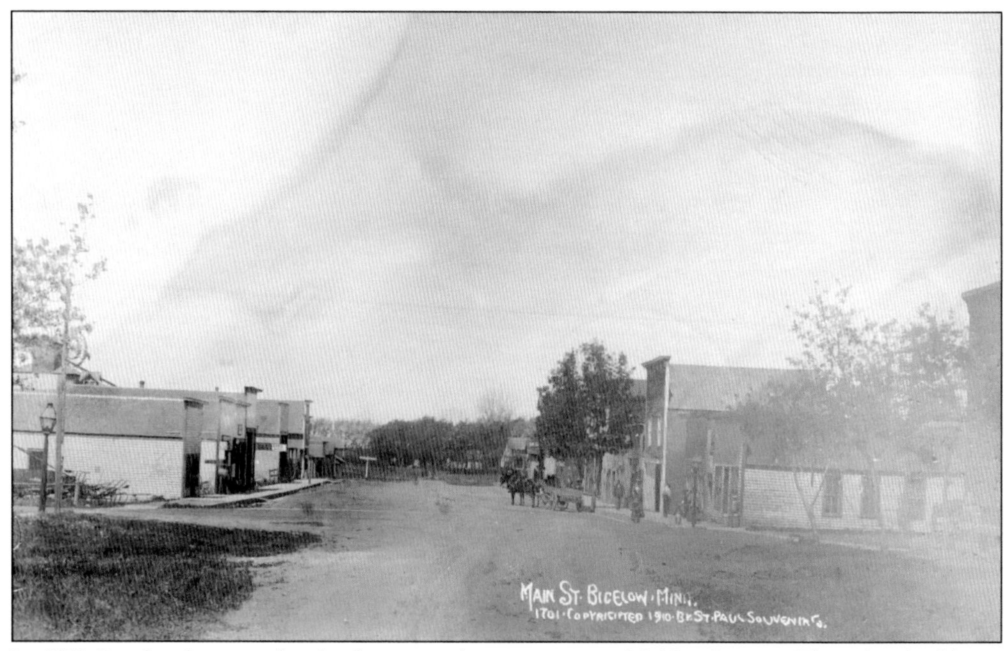

In 1872, Bigelow became the third organized community in Nobles County. Though it had been planned as a railroad outpost at the same time as Worthington and Brewster, inhabitants were a little slower to settle here. This postcard, taken in 1910, reflects a somewhat quieter downtown business area.

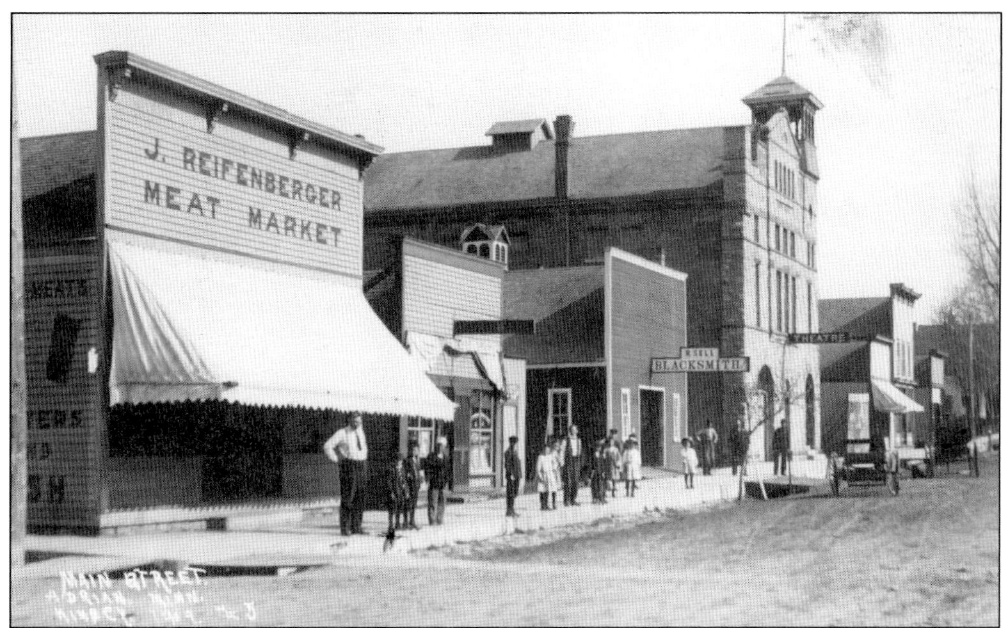

Like most Nobles County towns, Adrian was the creation of the developing railroads and the settlers they brought to the region. Originating in 1876, it was the first community in the western half of the county. These buildings, on the street's west side, include a meat market, a blacksmith shop, and the town's imposing city hall. This large structure was constructed in 1888 at a cost of $15,000; the upper story was an opera house that could seat 400 people.

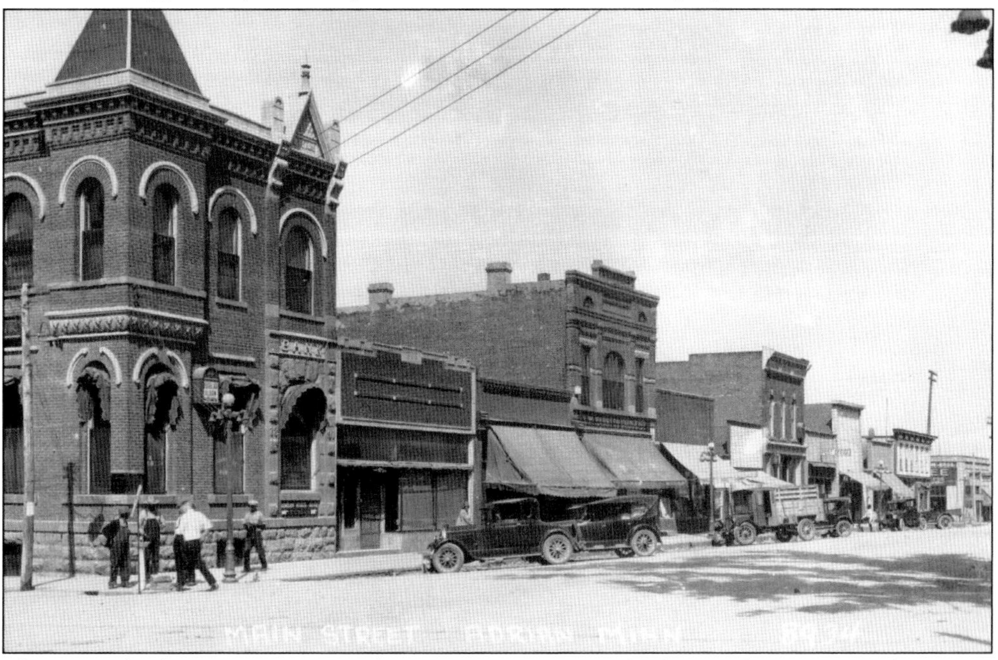

This view of Adrian's Main Street taken 10 to 15 years later also features businesses on the street's west side, just a block or two up the street from the previous photograph. Many of the brick storefronts had replaced the wooden structures that were more prevalent in the earlier image. The Adrian State Bank, erected in 1891, was one of the larger business establishments on Main Street.

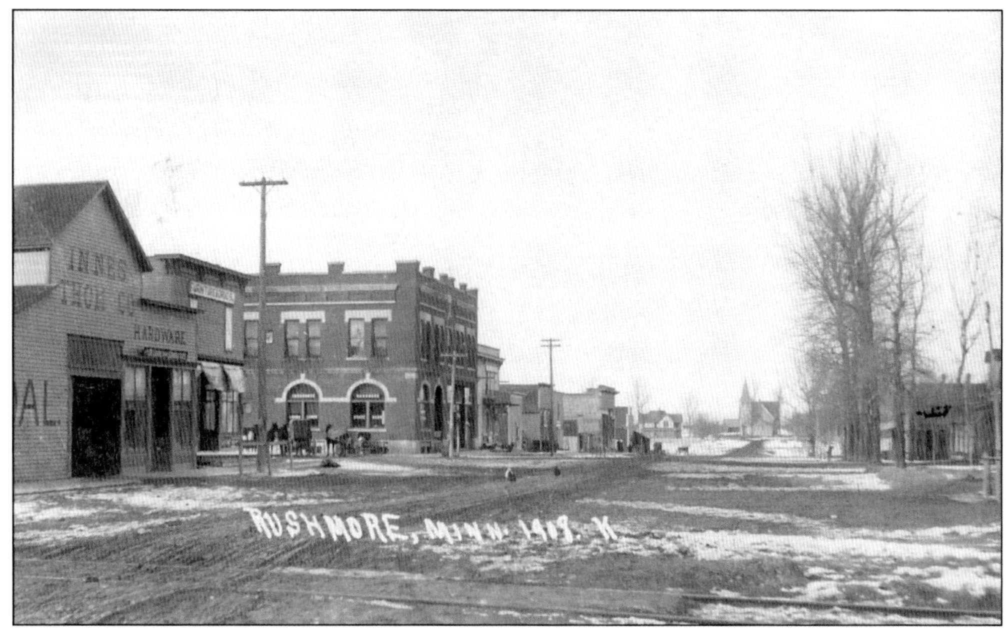

There was a need for a train station a few miles west of Worthington. It was named Miller Station after ex-governor Stephen Miller, who was a railroad land agent. Two years later, in 1878, a group of people from New York relocated here to establish a community. They renamed the townsite after their leader, S.M. Rushmore. County historian A.P. Rose described Rushmore as having broad streets lined with large shade trees, as evidenced in this 1908 main street photograph.

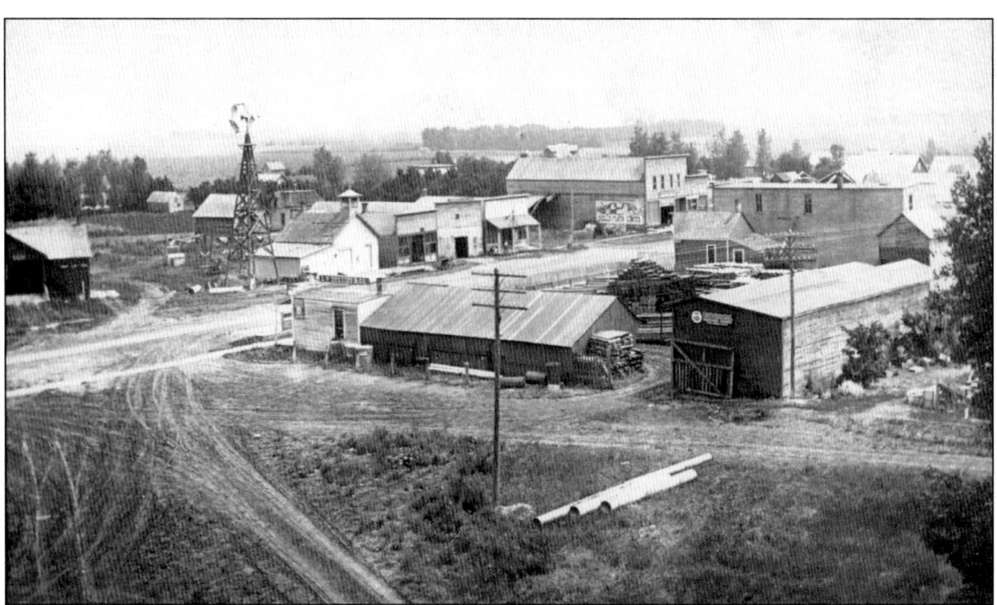
The first residents moved into the northeast corner of the county shortly after the Civil War. However, a settlement was not organized until 1879, when the townsite was designated as a train station known as Warren. Within a few months, it was renamed Dundee after the city in Scotland. This elevated view of the main street shows a thriving business area in the 1900–1910 era.

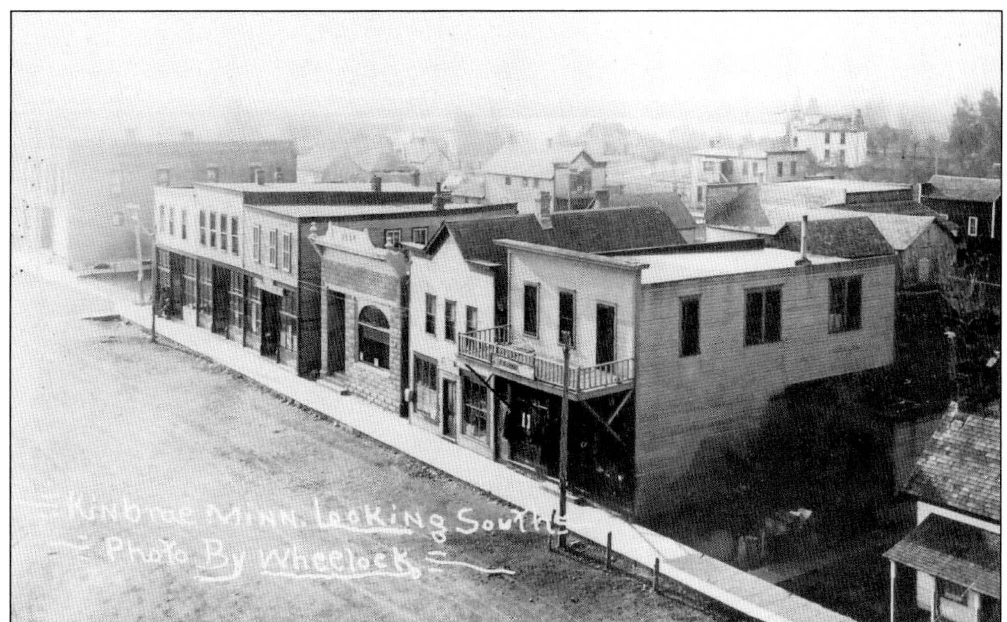

To compete with the Sioux City & St. Paul Railroad's line and depot in Dundee, the Southern Minnesota Railroad opened its own rail station and line less than two miles away. It was initially called Airlie but was rechristened De Forest when the site was surveyed in 1879. For a few years, the depot was referred to as De Forest Station while the post office was known as Airlie. In 1883, both structures and the town itself were all renamed Kinbrae.

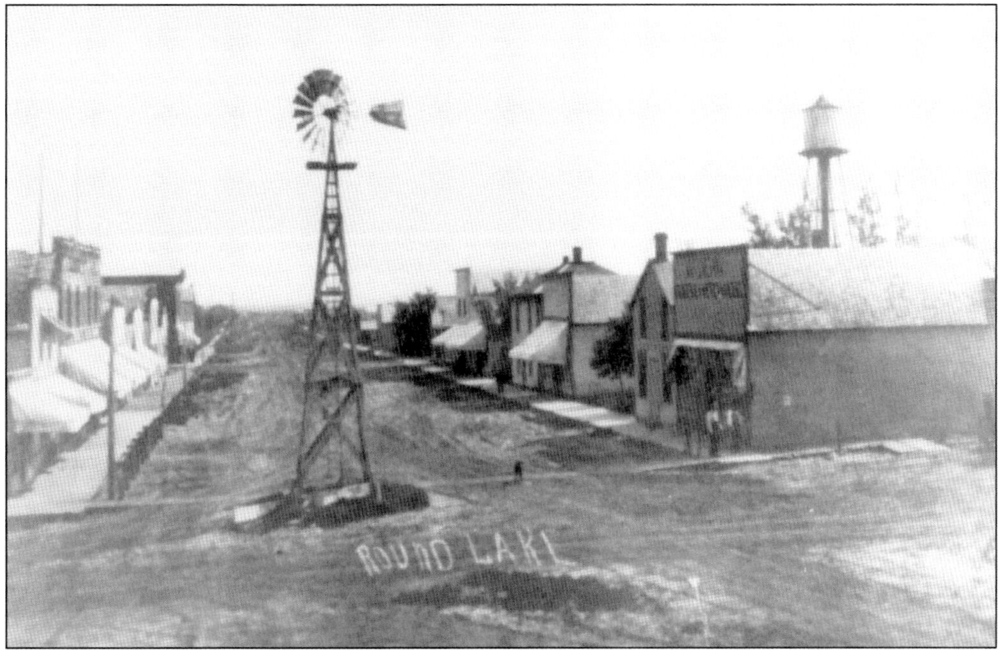

Still another railway company, the Burlington, Cedar Rapids & Northern, became engaged in community building. To support its southerly routes, it located a station southeast of Worthington in Indian Lake Township. It decided to call the proposed town Indian Lake but later changed the name to Round Lake for the nearby lake in Jackson County.

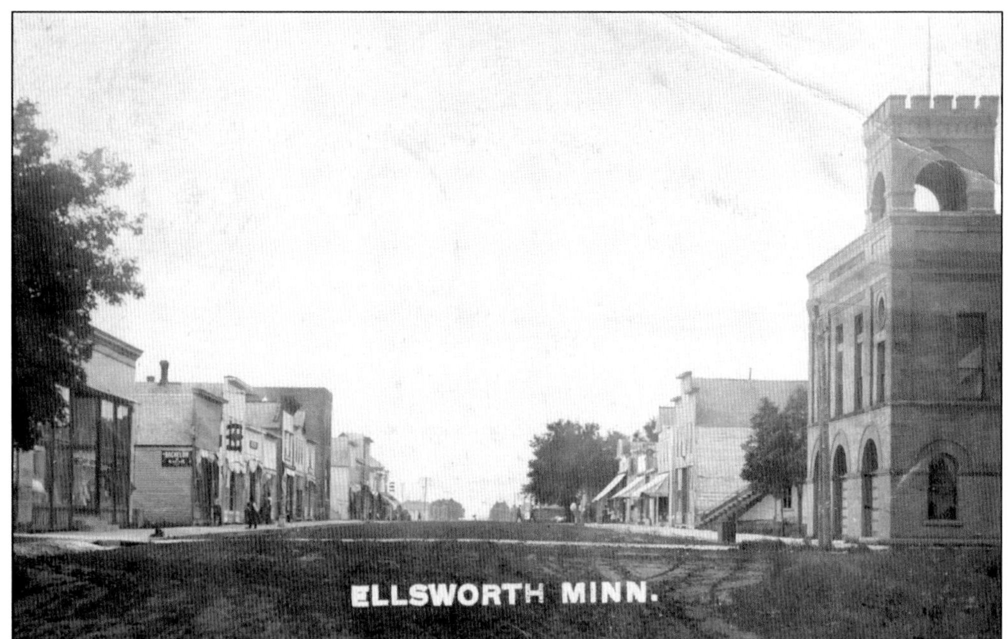

Although the first settlers in Grand Prairie Township came as early as 1871, it took another 13 years before the village of Ellsworth was established. The town's creation was the result of the Burlington Railroad's decision to expand rail services into the area. It built a five-stall roundhouse, a turntable, and an enlarged depot. By 1900, Ellsworth had become the county's third largest town.

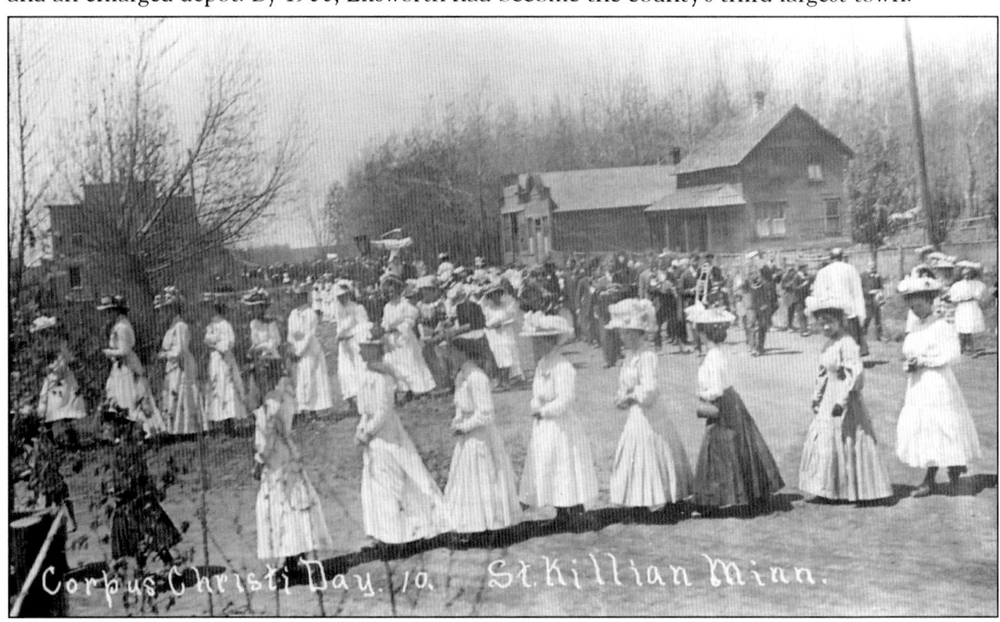

St. Kilian grew up around a church rather than a train depot. In 1887, a group of German farmers living in the area built a church named after an Irish monk who preached the Catholic faith in their native country. Within a few years, there was a general store, a saloon, and a post office. However, in 1899, all hopes for a prosperous town were lost when the Burlington Railroad selected a neighboring community for its rail expansion plans. St. Kilian's limited main street is visible in the background of this 1915 Corpus Christi celebration. (AB.)

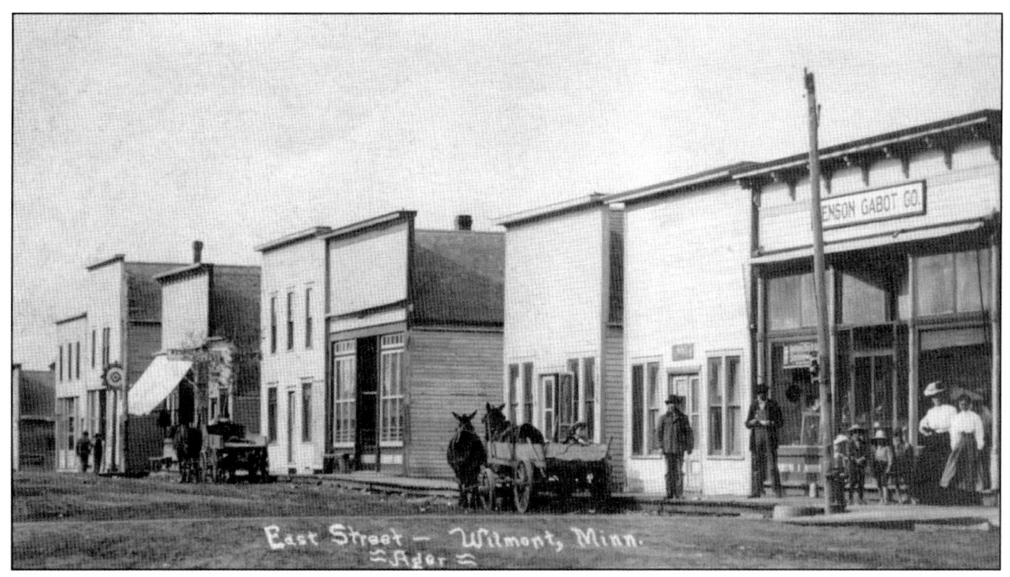

In 1899, the Burlington Railroad began making plans to expand services into the county's northwestern corner. Rather than using its rails to link Worthington to St. Kilian, an already established village, it opted to create a new townsite. Wilmont was born, and within six years, it had become the county's fourth largest town. These two images of Wilmont's downtown show a well-established row of businesses on both sides of the town's main street. In A.P. Rose's *An Illustrated History of Nobles County, Minnesota*, he describes Wilmont's main street as a "thoroughfare nearly a mile long."

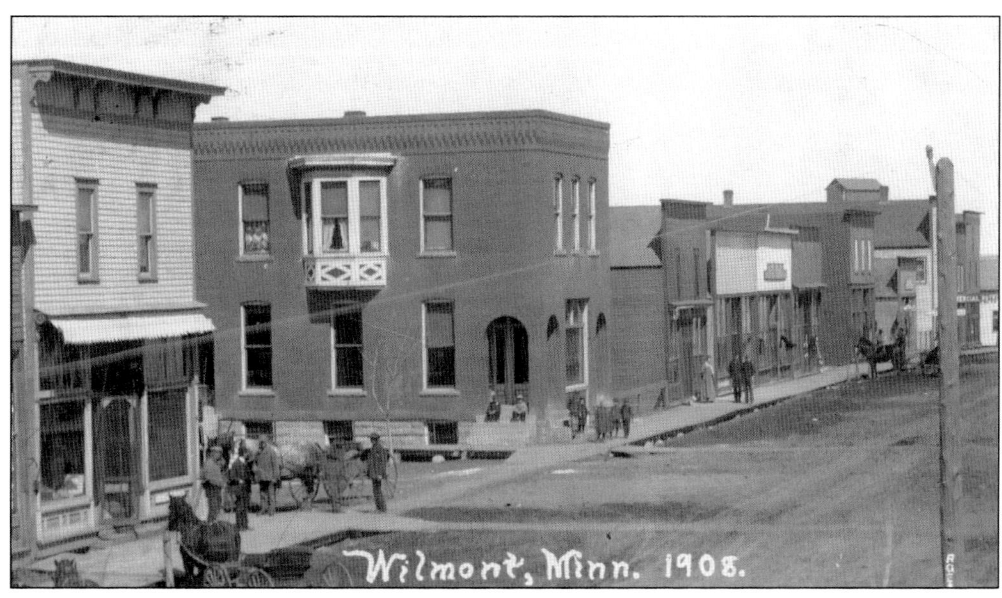

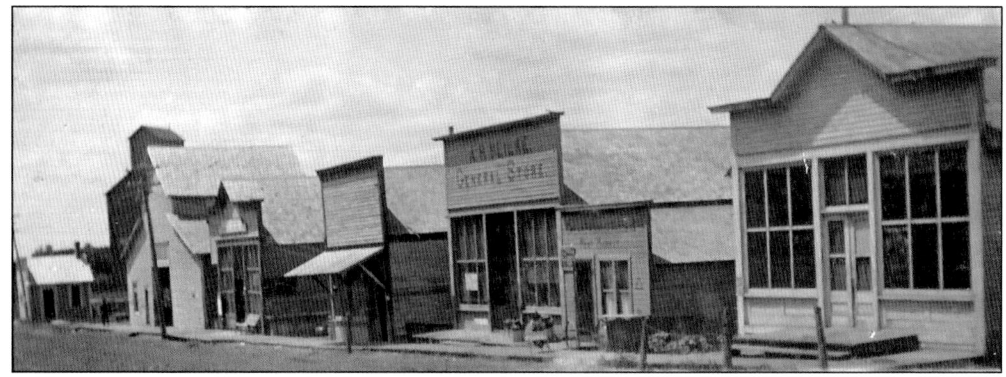

Reading is the town closest to the county's geographic center. Some of the first residents settled here as early as 1876. However, it took another 20-plus years and the Burlington Railroad's decision to expand its rail services before an actual village was established. Reading became the first community on the Burlington line to Wilmont and beyond. The town was named after H.H. Read, who sold the land to the railroad. (BSF.)

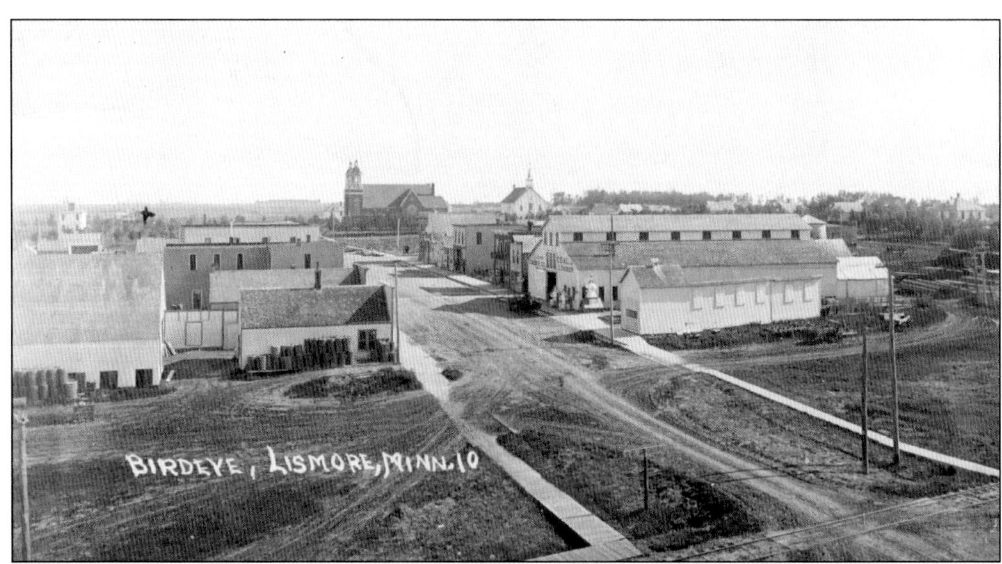

Lismore was the last Nobles County town to be organized, in 1900. It grew out of the Burlington Railroad's desire to locate a stop between Wilmont and the company's rail junction. This move also met the area settlers' need to gain better access to local trade markets. The two parties worked closely together to get the community established. They called the town Lismore after the township, which was named for a village in Ireland.

Two

Tilling the Soil, Harvesting the Crops

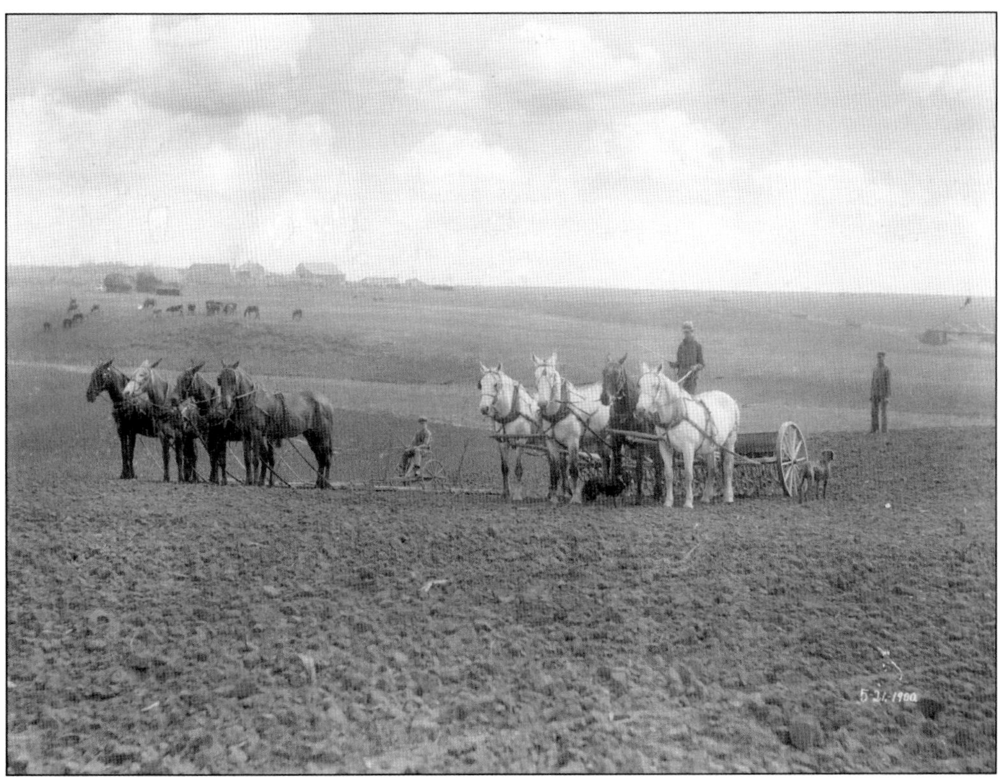

In this photograph from May 21, 1900, much work is being done to get the fields ready for planting on the Daniel M. Holland farm. The four-horse/mule team on the left is pulling a drag, while the other four-horse hitch is pulling a grain drill. The Holland farmstead can be seen in the left background; on the far right, a bridge over Elk Creek is visible.

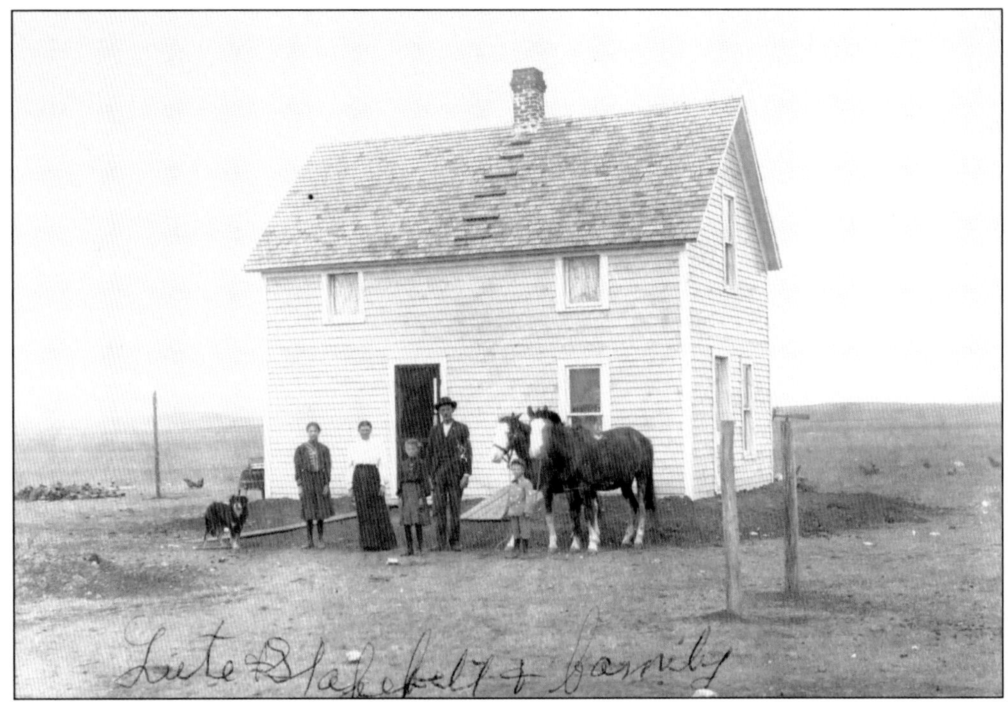

When families made their original homestead claims, often they were getting a piece of prairie land that had never been worked. This image of the Lute Slabebelt family shows their house in a rural setting completely devoid of trees. Little is known about where and how they lived and whether they were actively engaged in farming.

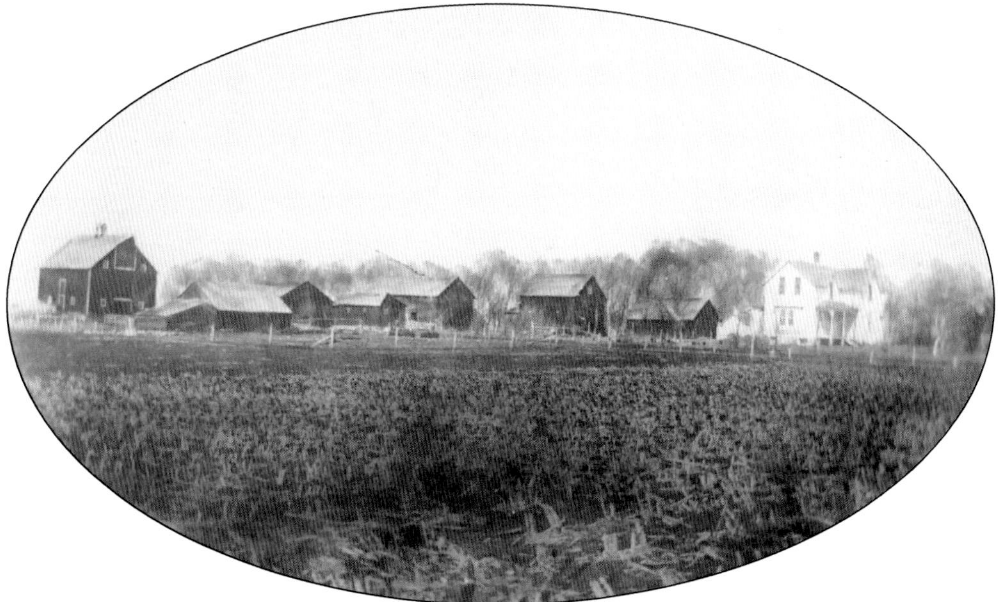

Contrast the barren look of the previous photograph to that of Anton Weber's well-developed farmstead in the Lismore area. As seen in this 1903 photograph, the Weber family farm featured a large house with a porch, several barns, sheds, and outbuildings, and a well-established grove of trees.

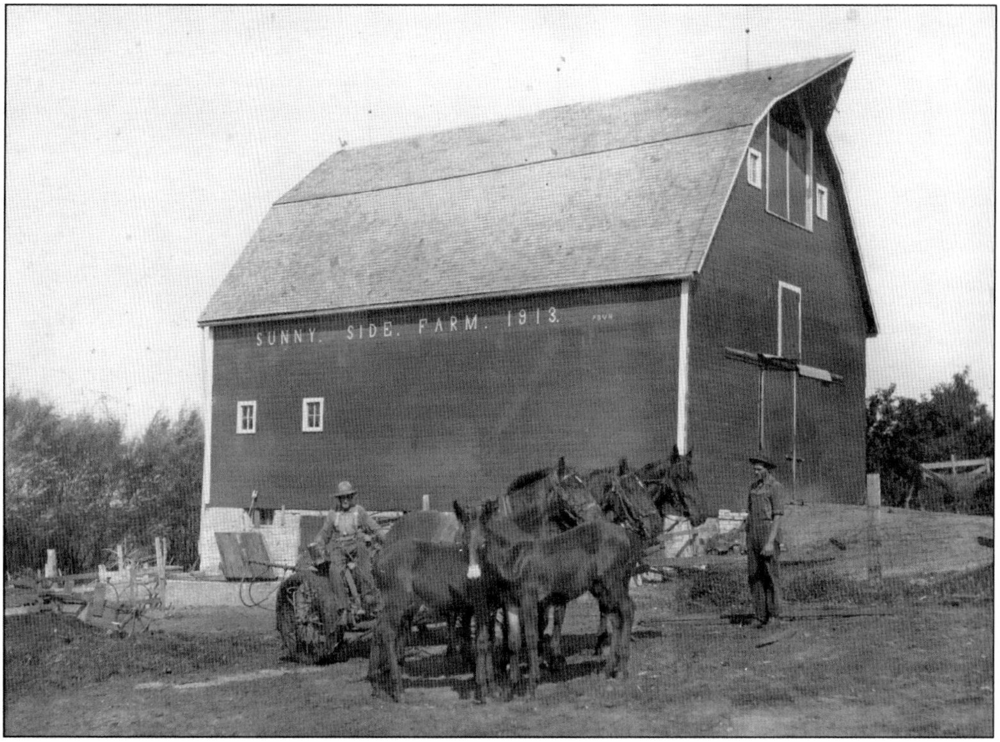

In the early 1900s, some people gave their farms a special name to help establish their identity. The farmstead in this picture is the Sunny Side Farm, as indicated by the sign on the barn. It was owned by J.W. and Ella Rogers and was located on Section 2 in Little Rock Township. Other farm names include Hillside, Clovercrest, Willow Lane Stock Farm, and Walnut Grove Stock Farm.

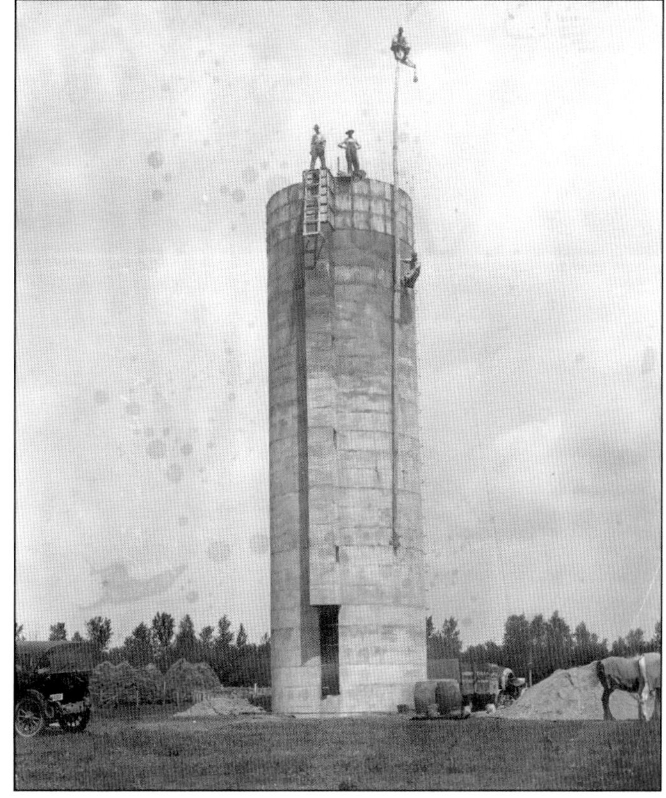

Silos did not appear to be common on the area's early farms. Nevertheless, this image shows one being erected around 1915 on the farm of T.C. and Margaret Thanning. It was located on Section 27 in Graham Lakes Township.

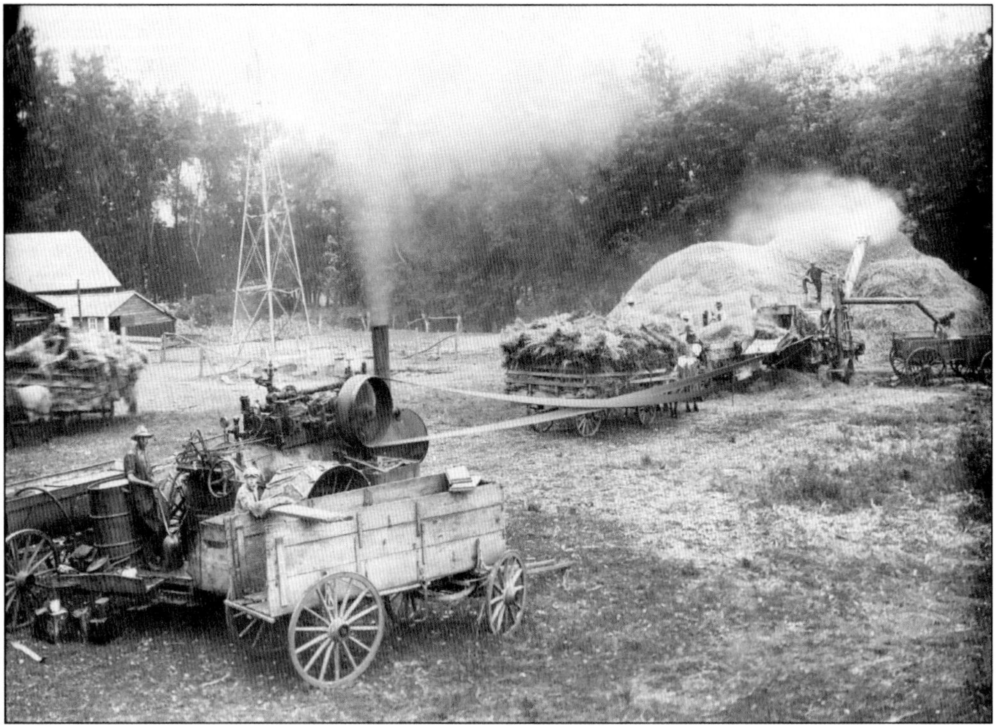

Threshing was a special occasion for farmers and their entire families. Given all the equipment required and the manpower needed to operate it, threshing typically involved many families working together to harvest the crops on one farm at a time. While the men were working in the fields, the women and children cooked and baked a host of foods to serve the workers throughout the day. This threshing scene occurred on the Nelson Metz farm.

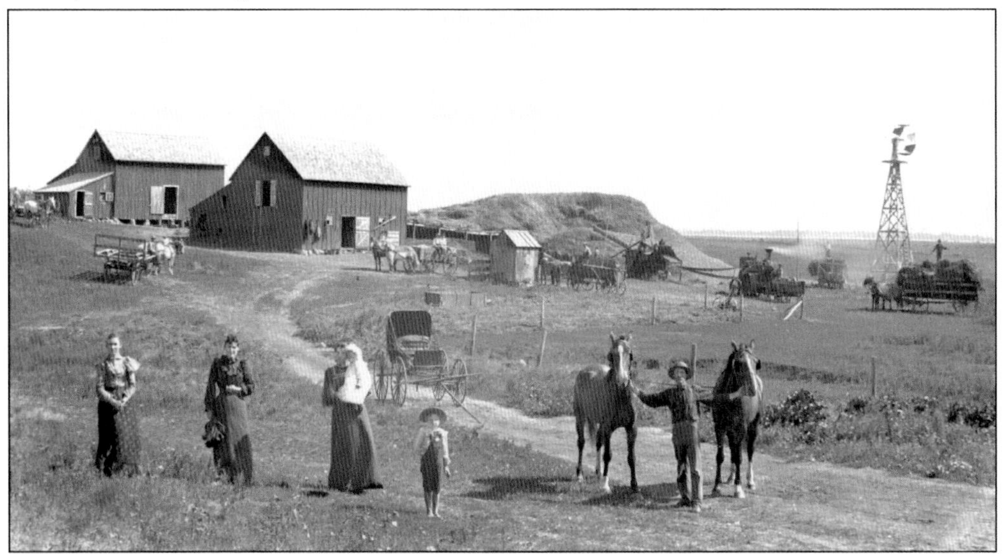

This threshing picture from the Worthington area was taken by E.F. Buchan around 1895. While the threshing crew is harvesting the crops in the background, the rest of the farmer's family chose to pose for the photograph in the farm driveway. They appear to be dressed up for the occasion, and they have even brought out the family buggy and a team of horses. (HDH.)

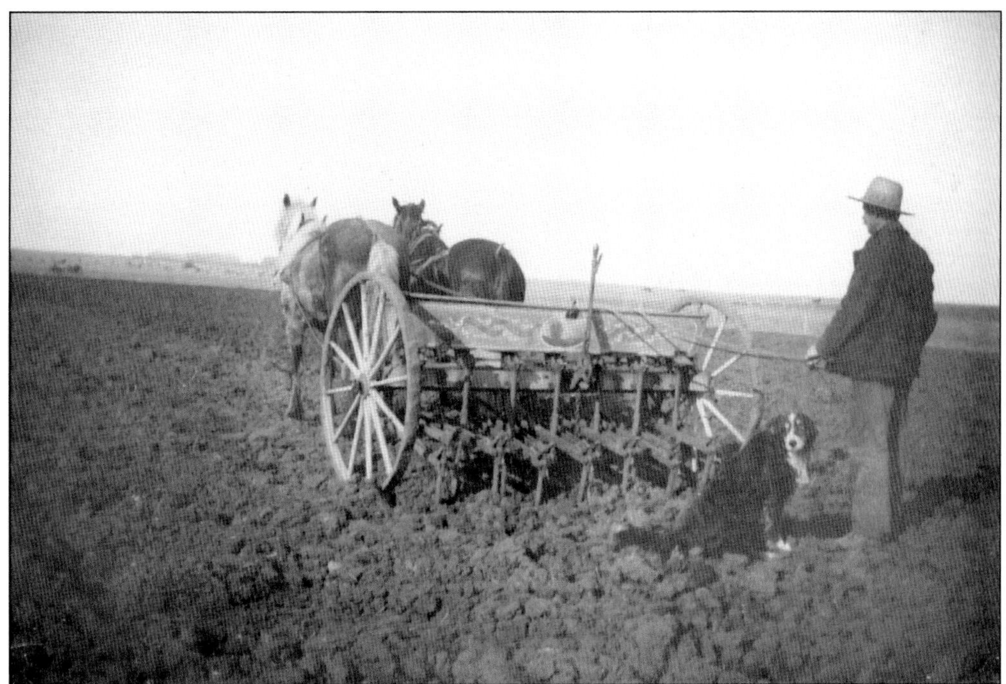

Jens Jorgensen can be seen around 1915 using a team of horses to pull a small grain drill in one of his fields. He could be planting a small grain, such as barley or rye. The Jorgensen land, Greenview Farm, was in Olney Township on Section 14.

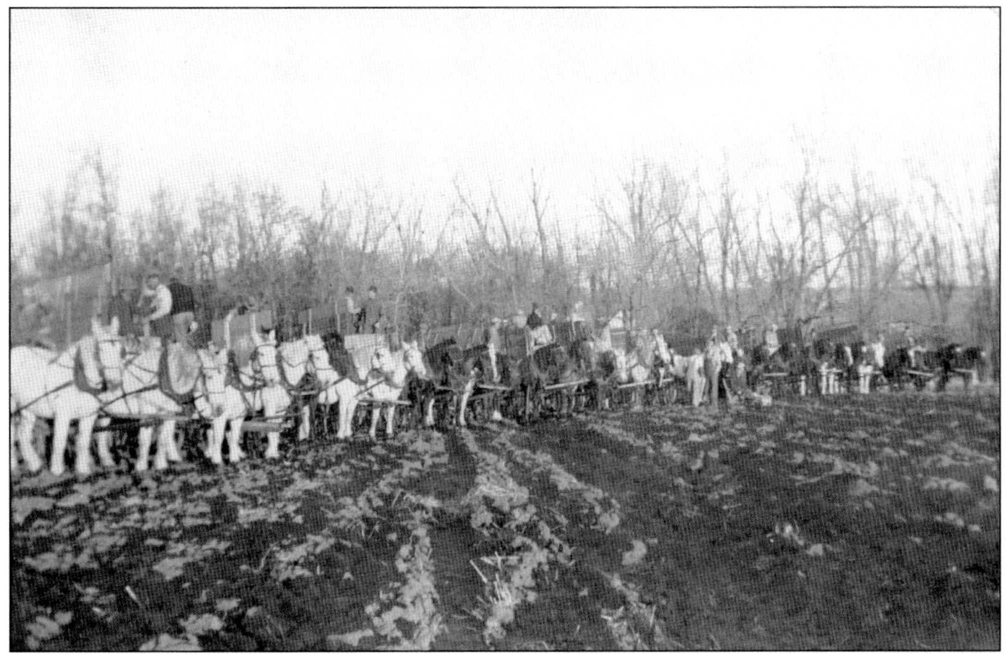

These farmers, with their teams of horses, have gathered to take part in a husking bee. The circumstances surrounding this get-together are unknown. It could have involved some sort of friendly competition, or they all may have decided to help a neighboring farmer who was unable to harvest his own crops.

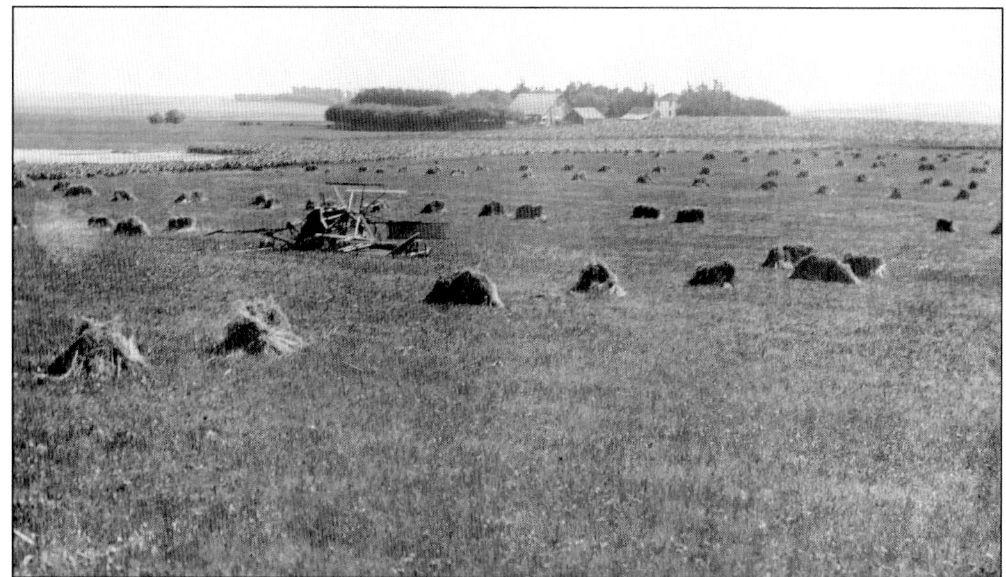

This Rushmore-area field, pictured around 1915, illustrates some of the processes involved in harvesting certain grains. The grain stalks were tied into bundles and then gathered into shocks. These in turn were thrown by pitchforks onto a bundle rack to be transported to the farmsite, where they would be processed through a mechanical threshing machine.

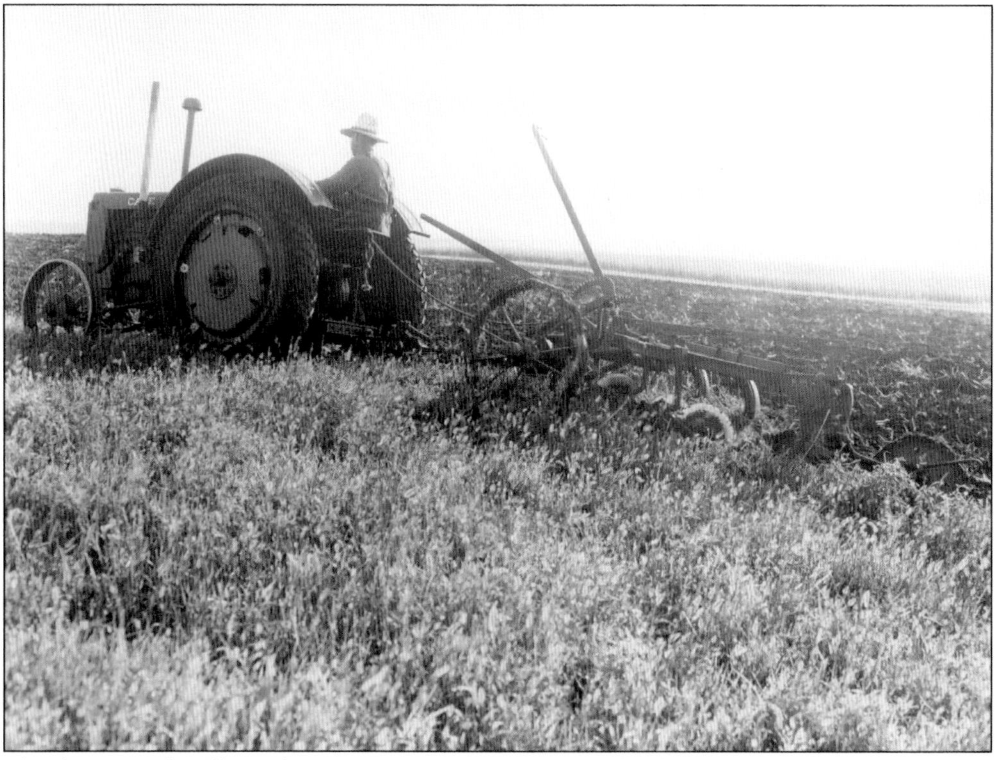

This farmer in the Ellsworth area is using a Case tractor and a three-bottom plow to prepare his field in Larkin Township around 1930. These smaller, gasoline-powered "row crop" tractors proved to be more versatile than their more unwieldly predecessors, the steam-engine tractors.

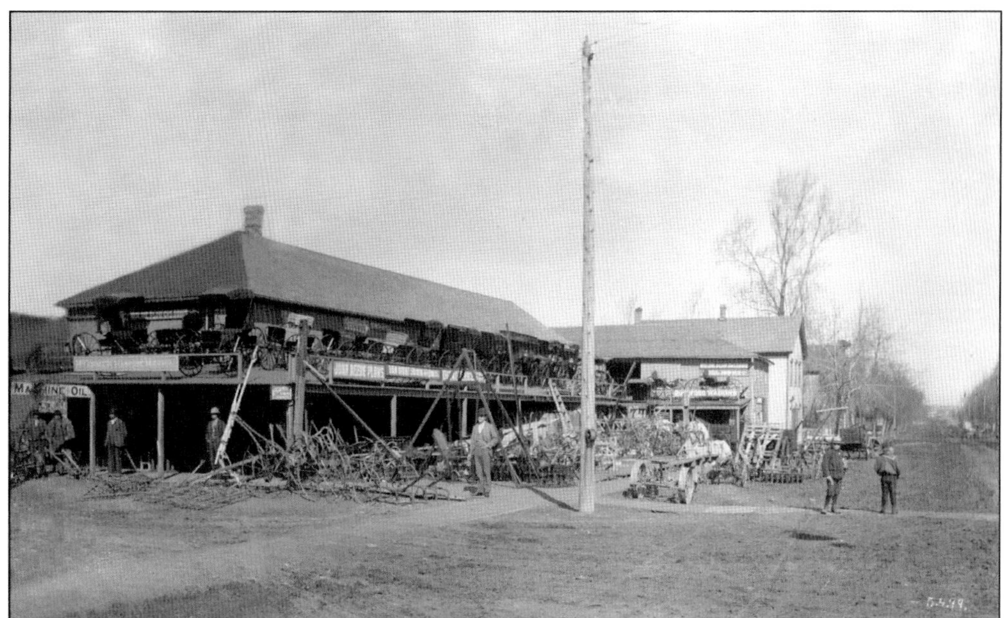

In the late 1800s, J.D. Humiston's implement store was situated in the center of downtown Worthington, across the street from the courthouse, currently the site of Mick's Repair. Humiston used any and all available space to display the equipment he had for sale, including a "showroom" on his second-floor awning. (HDH.)

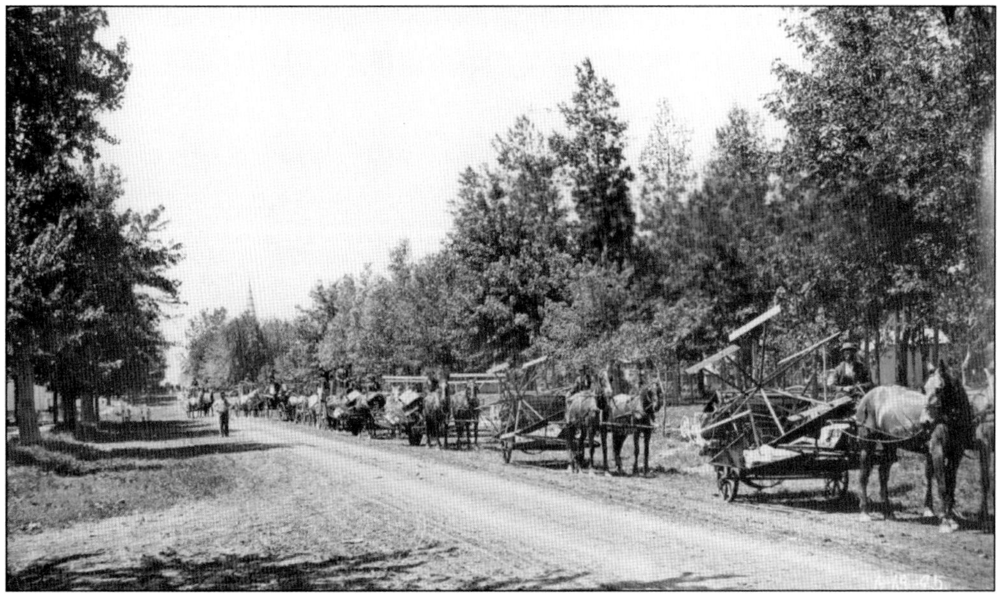

Some people called J.D. Humiston the "prince of implement merchants." The Parade of Implements on June 19, 1895, earned him this accolade. According to historian Ray Crippen's description, "sixty five well-dressed and happy-looking toilers of the soil, driving horses both sleek and fat, began a procession which stopped all traffic, horse and pedestrian." Each farmer drove a team of horses pulling a wagon loaded with McCormick machinery. The Worthington band led the parade. At the end of the day, Humiston had sold four carloads of McCormick equipment.

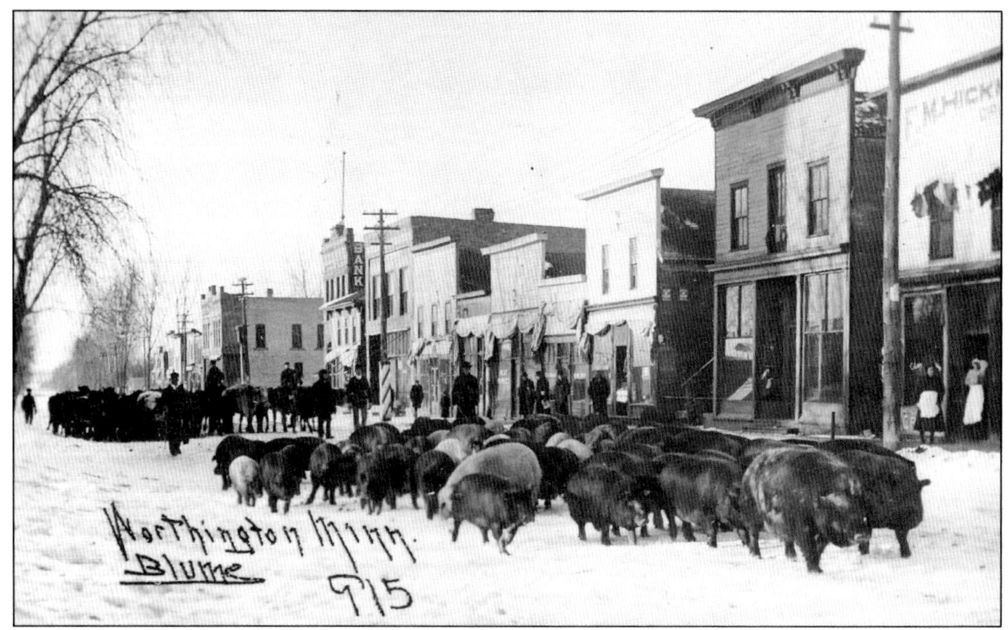

It is hard to know where these hogs are going. It appears they are being driven south down Worthington's Tenth Street, possibly towards the railroad stockyards. Behind the hogs, there is a herd of cattle with several herdsmen guiding them, including two on horseback. Some of the store clerks have gathered on the sidewalks to view the spectacle. (TG.)

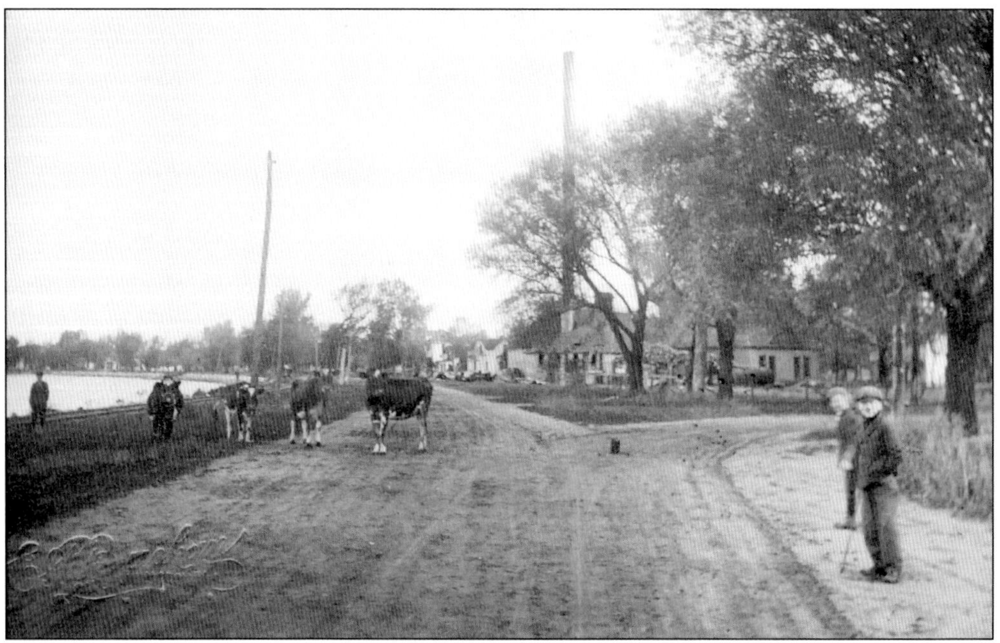

The boundaries between town and the rural area were often blurred. Sometimes there were small farms on the edge of town, so it probably was not surprising to see cows within the city limits. Here, a few cows have paused in the street on the southeast side of Worthington's Lake Okabena.

Three

Entrepreneurial Spirit

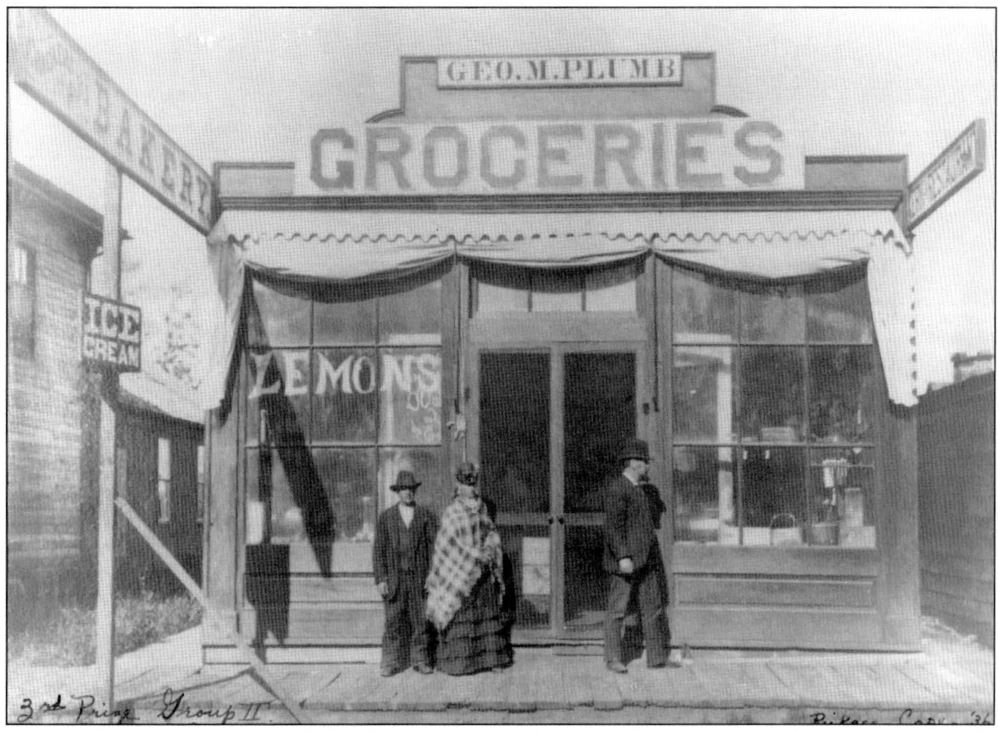

As Nobles County's towns developed and their main streets took shape, a host of businesses were established. This is a photograph of the George M. Plumb grocery, located on Worthington's Tenth Street across from the courthouse. Taken in 1874, this is the earliest photograph of a retail store in the historical society's collection.

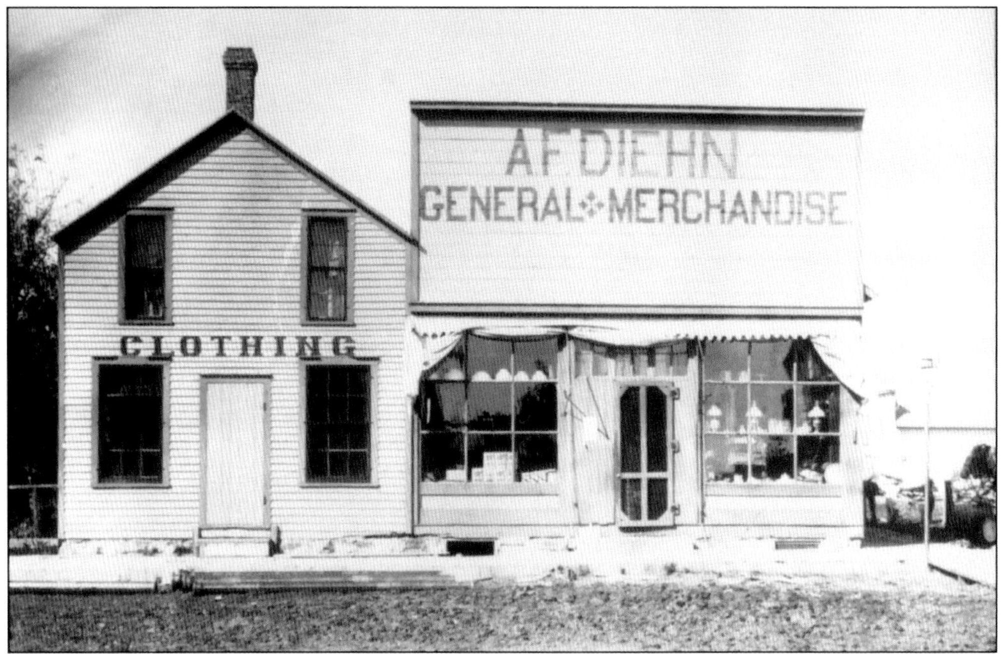

When people first settled in their new communities, they needed food, clothing, household supplies, and hardware. Sometimes these different items were all sold by one retail merchant—a general store. In October 1891, August Diehn bought partial interest in a Round Lake general store that he operated with his partner, Herman Moeller. A few years later, he became the sole proprietor of the business, which he continued operating until 1919.

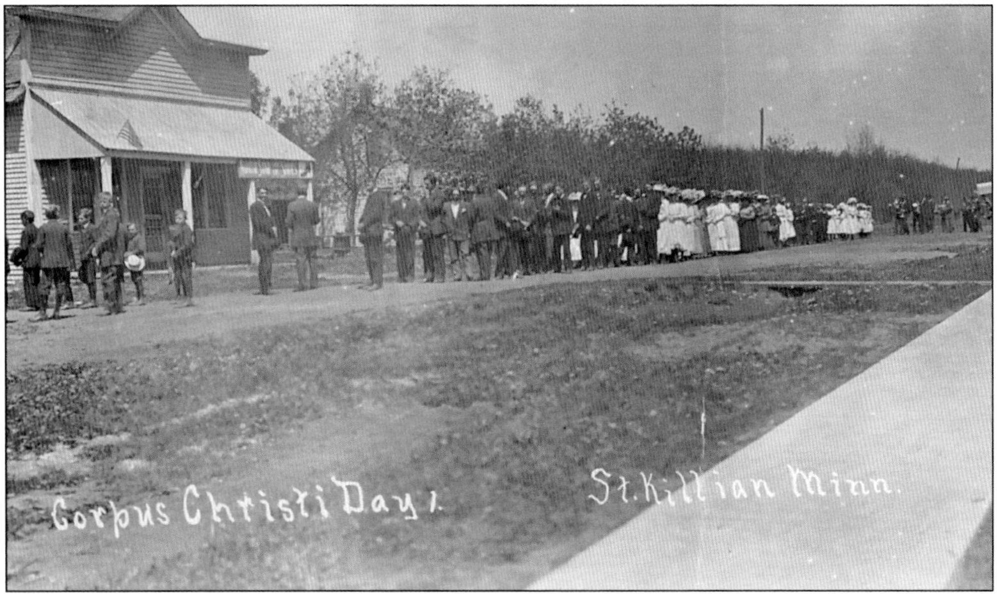

John Mock's General Store was St. Kilian's first building after the construction of the Catholic church. Mock's shop led to the establishment of other businesses, and the town's post office was set up in his store. By the early 1900s, almost all of St. Kilian's shops had closed, with the exception of the general store, which can be seen at left in this photograph of the community's 1915 Corpus Christi celebration. (AB.)

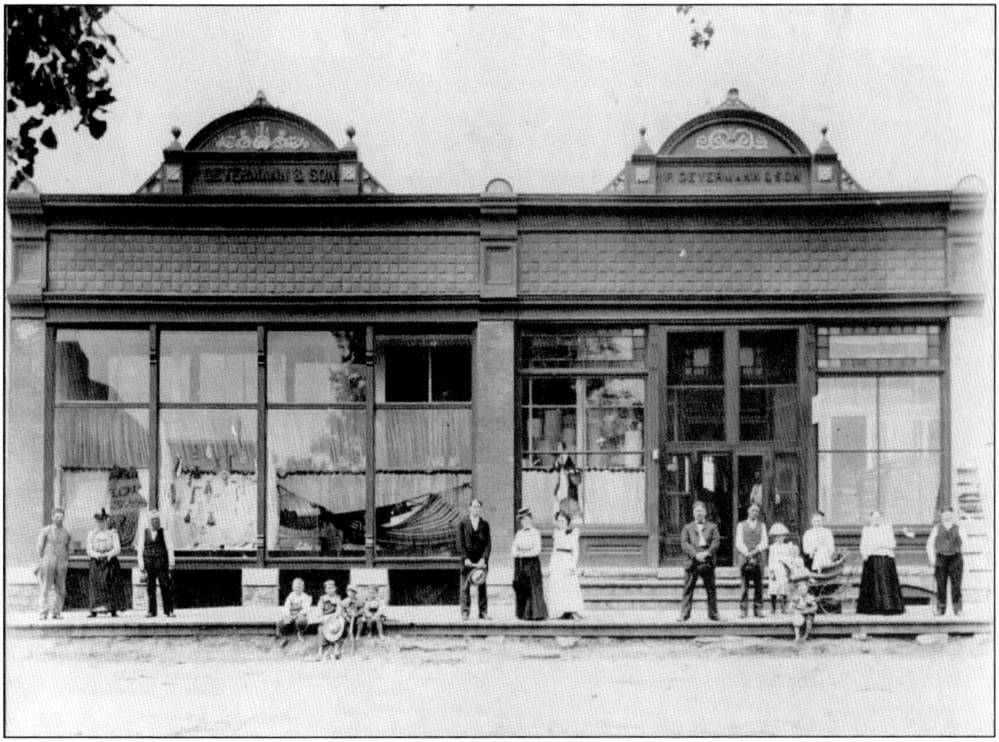

In 1881, Peter Geyerman moved from Shakopee to Brewster to open a mercantile store. His sons, Edward and Rudolph, later went into partnership with him. In 1892, they built the first half of the big store, and the second half was constructed in 1901–1902. By 1907, they employed 12 clerks, and hired salesmen who traveled throughout the area selling and delivering groceries and other goods by horse and buggy.

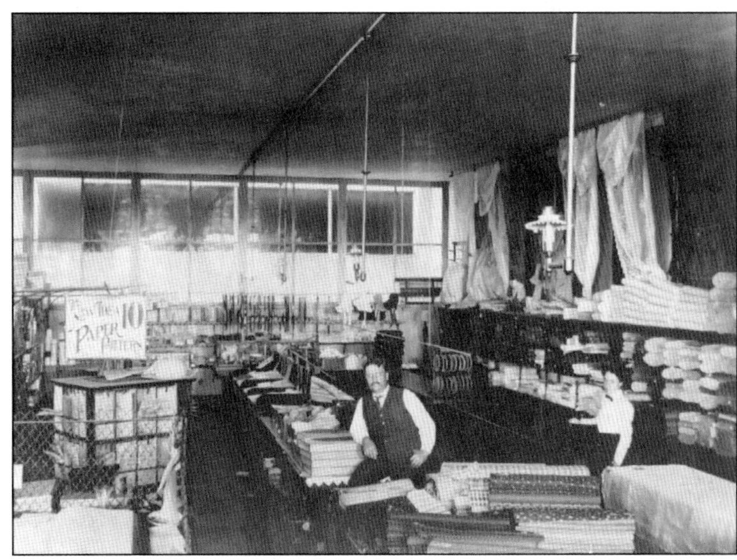

As is evidenced by this interior photograph of the Geyerman & Sons dry goods store, they offered customers an extensive selection of clothing, curtains, fabrics, and sewing patterns. Beyond these dry goods, residents could purchase groceries, including milk, cheese, and cold meats kept fresh in ice boxes, as well as dishes, jewelry, shoes, suits, and coats.

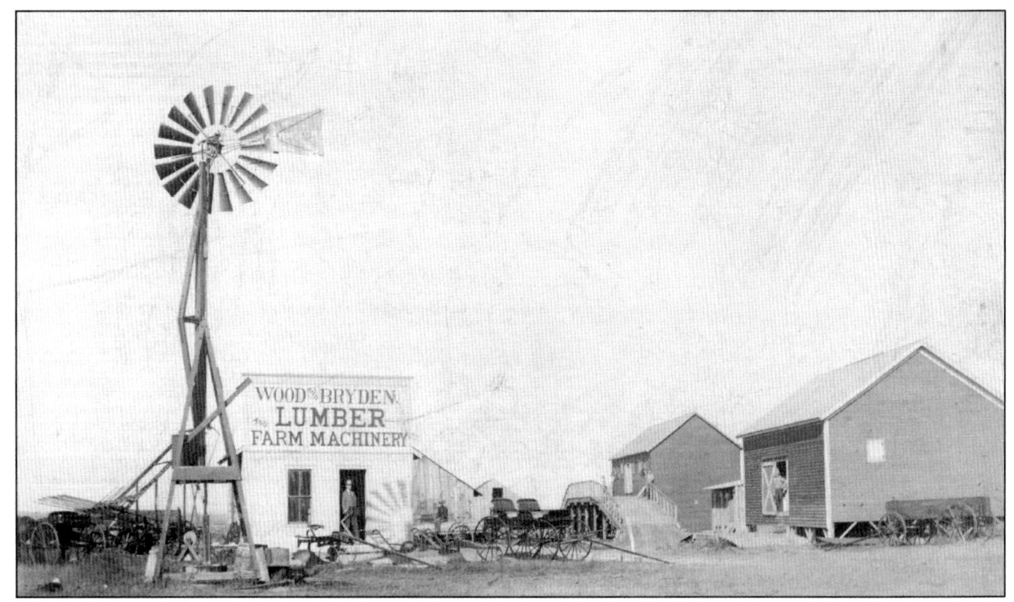

This photograph was taken between 1891 and 1903. S.T. Wood and J.H. Bryden had originally purchased Rushmore's Lumber and Fuel Company in 1891 from S.B. Bedford. They managed the business as a partnership until 1903. Sometime during those 12 years, they added farm machinery as one of the products they carried.

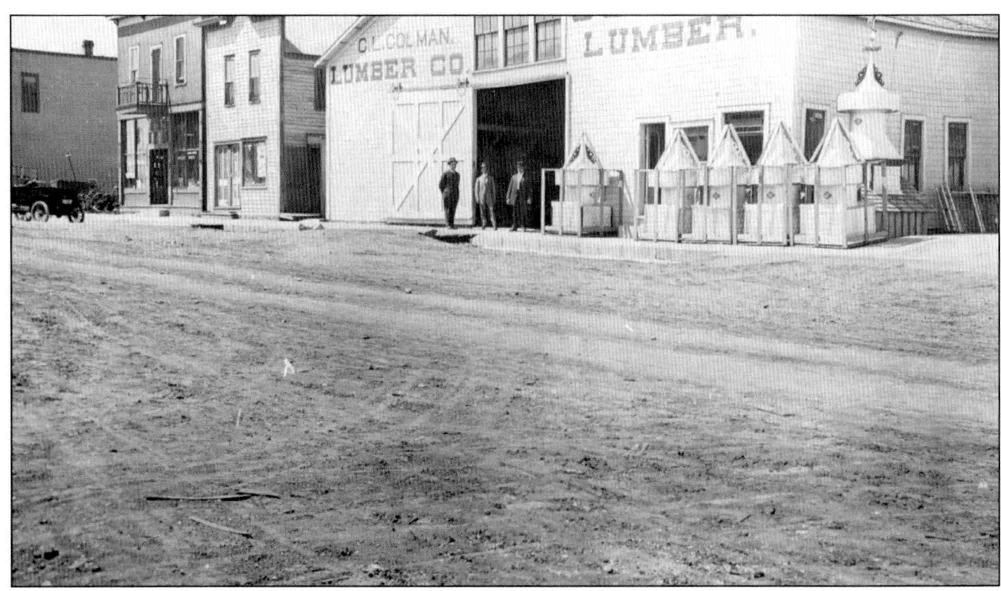

When communities were first organized, some of their initial stores were established as satellite locations of businesses that were already operating in neighboring towns. For example, C.L. Colman Lumber Company had a lumber yard in Worthington before opening this one in Lismore.

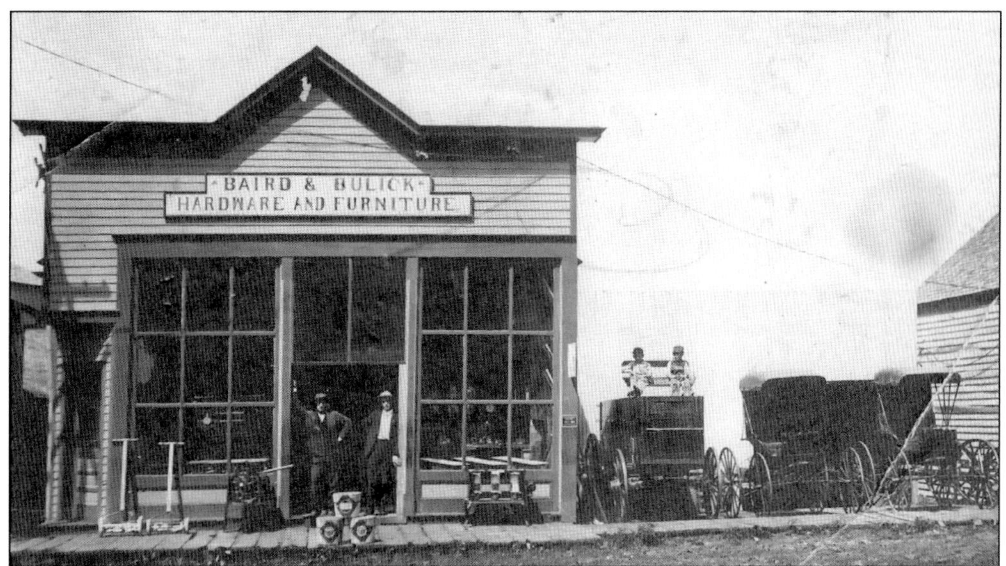

The first retail store built in the village of Reading was a hardware store owned by Charles Woodworth and Robert J. Jones. Erected in 1899, their shop was located on the west side of the main street. They used an adjoining vacant lot to store the larger equipment they had for sale. In 1909, John Baird and Frank Bulick purchased the business, which they operated until they sold out two years later. (BSF.)

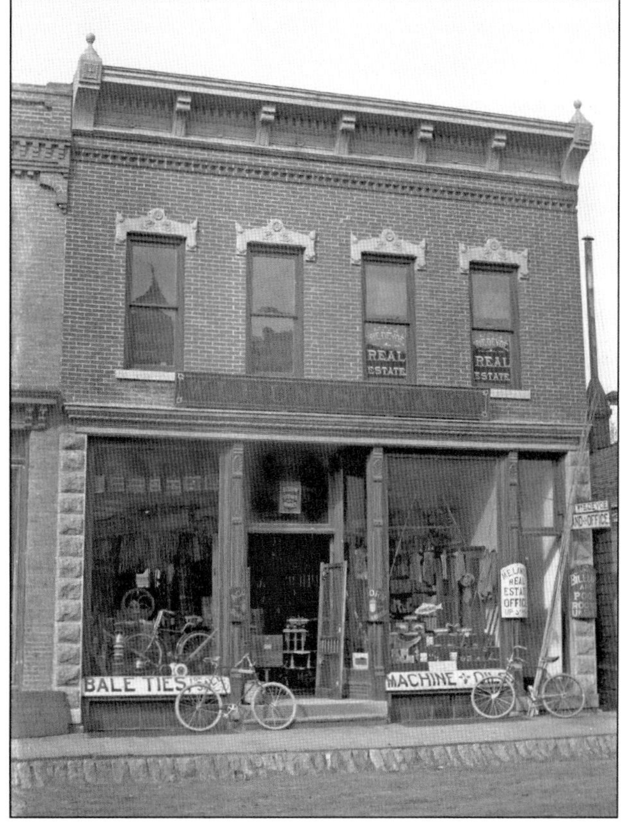

One of the earliest families to settle in Worthington was the Humistons. Will I. Humiston arrived with his family in 1872 at the age of 11. He was educated in local schools, attending classes in the winter months and herding cattle during the summers. In 1885, he went into the hardware business. The W.I. Humiston & Co. store at right, which was constructed in 1892, was located on Worthington's Tenth Street where the Daily Apple Store is today. (HDH.)

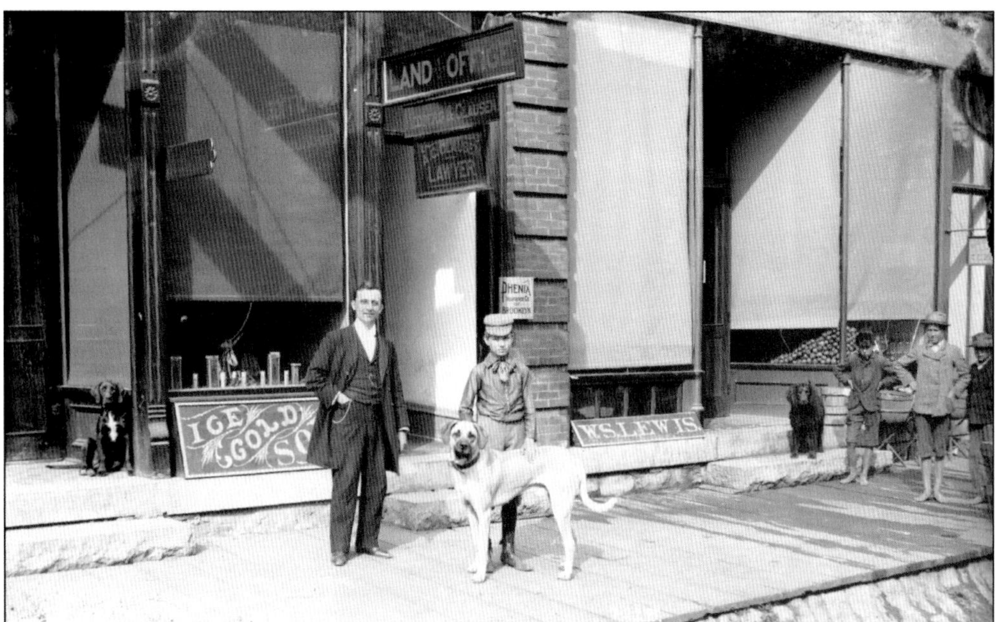

Another of Worthington's early retail merchants was W.S. Lewis, who had a grocery business. He and his family relocated to Worthington in September 1883. Shortly after his arrival, W.S. purchased a grocery store from A.S. Husselton, which he owned and operated for 13 years. His store, pictured here, was on the west side of the main street, three storefronts south of the corner bank building. (HDH.)

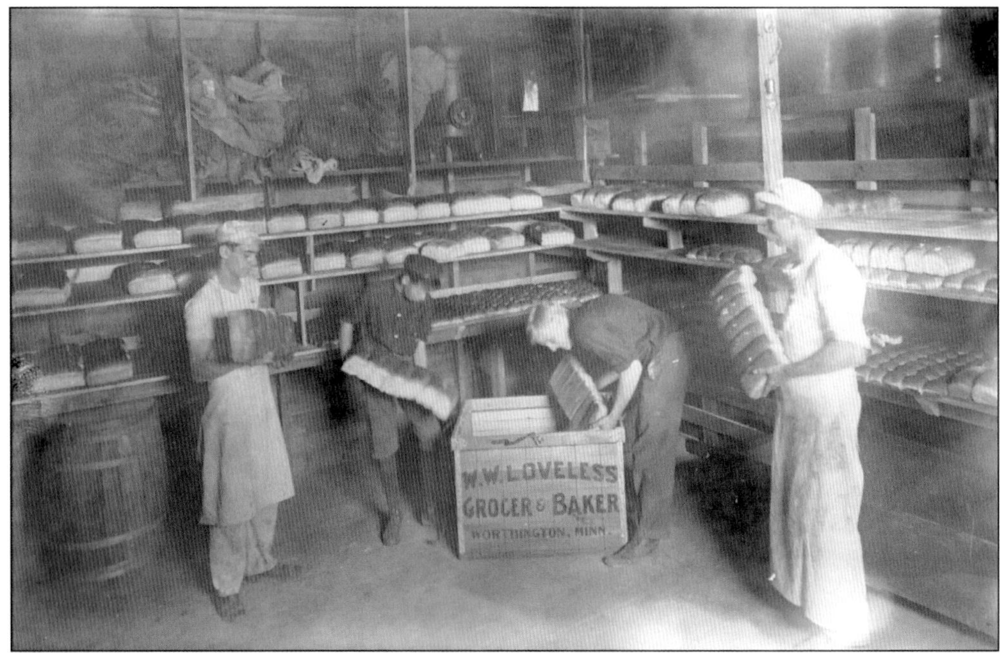

After completing two years of college at 13–14 years of age, William Loveless moved to Worthington with his family in 1872. He helped in his father's hotel and clerked for other merchants until he went into business for himself in 1892, when he opened a grocery store. In addition to groceries, Loveless's business included a bakery.

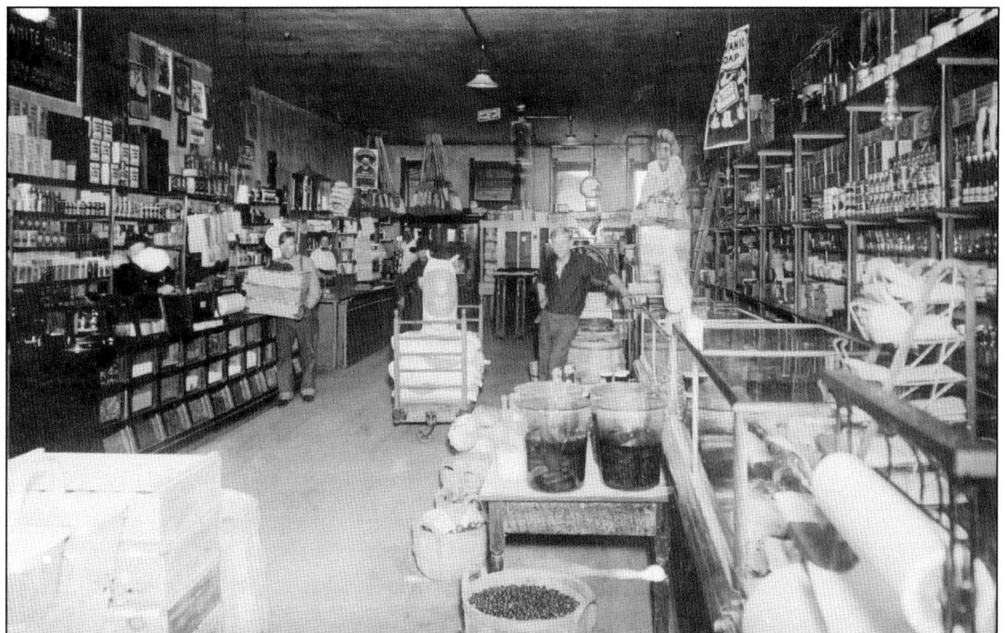

To promote and expand his growing business, Loveless decided to construct a new brick building to house both his grocery store and bakery operation. This structure, built in 1898, was located on Worthington's Tenth Street across from the courthouse. In this photograph of the store's interior, many of the products are packaged in bulk. Shown among the workers are Carl Larson, Nellie Crever, E. Church, and William Loveless Jr.

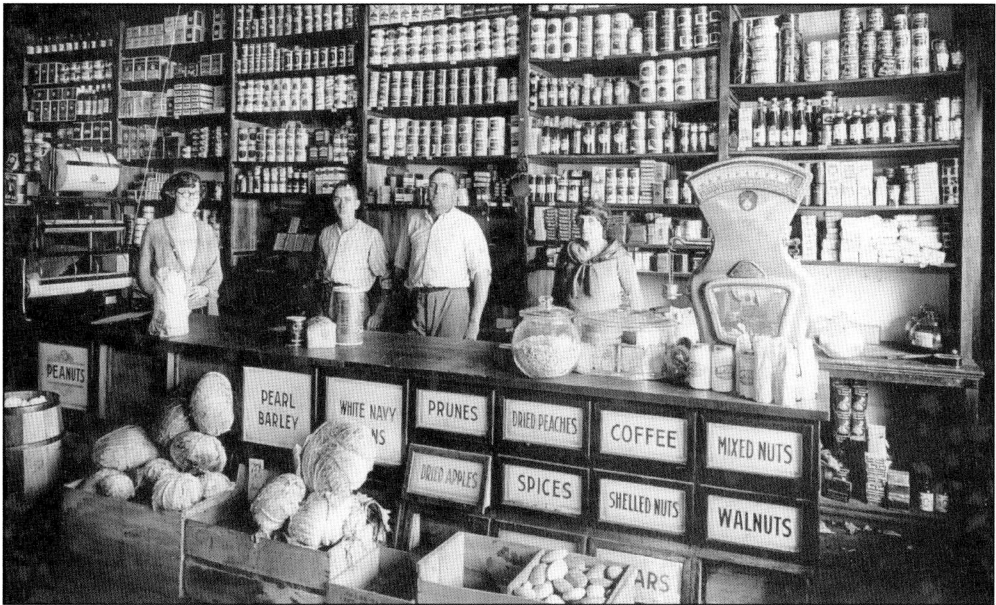

The Dundee Coop Store was unique. It was established in 1909 by approximately 100 men who formed a cooperative to share the costs of operating the town's general store. Shareholders received a dividend on their purchases and a share of the profits; other customers received a rebate on their purchases. The store sold a variety of goods such as groceries, crockery, glassware, furnishings, shoes, clothing, kerosene, and notions.

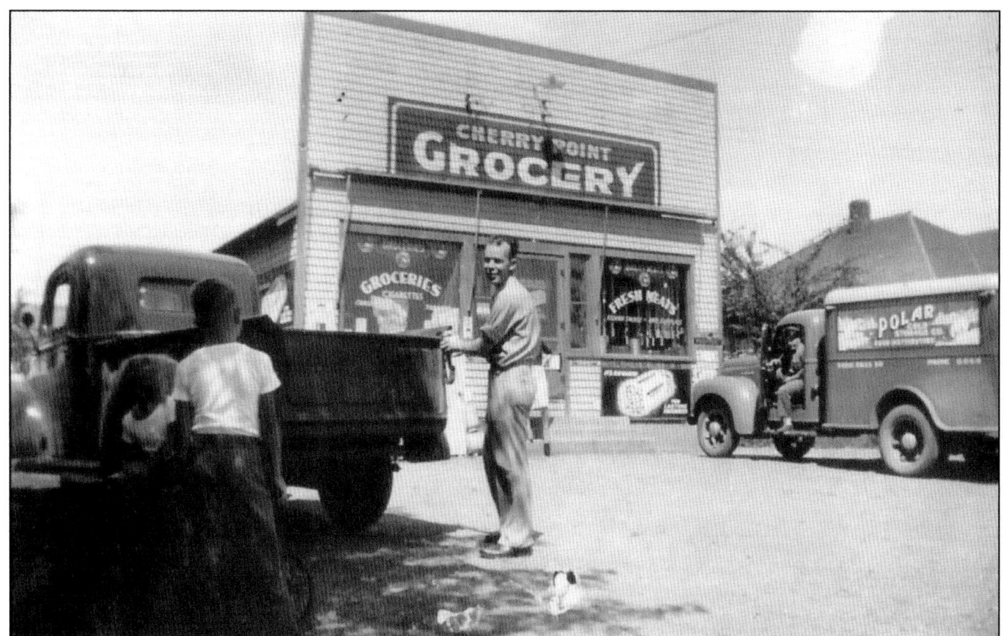

As Worthington grew, a new type of business developed—the neighborhood store. These small shops were located in residential areas to offer families convenient access to daily staples. The Cherry Point Grocery was started in 1936 by Ralph and Myrtle Gregorson on the north side of Lake Okabena. Customers could also purchase fishing bait, fishing gear, shotgun shells, and pocket knives, or they could rent a rowboat. (DG.)

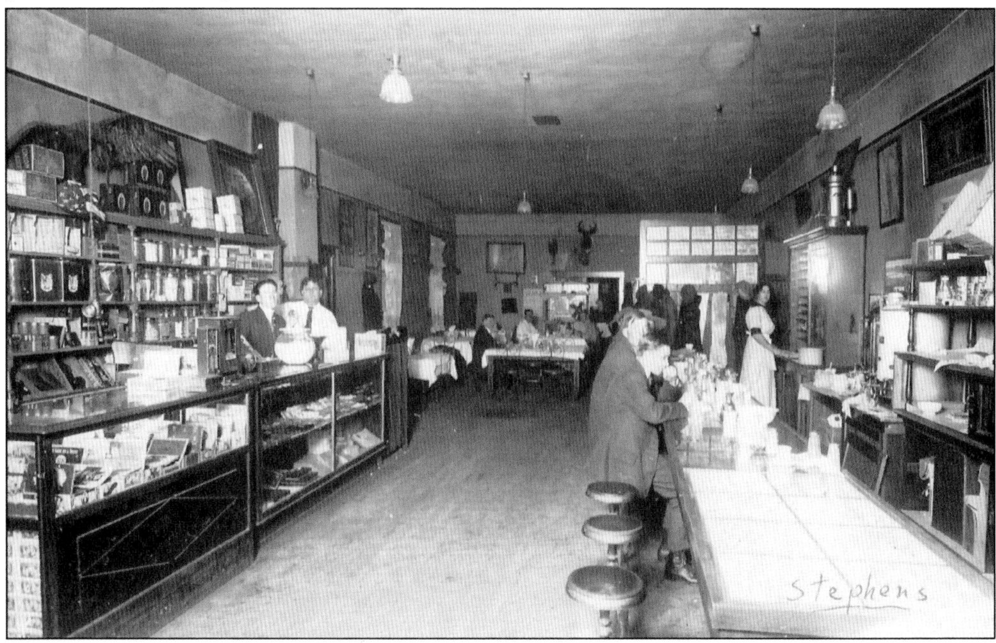

This interior photograph of a Worthington restaurant was taken around 1912. Though this eating establishment's precise location within the downtown area is unknown, it was believed to have been managed by H.W. Steffens. He purchased the café in 1907 from William Devaney, who had recently bought Chris Hogan's billiard and pool hall. (LFi.)

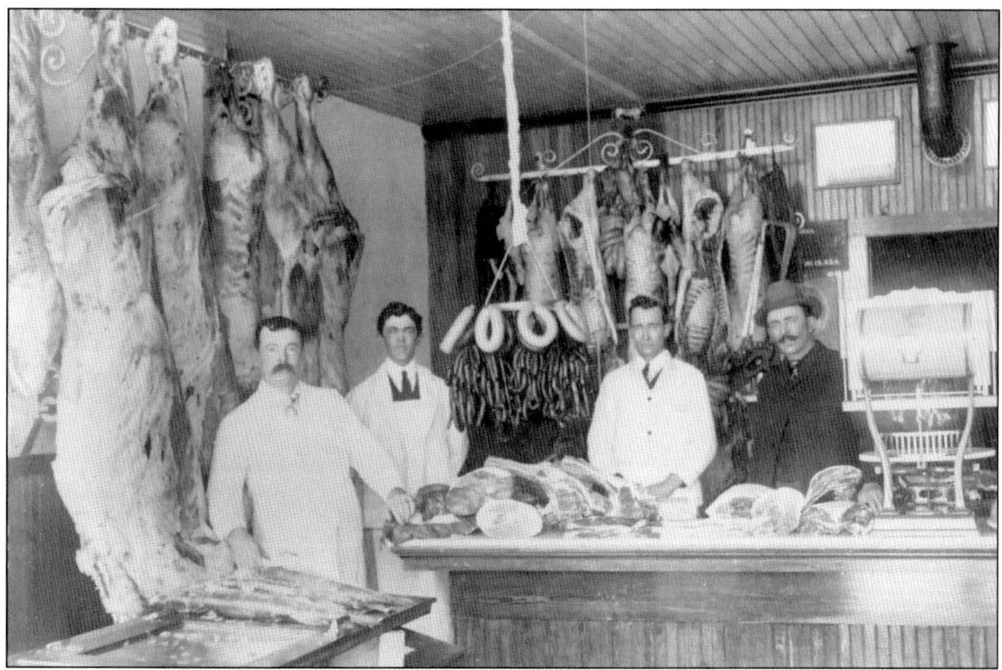

Occasionally, two separate but related businesses were owned by the same individual. In Wilmont, Tom Hayes and Jack Reilly managed a livestock yard where they bought and sold cattle and other farm animals. It seemed logical for them to open the town's first meat market. Pictured in their butcher shop are, from left to right, William Higgins, Jack Carey, Jack Reilly, and Tom Hayes.

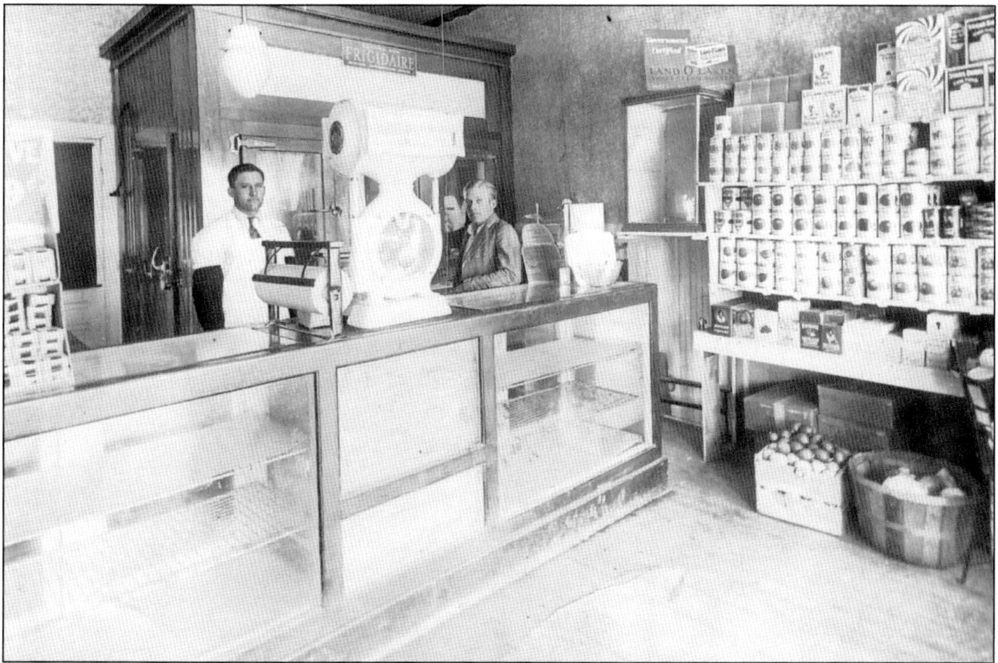

Pictured some 20 years later is the butcher shop in Lismore known as the Baltes Meat Market. Located in the Bach Hall building, the store was owned and operated by the two Baltes brothers, Leo and Matt. Standing behind their meat counter are Leo "Butch" Baltes (left) and Matt Baltes. (DL.)

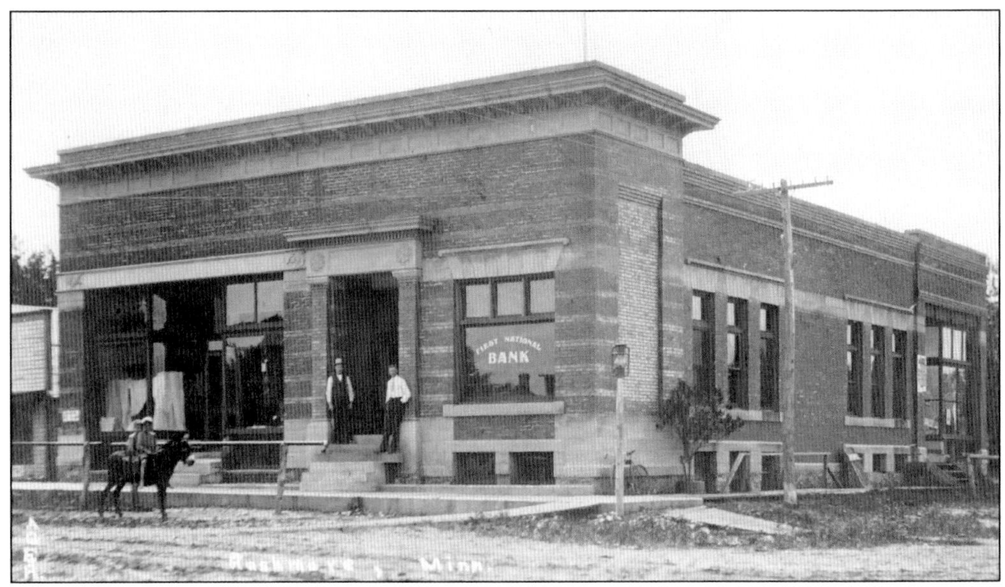

As the suppliers of monetary resources for families, farmers, and commercial businesses, banks played an important role in the growth and development of early communities. Rushmore was fortunate to have two such institutions. Established in May 1903, the First National Bank was an imposing brick structure on the corner of Main Street and Second Avenue. The building also housed the Rushmore Mercantile store and the town's post office.

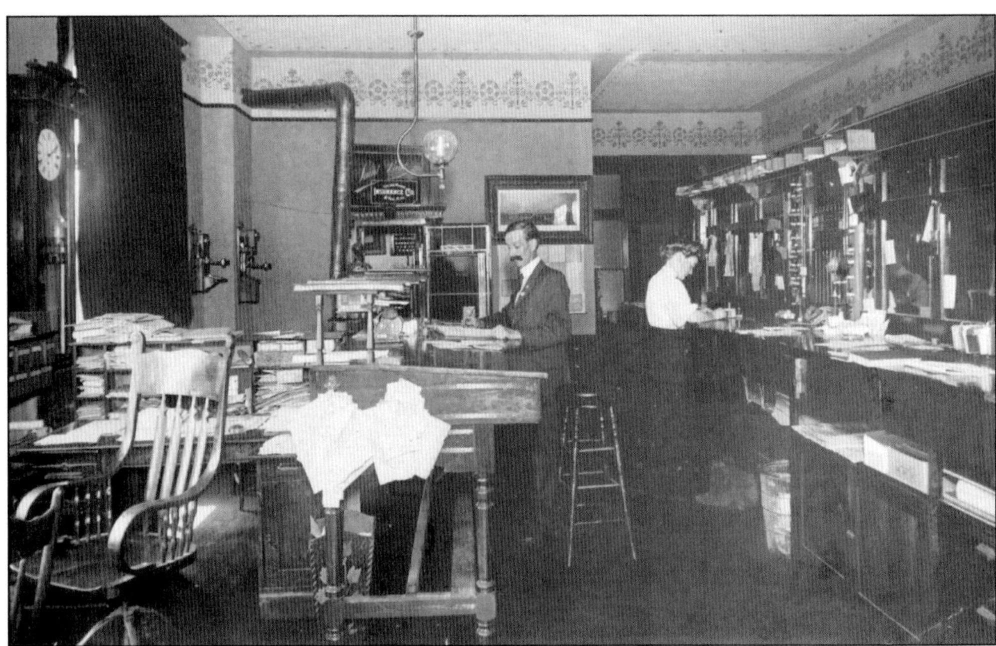

Just a block down Main Street, on the corner of First Avenue, stood the State Bank of Rushmore. Like its competitor, it was constructed in May 1903. Pictured conducting financial business are the bank's cashier and president, Salthiel Bedford, and a female teller. The State Bank building also provided space for other enterprises, including Constable's general store, the town's telephone exchange, an opera house, and a livery.

Hotels sprang up in the county's towns to provide sleeping accommodations for travelers, salesmen, or townspeople without other housing. In Adrian, George Slade purchased the Central Hotel, which he operated for five years before tearing it down. In 1891, he erected a new brick building, the Slade Hotel, on the same site. In addition to the lodging rooms and dining facilities, the Slade building housed a saloon and billiards parlor, a bank, and sample rooms for traveling salesmen. This property was listed in the National Register of Historic Places in 1975.

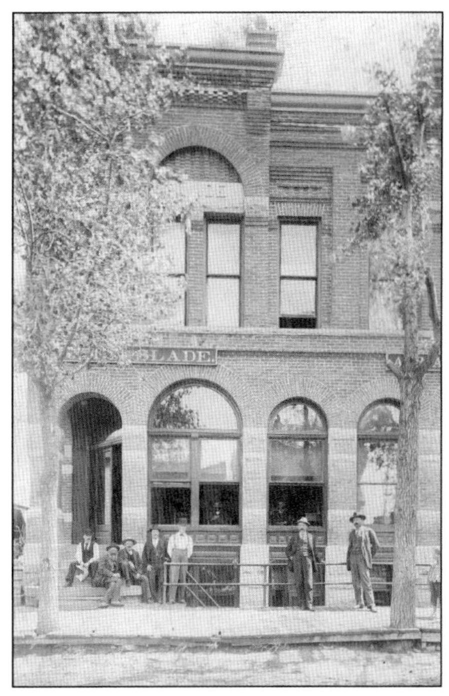

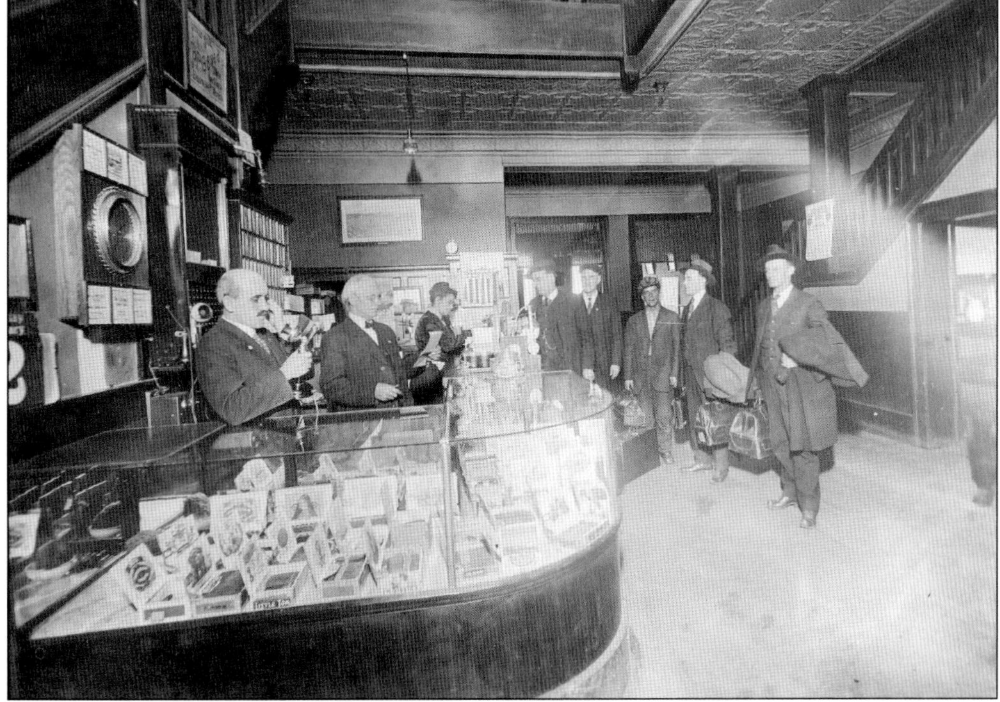

When the Thompson Hotel opened in 1912, it was the finest hotel between Sioux City and Mankato. The building had four different levels: the basement and street levels housed various retail shops, while the top two floors featured the guest rooms and a banquet hall. Behind the hotel's front desk are, from left to right, day clerk George Ireland, owner Peter Thompson, and his daughter Hannah. This property was listed in the National Register of Historic Places in 1984.

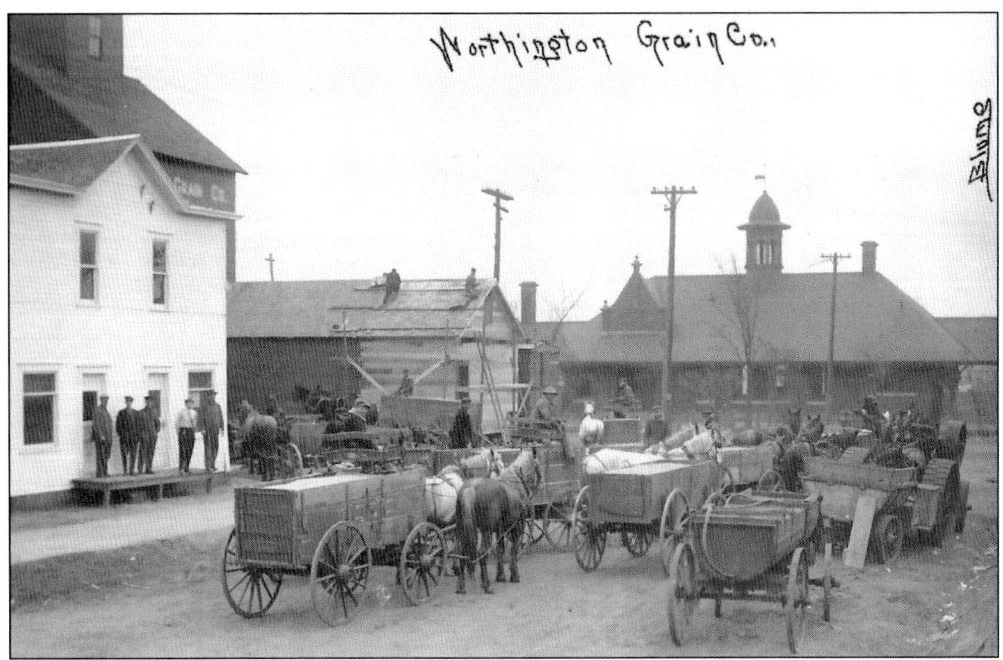

Grain companies preferred to locate their elevators close to railroads to make it easier to transport the farmers' crops to other markets. Here, several farmers are waiting to unload their wagons of grain at the Worthington Grain Company. In the meantime, a crew of workers is busy constructing and shingling another storage building.

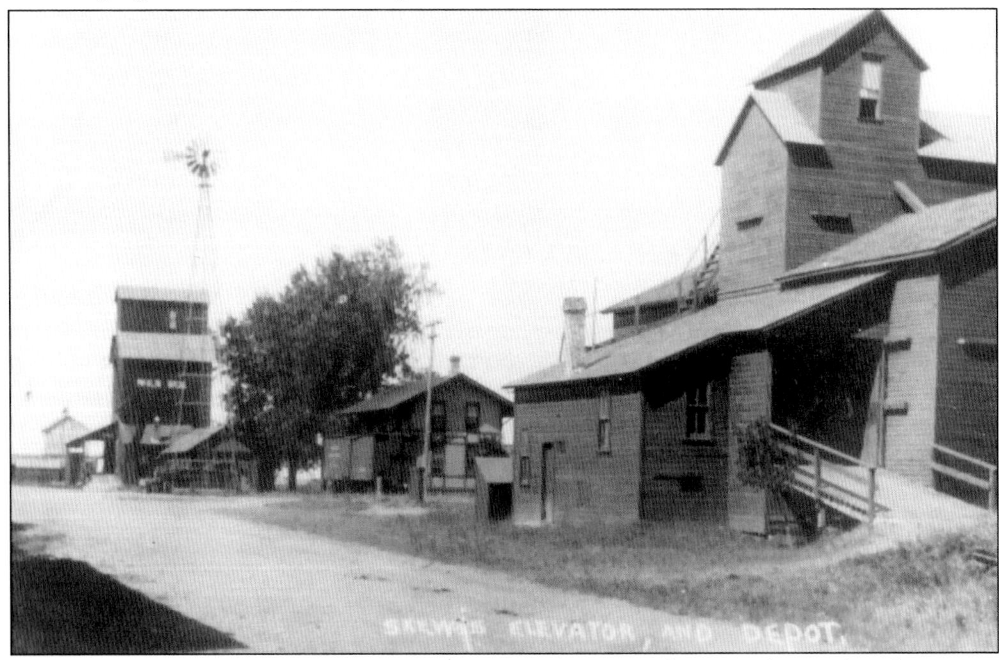

The Skewes Grain Elevator was one of the two grain elevators to be erected in Kinbrae by 1900. It was one of the enterprises established to take advantage of the townsite's location as a stop on the Southern Minnesota Railroad, which had extended its line from Heron Lake to Fulda. The elevator could purchase the harvested crops from local farmers and ship them on to larger markets.

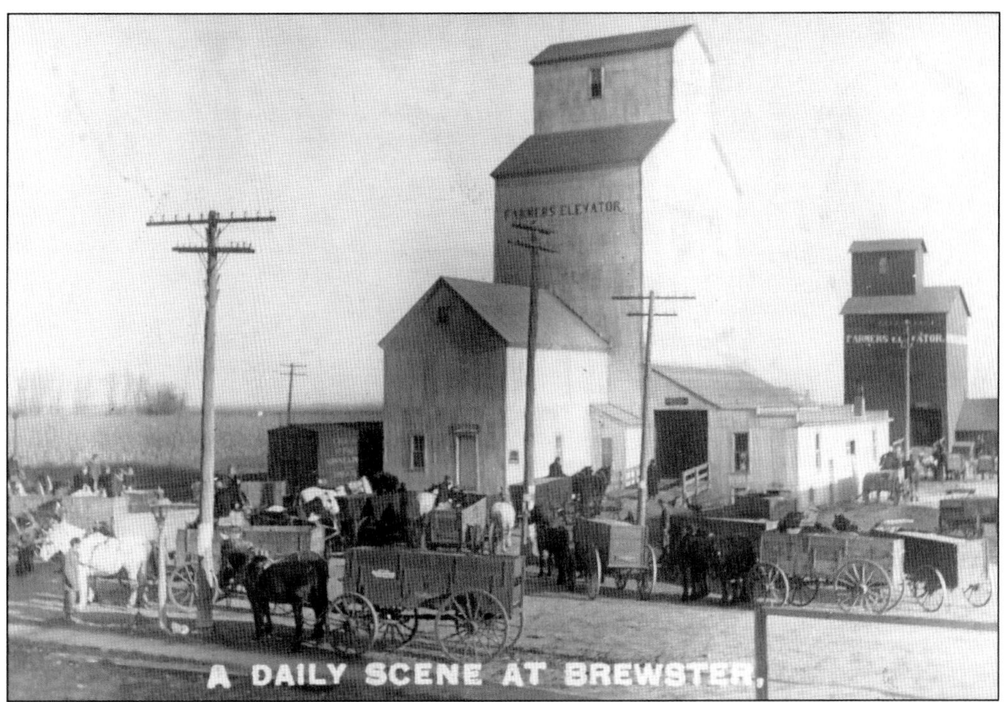

Even in the early 1900s, a good fall harvest day would bring farmers to the local elevator. Shown in this scene at the Brewster Farmers Elevator is a line of farmers with their horses and triple box wagons waiting to unload their crops so they could be stored or sold.

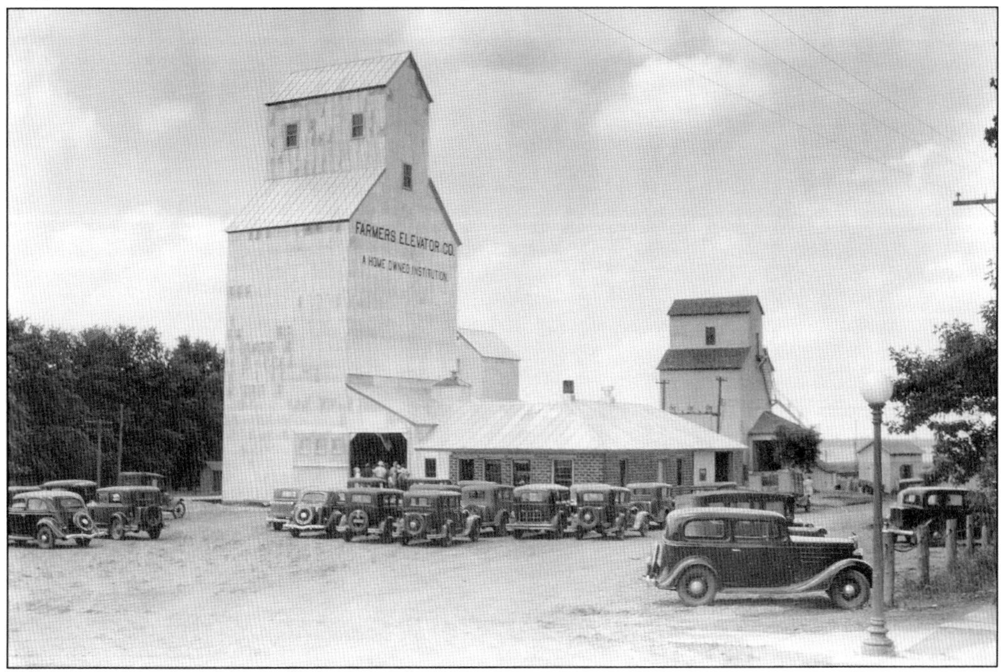

This photograph of a grain elevator was taken some 30 years later than the previous photograph in Brewster. It shows the Bigelow Farmers Elevator with a parking lot full of cars. What brought all these people to the elevator on this particular day is unknown.

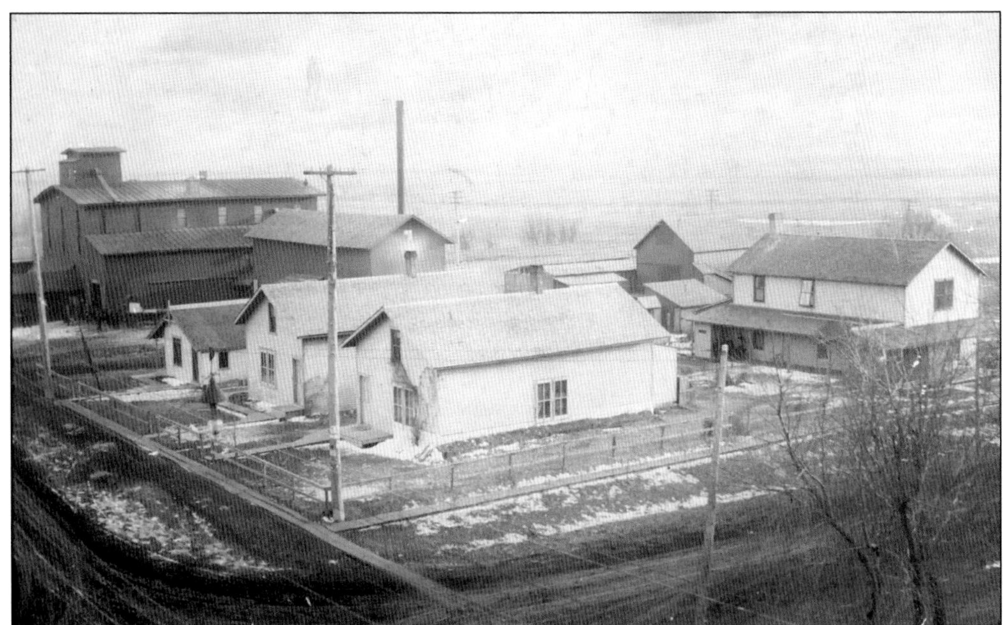

This multi-building complex was the site of the Worthington Milling Company, which was located in the vicinity of the current Vast Cable TV office. It was the county's oldest milling operation, capable of producing 150 barrels of flour and 50 tons of feed daily. Its products included several types of flour, including whole wheat, graham, buckwheat, and rye. Co-owner and miller J.D. Matteson came to Worthington after working in the milling business in Minneapolis.

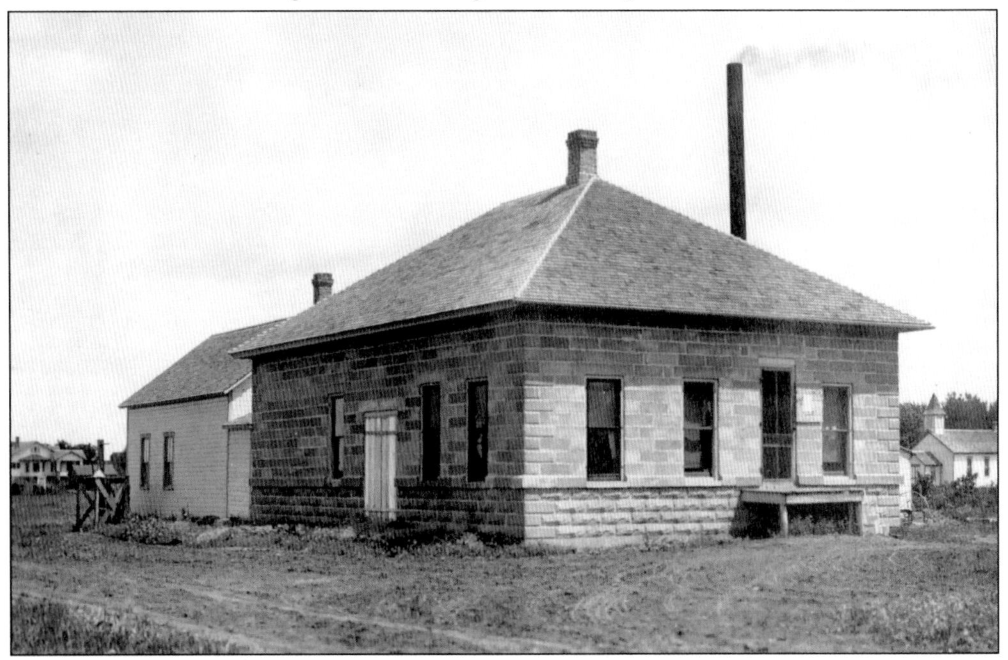

Creameries were established to process cow's milk into a variety of dairy products, including butter and cheese. This is the Rushmore Cooperative Creamery, which was established in 1894. Its first butter maker of record was G.W. Wheeler. In 1918, the creamery was purchased by E.O. Olson, who already owned the Worthington Creamery and Produce Company.

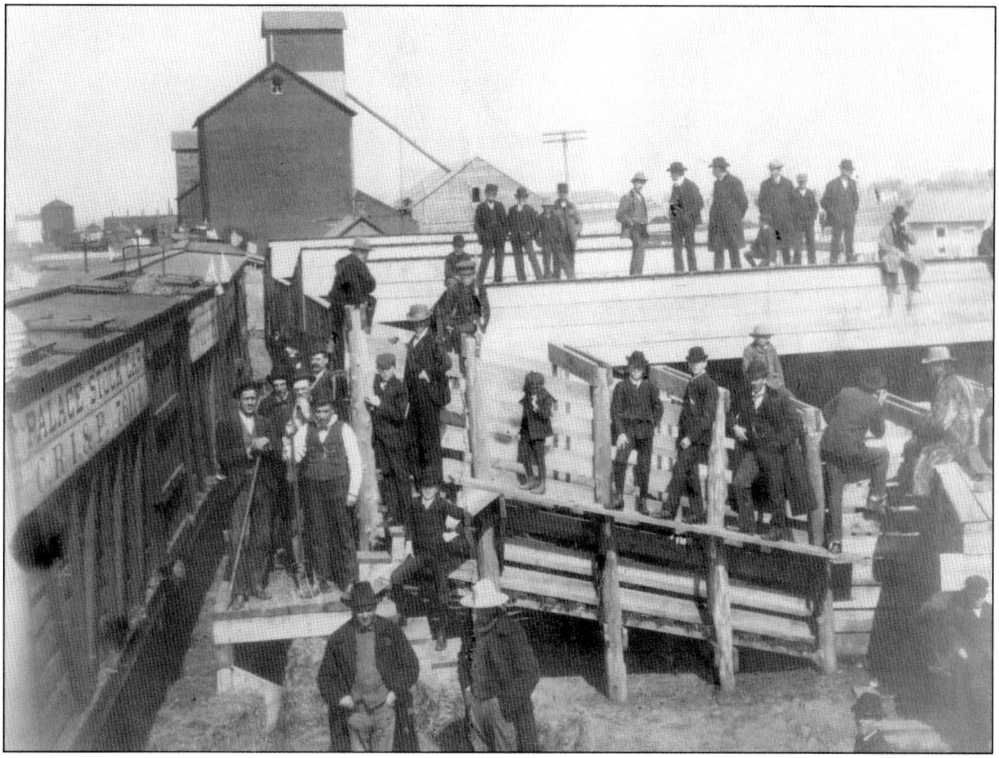

By the early 1900s, Ellsworth had become a big shipping center for cattle. Every two weeks at the local stockyard, hundreds of cattle would be loaded onto the Rock Island trains for shipment to the markets in Chicago. Some of the area's cattle ended up as far away as Montreal and England. Given the amount of cattle that were shipped, Ellsworth was often called the "Wichita of the north."

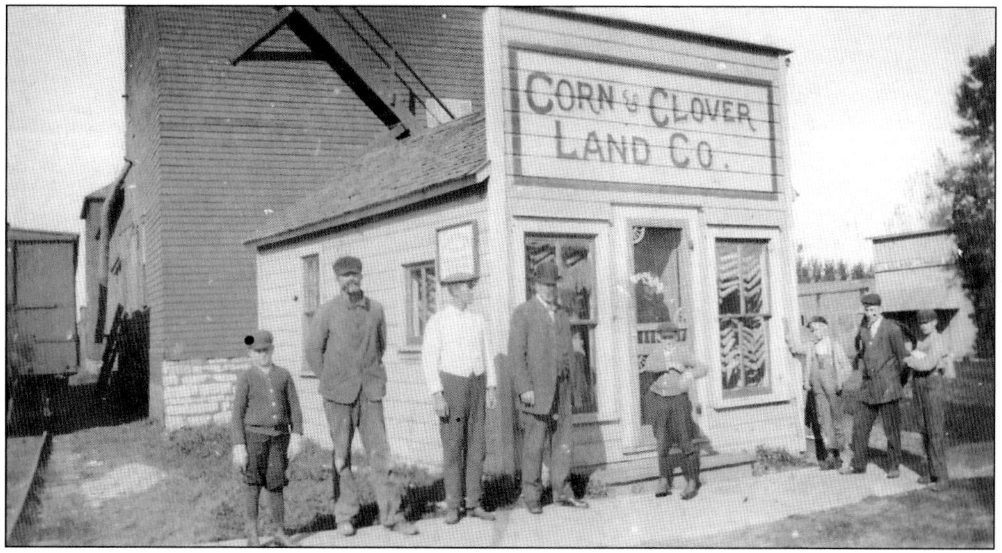

With settlers moving into Nobles County to acquire property for farming, land was frequently bought and sold. Land agents played an important role in managing these transactions. It appears this agent had his own private office known as Corn & Clover Land Co. While little is known about this Worthington business, it is believed to have been located close to a grain elevator.

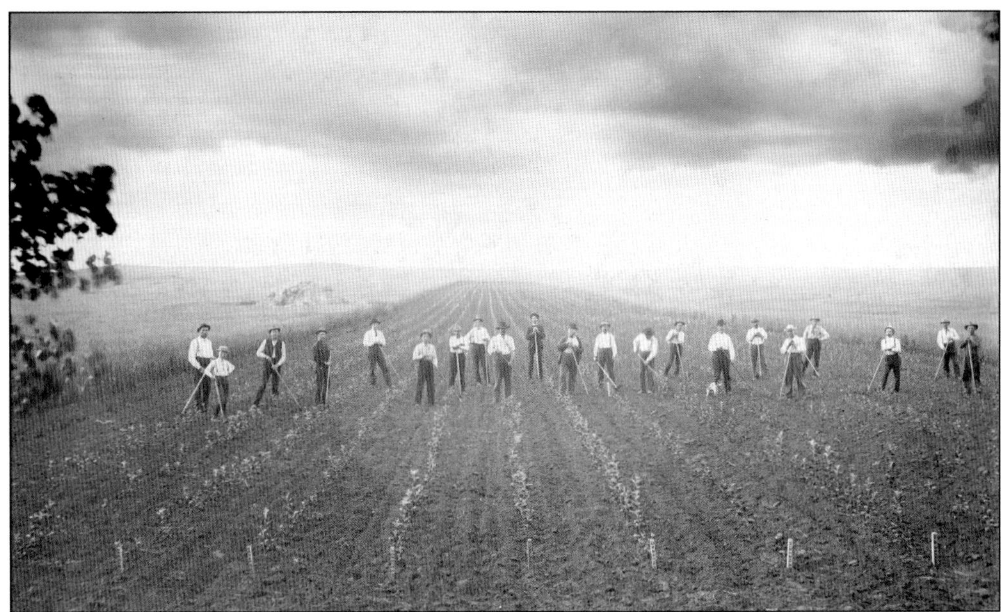

As new settlers established their farmsteads, there was a demand for seedling trees. Farmers wanted to plant tree groves to protect their farm buildings from the prairie winds. One of the area's earliest nurseries, the Kanaranzi Nursery, consisted of 15 acres of land west of Adrian. Established in 1894, it offered a full line of nursery stock, including 20 varieties of apple trees.

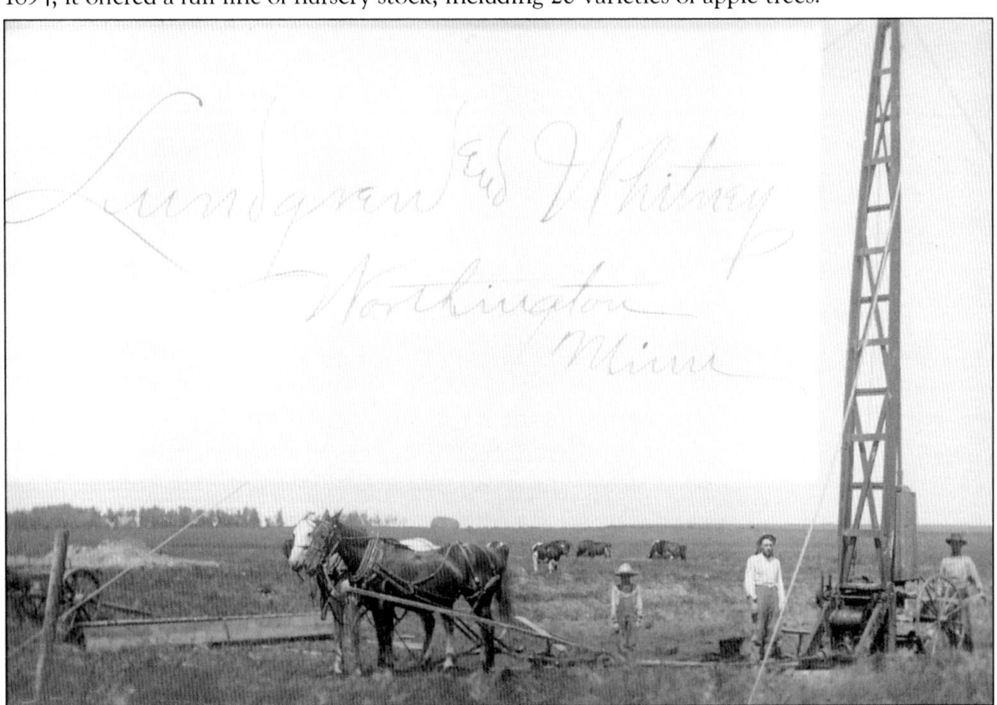

In the early days, since there was no running water available in rural areas, farmers would have to come up with their own source of water. The only option was to have a well dug. Water could then be pumped for household use or given to livestock. This photograph postcard was apparently sent to prospective customers by Lundgren and Whitney to promote their well drilling business.

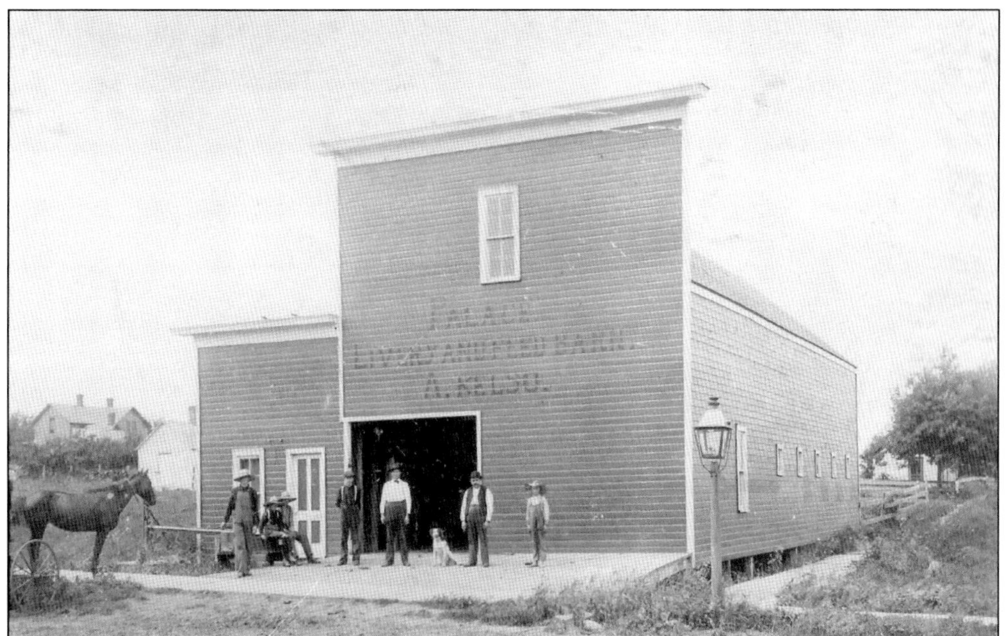

Before the advent of the automobile, horses were the primary mode of transportation. Livery barns were established to offer a place that could feed and care for people's horses while they were in town conducting business. In Wilmont, individuals could "park" their horses at the Palace Livery and Feed Barn, which was owned by A. Kelso. In 1919, the building was destroyed by fire.

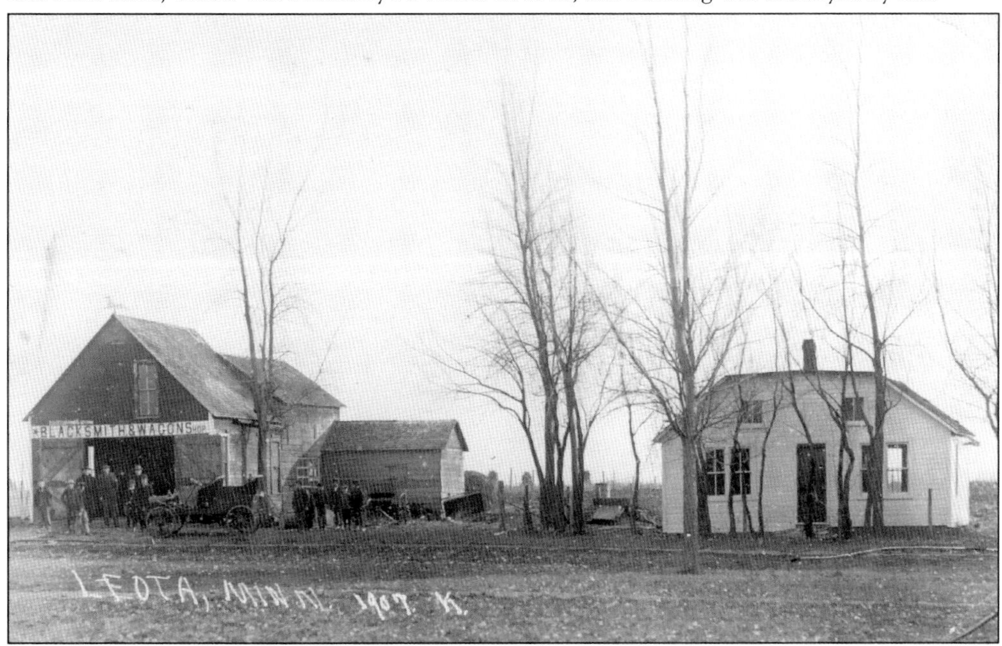

One of the earliest businesses established in nearly every town was a blacksmith shop. These tradesmen could repair the equipment needed by farmers and others to do their daily work. This is a picture of Leota's blacksmith shop, which was started by a young Dutchman, Jan Kallemyen, in the early 1900s. His father, Martin, was the person most responsible for encouraging Dutch families from northwest Iowa to resettle in Leota.

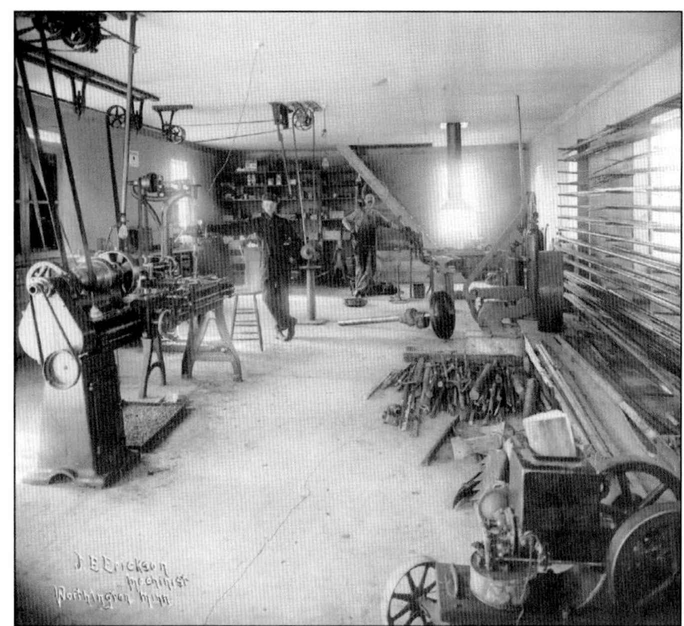

J.E. Erickson and his partner, Oscar Blood, established the Worthington Plumbing Company in 1905. This undated photograph is entitled "J.E. Erickson, Machinist." Without more complete records, one is left to wonder. Had Erickson and Blood dissolved their partnership by the time this photograph was taken? Had Erickson left the plumbing business to become a machinist? Did the photographer simply mislabel the photograph? Though a picture can be worth a thousand words, it still may not answer all the questions.

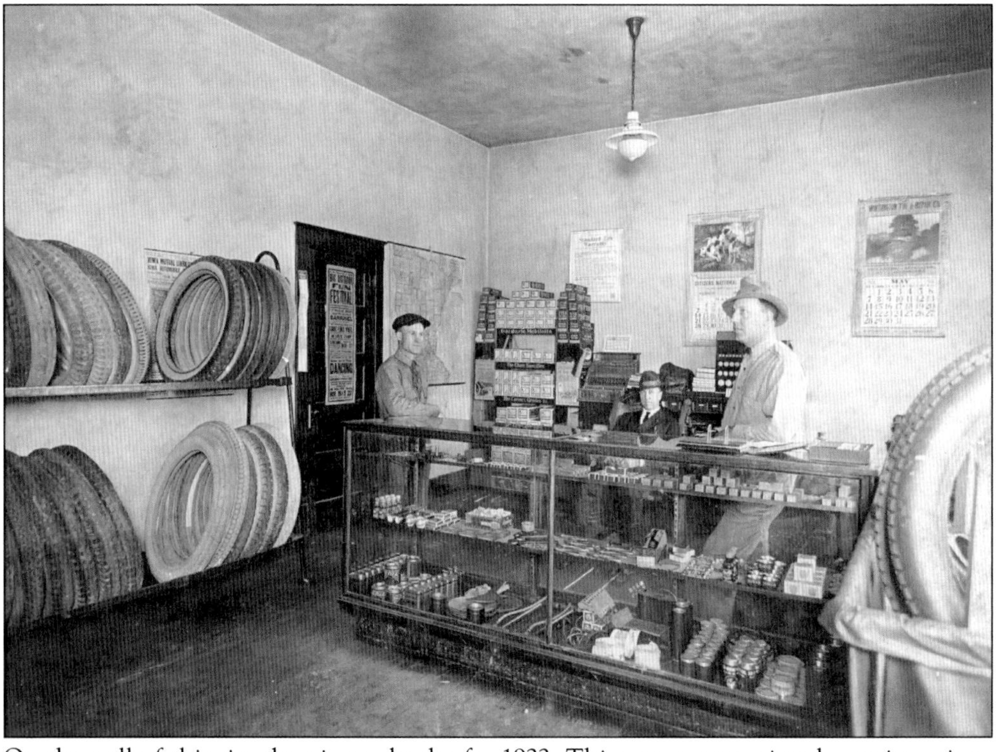

On the wall of this tire shop is a calendar for 1922. This was a promotional premium given away by the Worthington Tire and Repair Shop, believed to be the same business shown in this photograph. It was located at 900 Third Avenue, which was immediately across the street from the former National Guard armory.

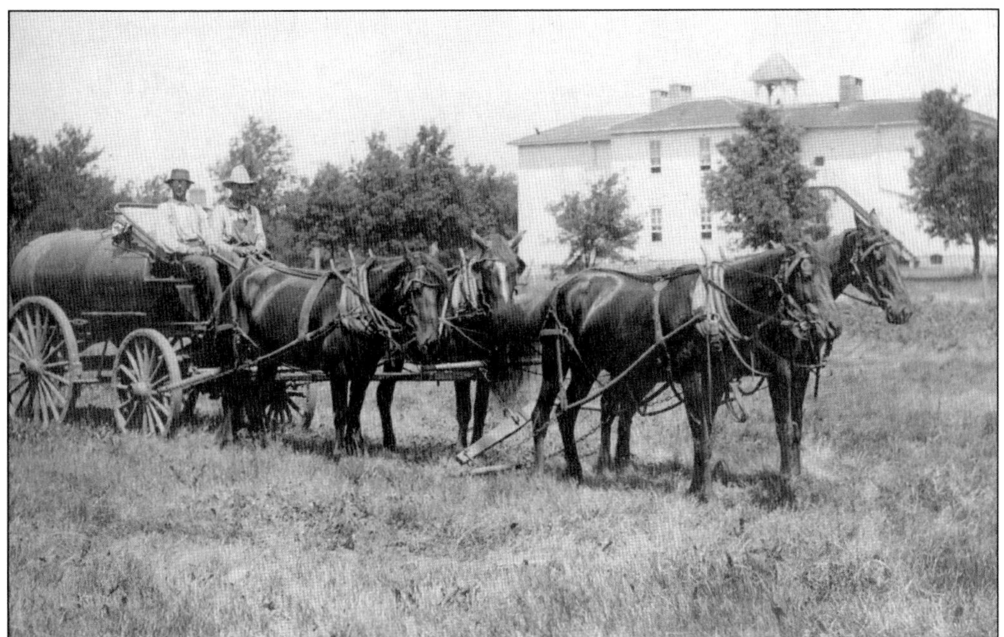

In the early 1900s, Henry Boyer ran a dray line service (to transport goods a short distance by means of a cart and dray horses) in the Round Lake area. He regularly transported farmers' milk to the creamery, unloaded coal from railroad cars, and hauled sand from Round Lake for construction purposes. In this photograph, he and his helper, Ed Jenkins, are delivering kerosene or gas for Standard Oil Company.

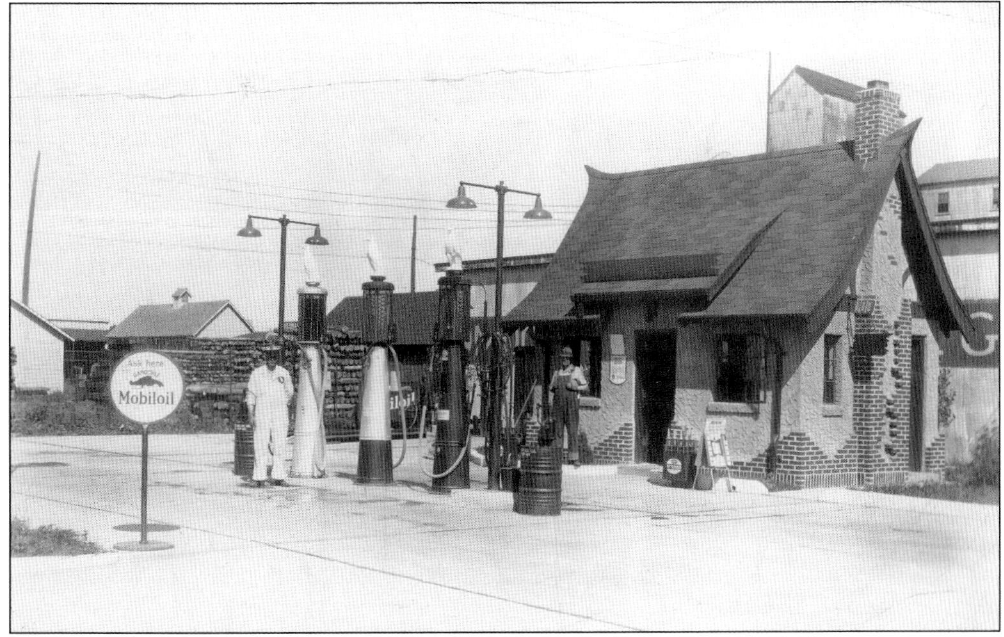

Early gas stations were not the oversized convenience stores of today. Pictured here are John Kingery, attendant, and T.P. Baker, agent, at the White Eagle service station on the southeast corner of Second Avenue and Ninth Street in Worthington. Notice the white eagles perched on top of the gas pumps. There was some brand of gas station at this site from 1932 to 1965.

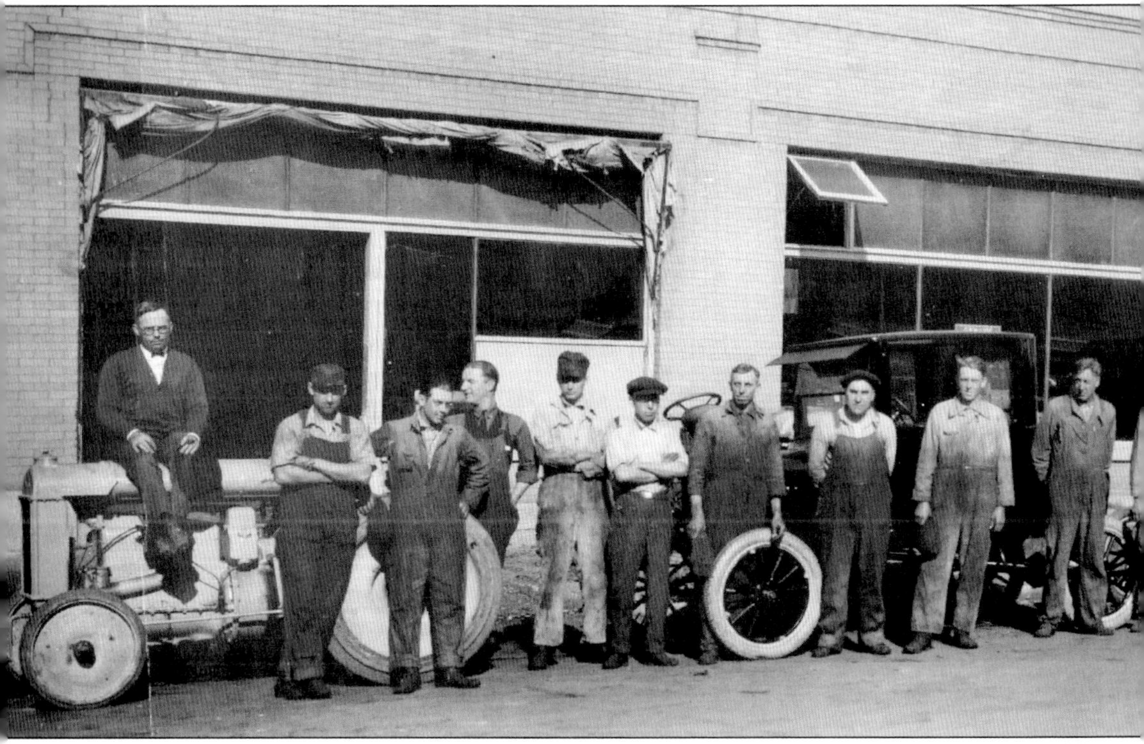

H.E. Tellander's automotive career began in the early 1900s. He first went into business for himself in 1912 when he set up a repair shop on Ninth Street across from the old YMCA, which at the time was the town's first armory. In 1917, to expand his enterprise, Tellander decided to lease the former Ullrich Garage building on Tenth Street, Worthington's primary thoroughfare. He now had ample room to sell new and used cars in addition to repairing them. Nine years later, in

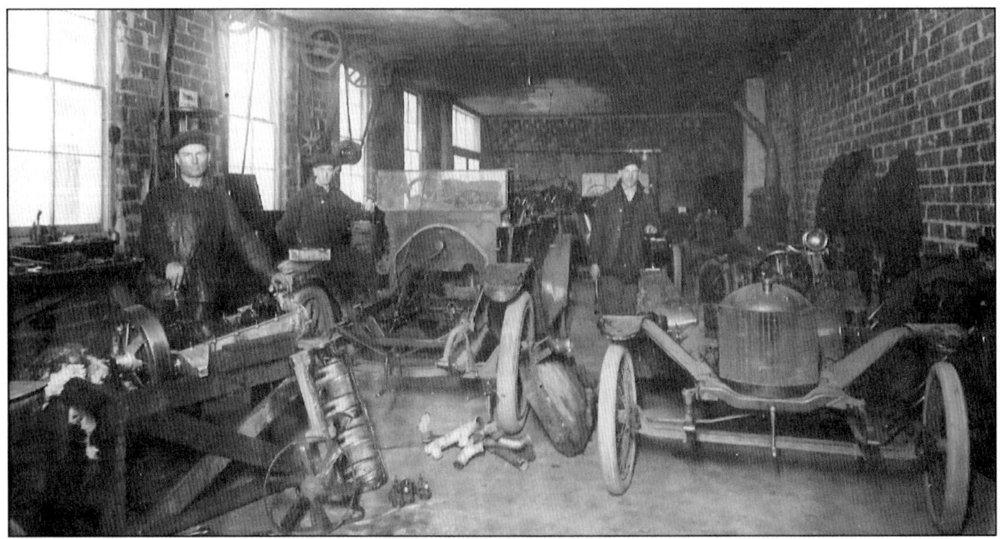

This interior view of the Tellander building shows three of the mechanics working to repair some of the cars. Working conditions, although probably good for the time, seem less than ideal. The cars are crammed into the available space, leaving little room for the workers to maneuver. There is a potbelly stove for heat, and the windows appear to be the primary source of light. (LG.)

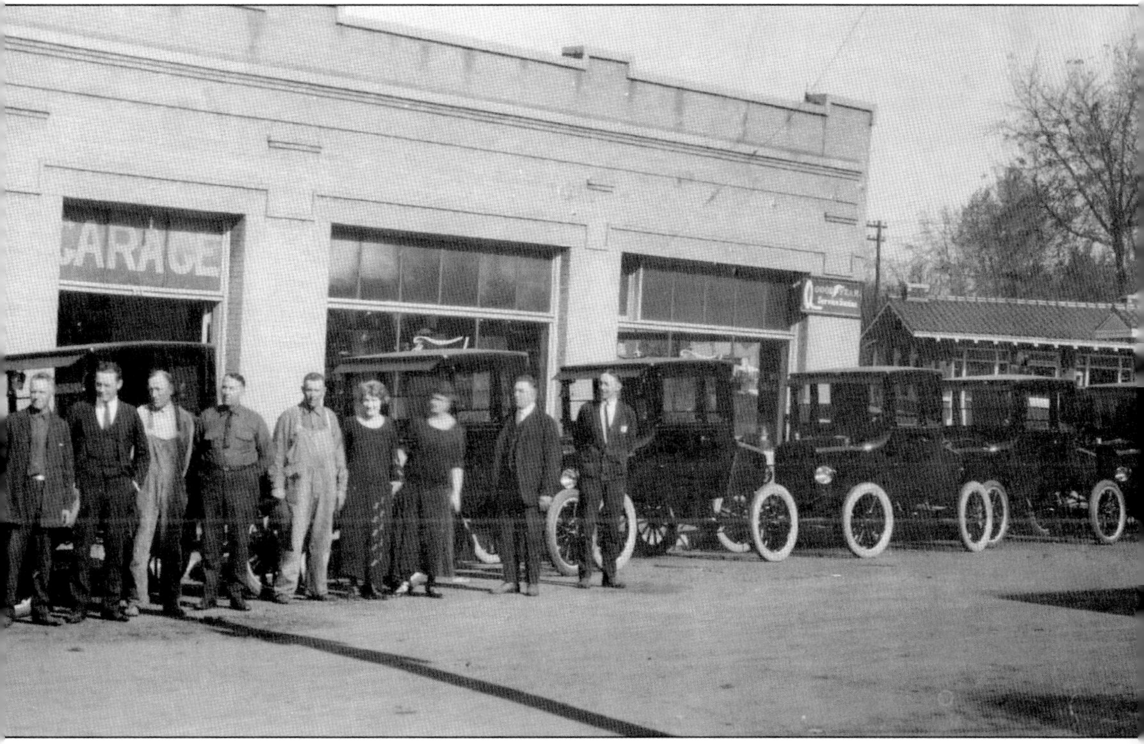

1926, he took on a partner, J.C. Hagge, and changed the dealership's name to Tellander-Hagge Ford. They built a gas station on an adjacent lot so they could offer more complete service to their customers. For years, the Tellander-Hagge business anchored the north side of Worthington's downtown. This photograph was taken around 1920. (LG.)

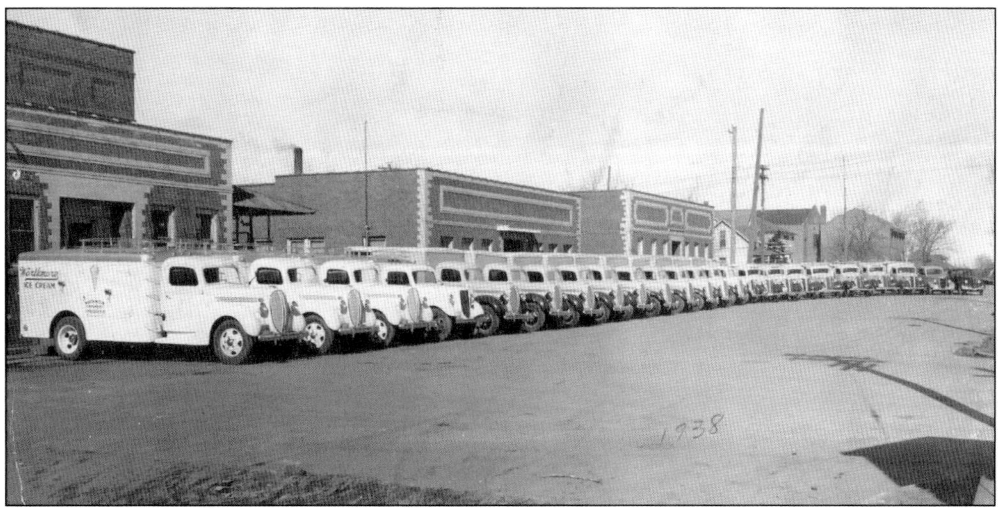

Undoubtedly, one of Worthington's cornerstone industries during the first half of the 20th century was the Worthington Creamery and Produce Company, founded by E.O. Olson. He built his business empire by expanding the markets for his day-to-day products: eggs, butter, chickens, and ice cream. Olson developed his ice cream plant during the Great Depression and coined a special brand name to market it—Worthmore. Here is the fleet of 1938 Ford refrigerated trucks he used to have it delivered. (LG.)

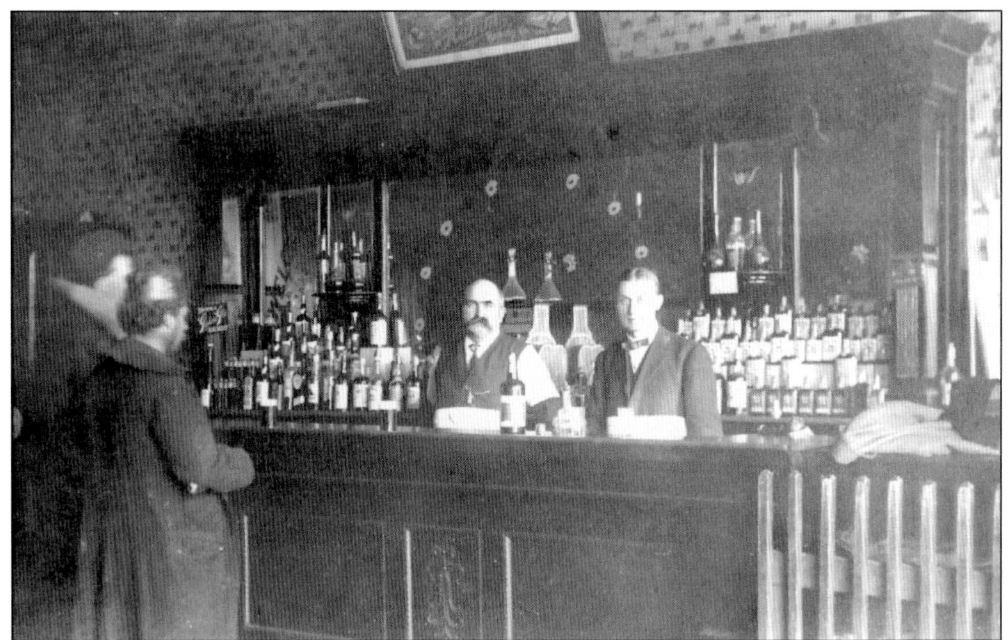

The term "saloon" can conjure up images of the drinking and gambling establishments of the Old West. This photograph of an early-20th-century prairie town saloon was taken in Wilmont around 1913. The bar, known as Broich Saloon, was owned and managed by Chris Broich. He is shown here at left behind the bar with bartender Thomas Henrichs.

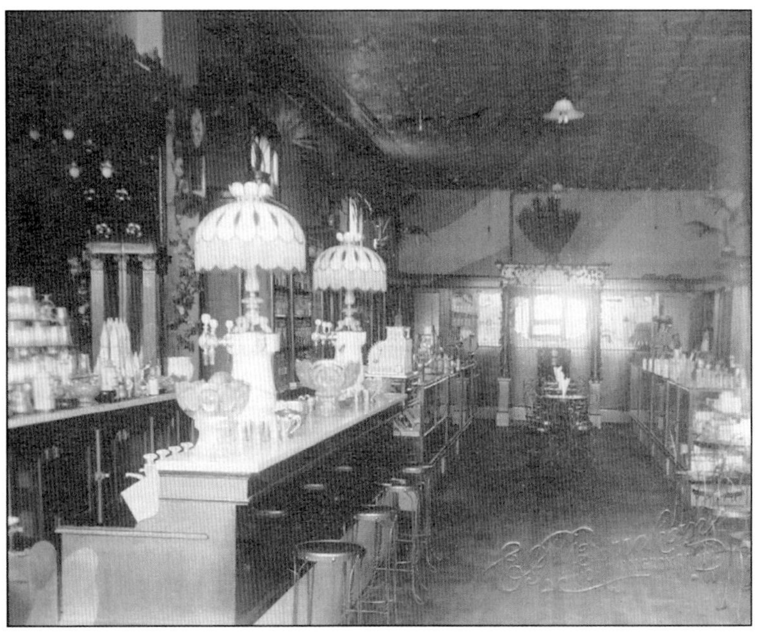

The exact location of this early Worthington soda fountain is not known. It certainly could have been in Caserato's Ice Cream and Confectionary Shop in the Thompson Hotel building. Another possibility would be one of the town's drugstores, which also offered ice cream sundaes and soda drinks.

Four

Horses, Trains, Planes, and Automobiles

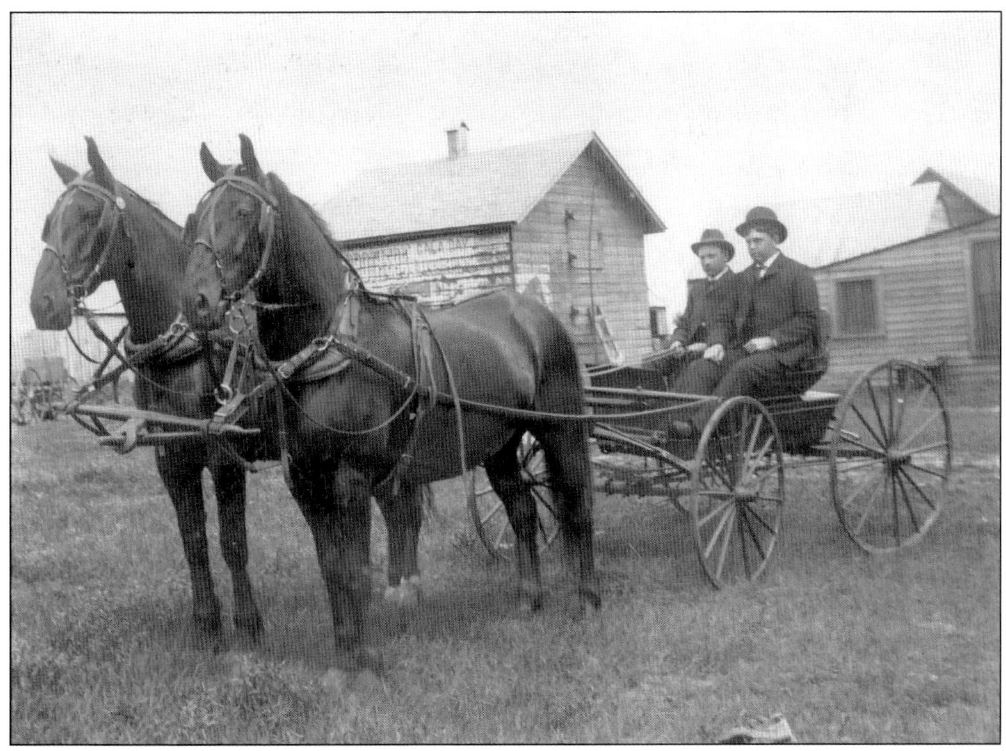

For the first 40 years of Nobles County's history, horses were the primary mode of transportation. More often than not, they pulled a wagon or buggy that could accommodate more than one passenger at a time. In this photograph, Round Lake residents James Bixby and his friend appear to be on their way to church or a formal meeting, given their attire.

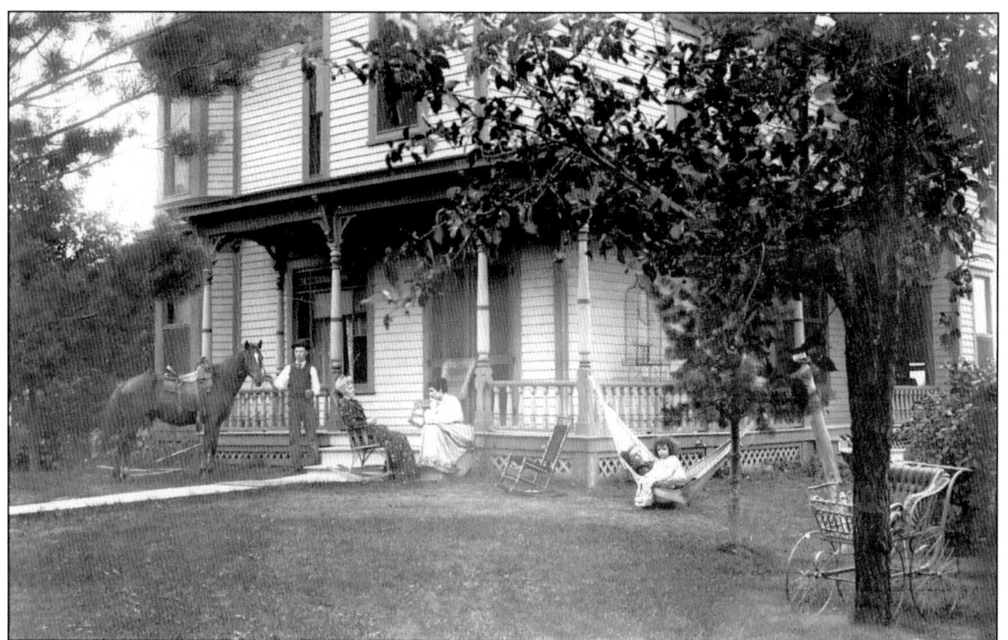

This photograph was taken by Worthington photographer E.F. Buchan in the late 1800s. The exact location of the house is unknown, as is identity of the subjects. The man of the house is holding the reins of his saddled horse, while the rest of the family members are relaxing. (HDH.)

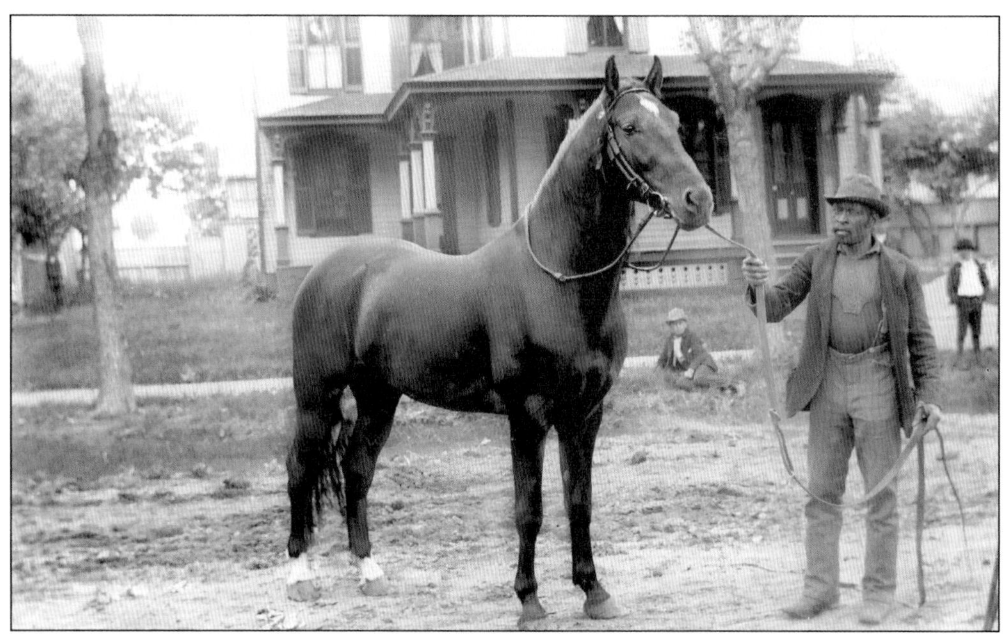

This picture was also taken by E.F. Buchan during the same period. Though the black man is unidentified, it is believed that this photograph was taken someplace in Worthington. According to census records, there were very few people of color living in the county during these early years. (HDH.)

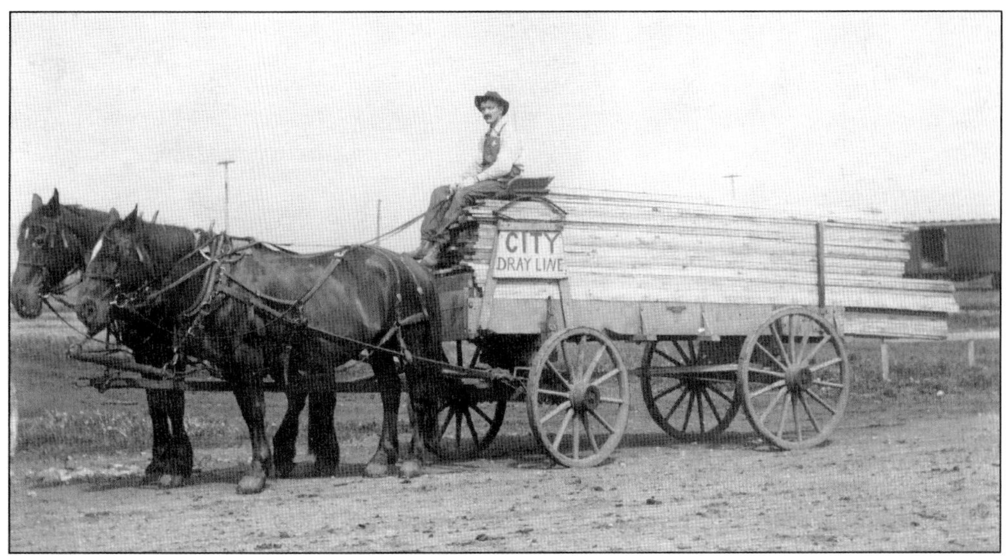

Prior to 1915, most short-haul work was handled by horses and wagons. Almost every town in the county had someone who offered dray line service. In Lismore, it was Jerome Hansen. Here, his hired man is hauling a load of lumber with a wagon that has a sign advertising Hansen's business.

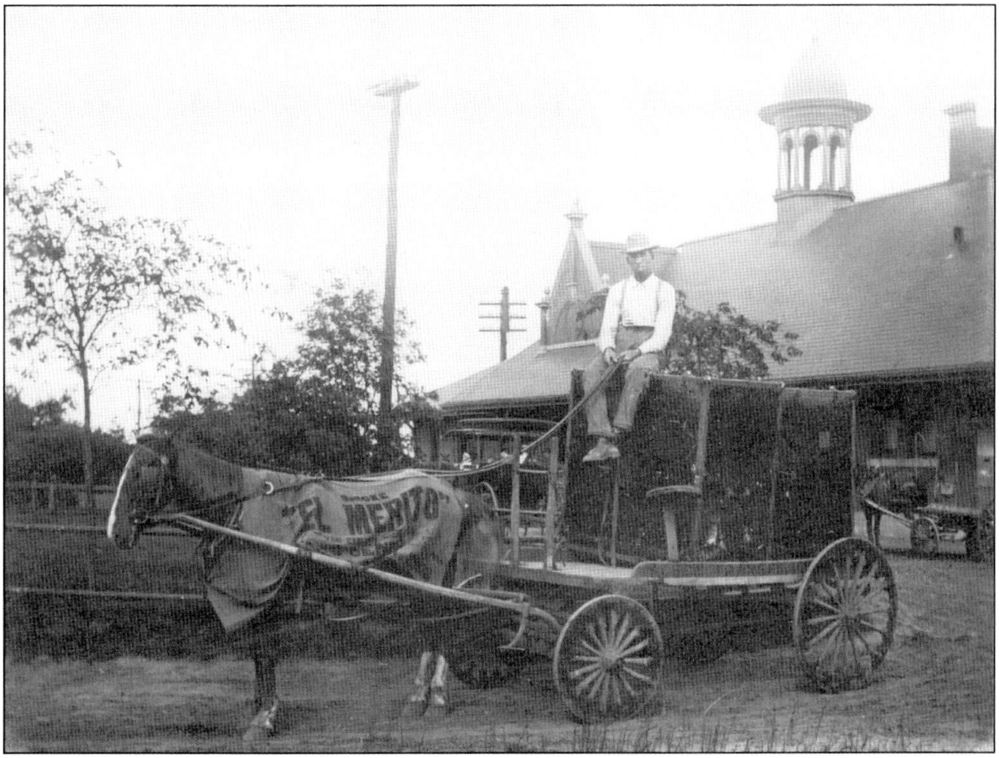

In this 1908 image, dray man Fred Rose is parked in front of the railroad depot on Worthington's First Avenue. He is sitting on the container used for storing the products he is hauling, which could have been delivered by train. His horse is wearing a blanket advertising El Merito cigars, a promotion probably paid for by a local merchant. Behind Rose's wagon is another dray cart parked in front of the train station.

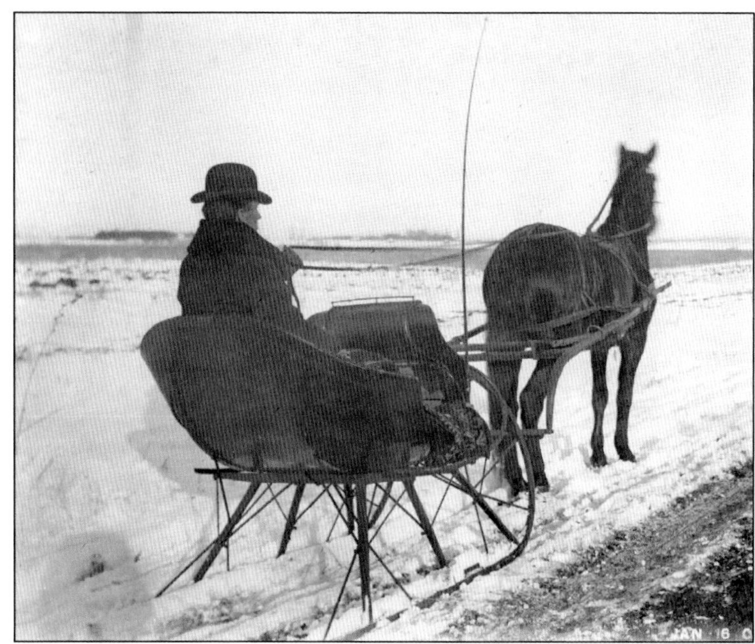

Given the challenges of road travel during the winter months, early settlers needed to have an alternative to a wheeled buggy to navigate deep snow. Sleighs or bobsleds pulled by a one- or two-horse hitch were a popular means of winter travel. This man could have been a local doctor making a house call to a patient; there appears to be a satchel resembling a physician's bag in the sleigh.

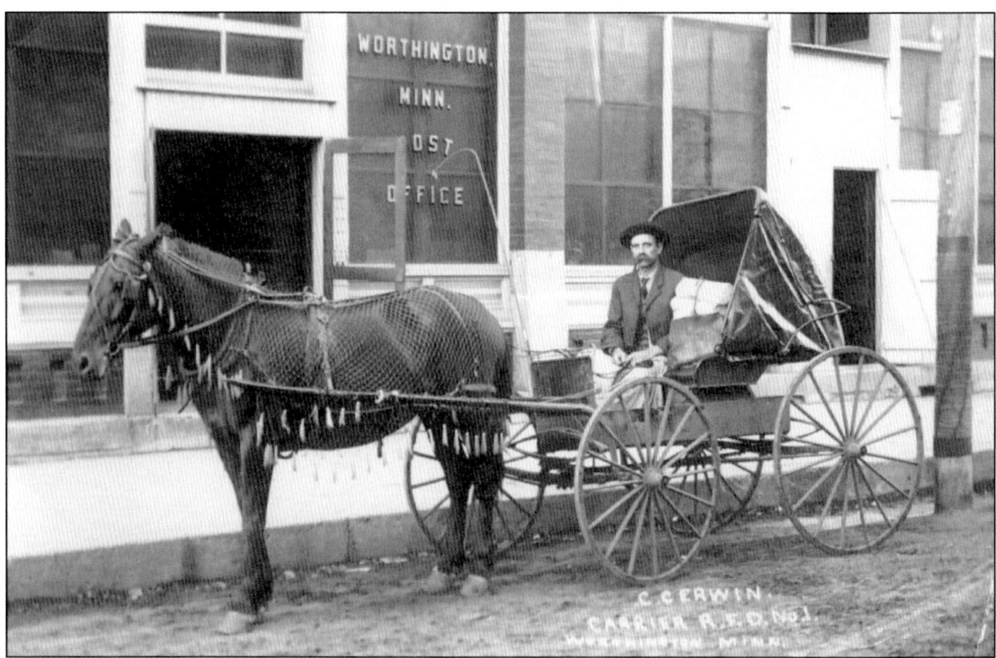

Even the mailman relied on horse power to get the mail delivered. C.C. Erwin, the rural mail carrier for Worthington's Rural Free Delivery Route No. 1, is parked with his horse and buggy in front of Worthington's post office, which was located in the back of the State Bank building. From the bundle of mail stacked in the buggy and on his seat, Erwin appears to be getting ready to make his daily mail run.

On July 25, 1900, E.F. Buchan took a photograph of several railroaders posing by steam engine No. 1 of the Chicago, Minneapolis, St. Paul & Omaha Railroad. It was parked on a sidetrack in the depot yard. One of the men pictured is Guy Otis Bigelow, a train engineer who was coincidently from the town of Bigelow. The station's water tank can be seen behind the train engine.

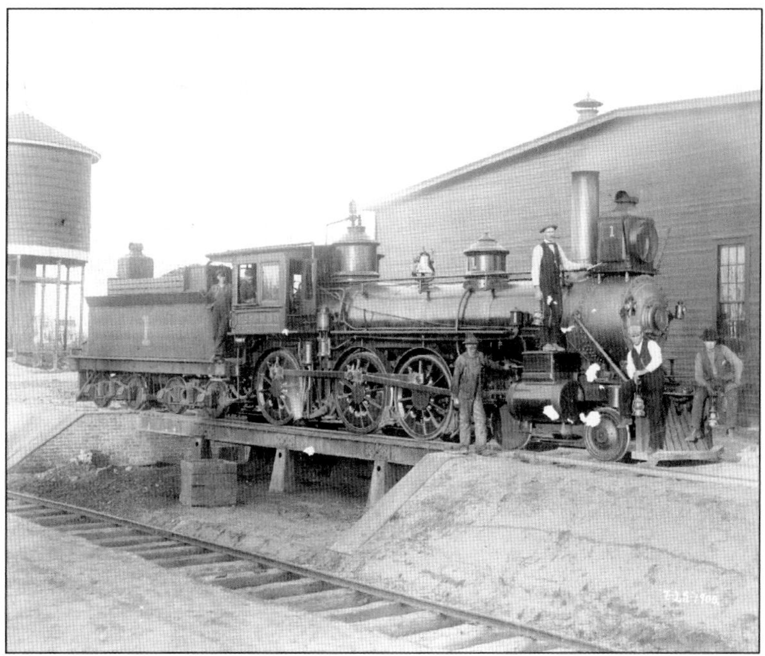

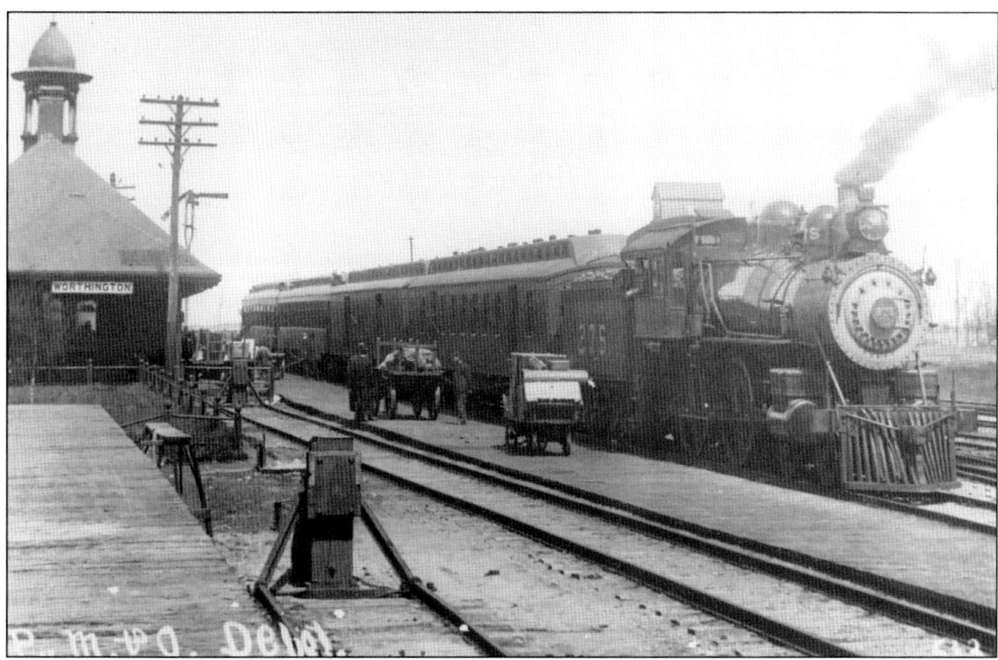

During the heyday of railroads, several trains a day could pass through a train station, especially in a larger town like Worthington. The Chicago, Minneapolis, St. Paul & Omaha Railroad's steam engine No. 275 is pulling a six-car train, including a coal car and four passenger cars. There are several rail carts being used to haul luggage to and from the train. The top of one of the grain elevators can be seen above the train engine.

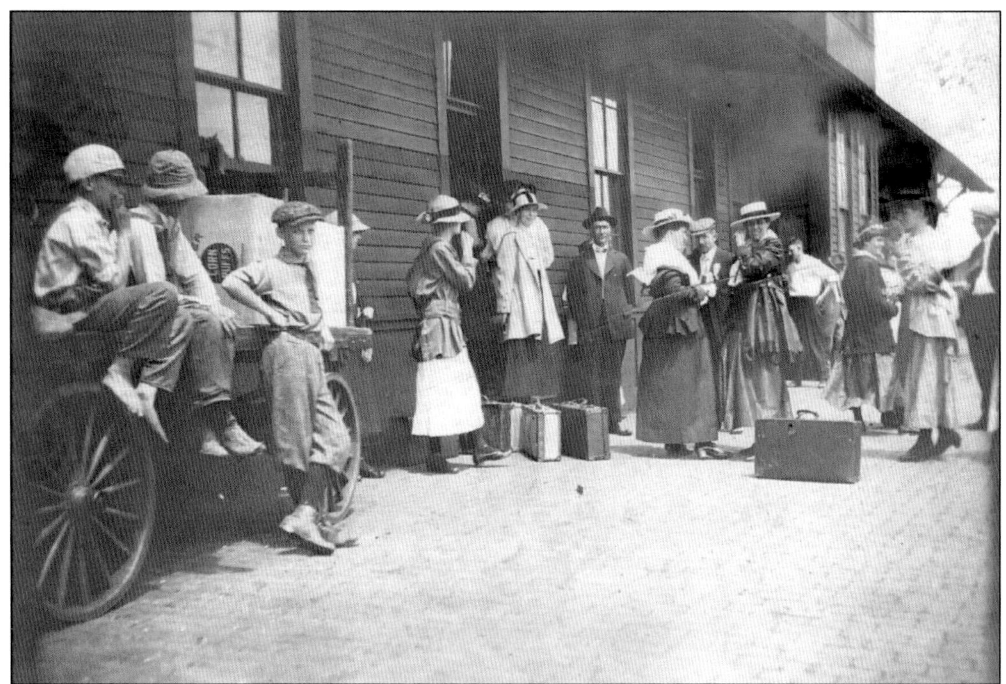

Given the popularity of rail transportation, depots could sometimes be filled with passengers or with people waiting to pick up travelers. The depots typically had several benches and chairs to accommodate those waiting. During pleasant weather, some people chose to wait outside the depot, as seen in this picture of the Worthington station. (TG.)

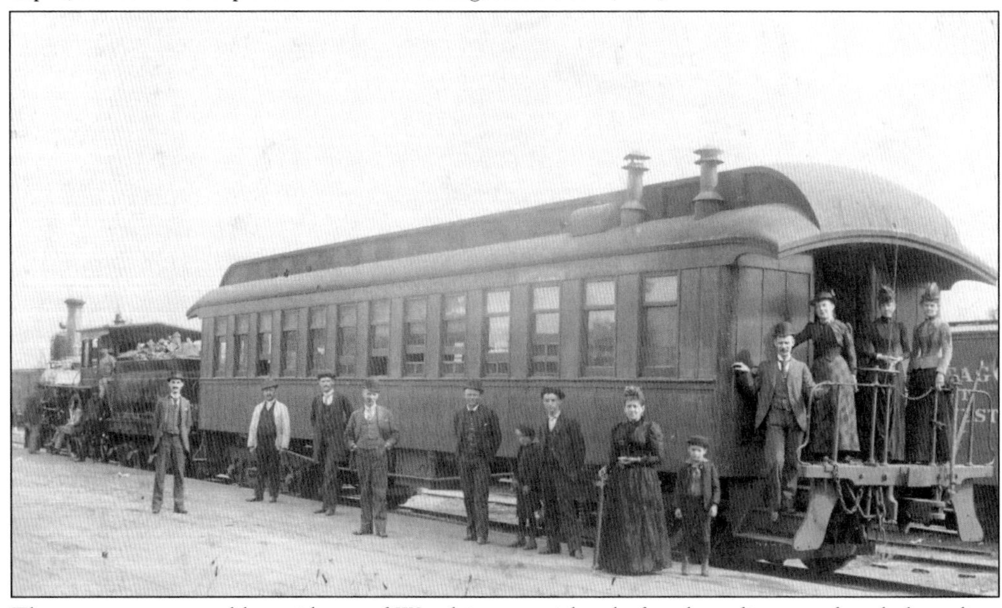

These are some notable residents of Worthington either before boarding or after de-boarding the train. Since the steam engine is pulling only one passenger car, it may have been arranged as a special trip for only this small group, like a charter trip. Some of the identified individuals include Charles Smallwood (far left), Jim Messer (third from left), Fred Parker (fifth from left), and Hannah Parker (eighth from left).

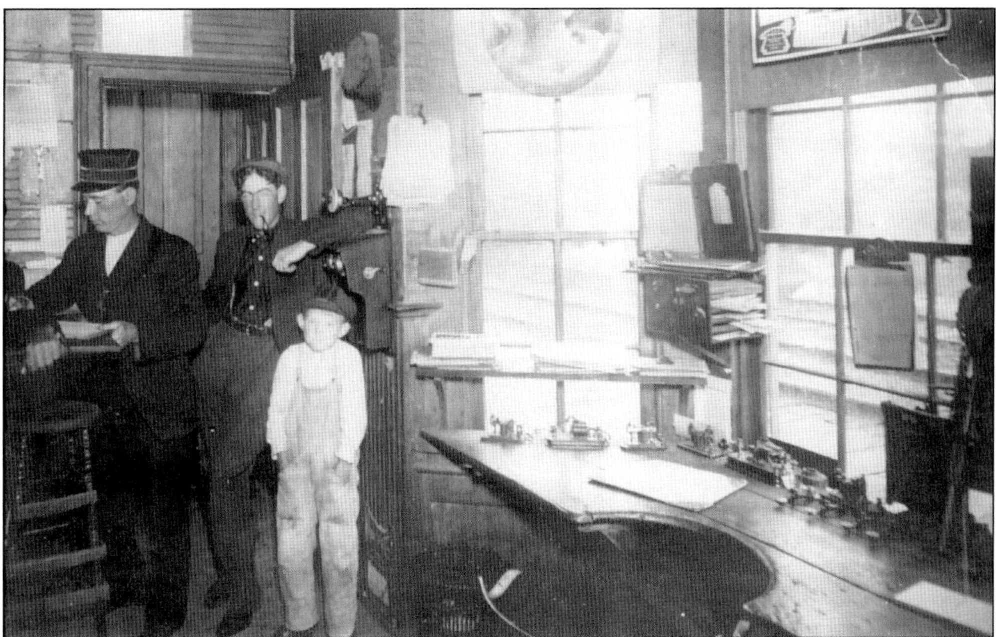

The first building erected in Bigelow was the depot for the Sioux City & St. Paul Railroad. The train station was an important hub in the railway transportation system. Passengers could purchase their tickets from the station agent and wait to board the train when it was time to depart for the next destination. Pictured in this interior photograph of the Bigelow depot is Fred Pingle, Alvin Pingle, and Rascal Tarrington.

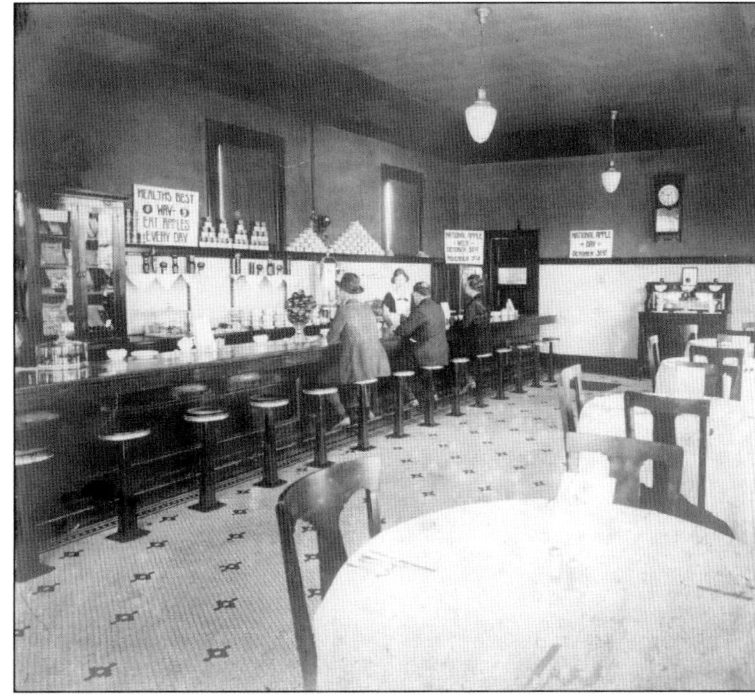

A few years after Worthington's second depot was erected, a small free-standing building was constructed on the west edge of the station's brick platform. This structure housed a café that offered travelers refreshments and food as well as other amenities, like newspapers. Over the years, the café was known by different names, such as Depot Lunch, the Beanery, Depot Café, and Tex-Ann's Café.

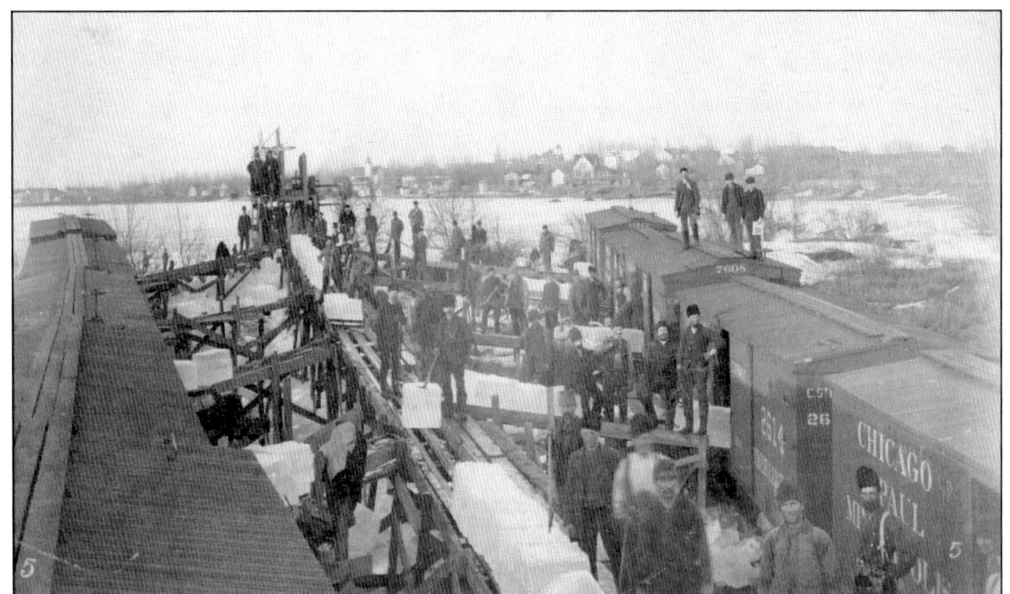

Before the advent of electrical refrigeration, ice was needed to preserve food for commercial and residential customers. Worthington's Lake Okabena provided the area with an ice source for 80 years, from 1872 to 1952. At one time, as much as 40,000 tons of ice was harvested in a single year. Using train boxcars, ice was shipped hundreds of miles to larger cities with meat-packing plants.

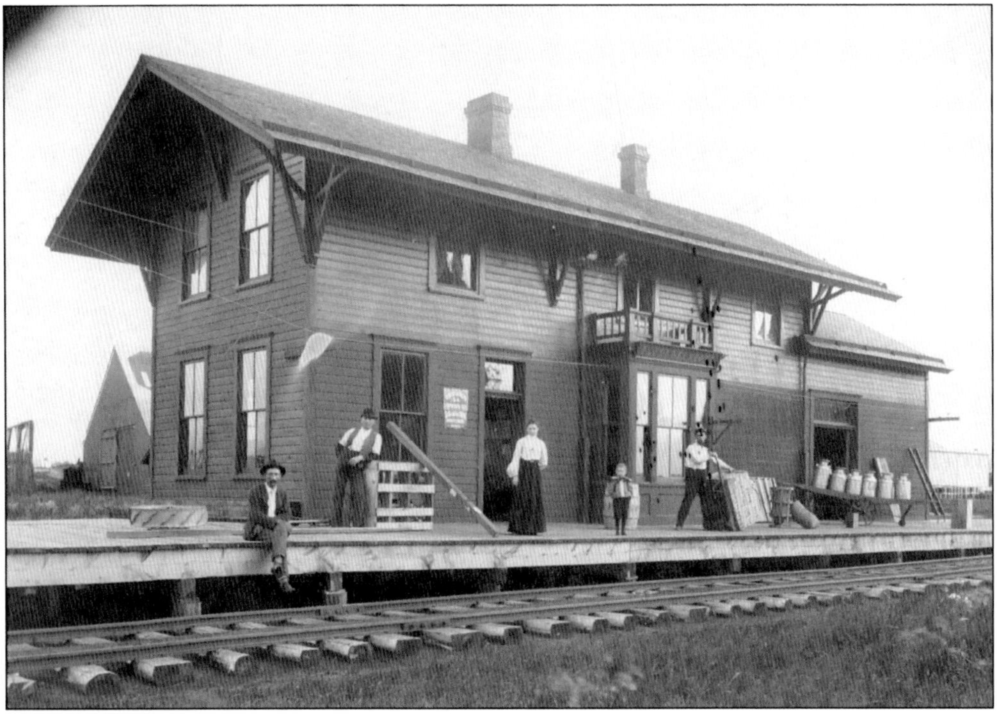

The Lismore depot was built by the Burlington Railroad in 1900. Fred Hofkamp, a Lismore resident, can be seen leaning on a crate while waiting for the arriving passenger train. He worked for the Lismore Bank and was also employed with the Olberding Store selling groceries and clothing.

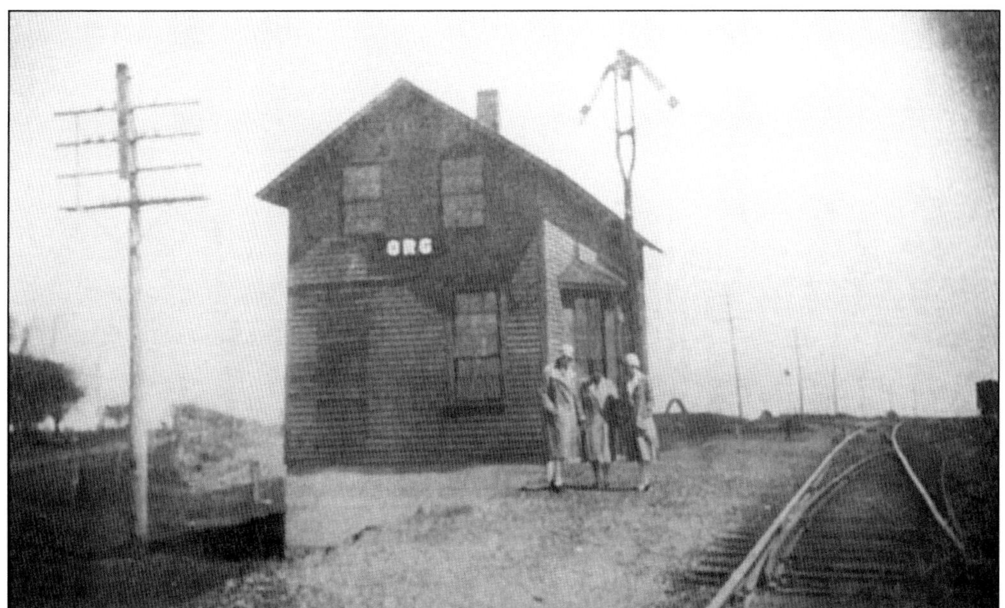

Org was never much more than a whistle stop on the railroad line, but it did have its own train depot, built in 1886. Pictured outside the station around 1930 are three women, including the station agent, Agnes Petersen (left), and her two friends Frances Bjornstad and Hilda Johnson. (BS.)

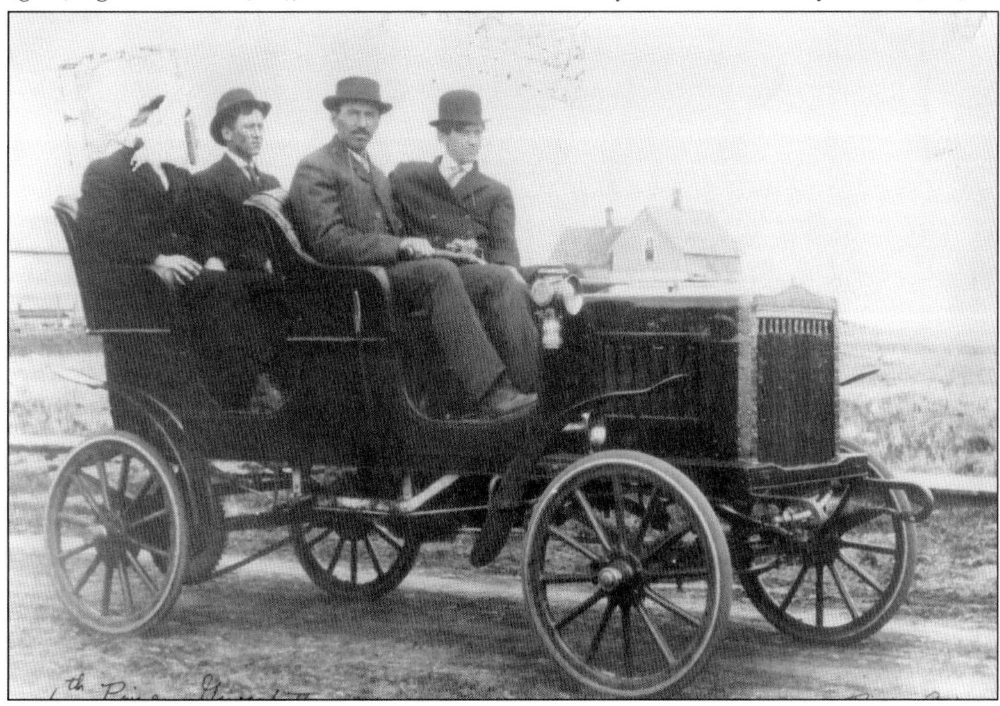

While Henry Ford was perfecting his automobile-making skills in Detroit, Peter Spartz was tinkering in his Wilmont garage. In 1900, Spartz reportedly built the first automobile in Nobles County, a chain-driven, two-cylinder vehicle. From left to right are Peter Spartz and his three brothers, John, Henry, and William. It took them approximately 10 hours to drive 180 miles to Clark, South Dakota.

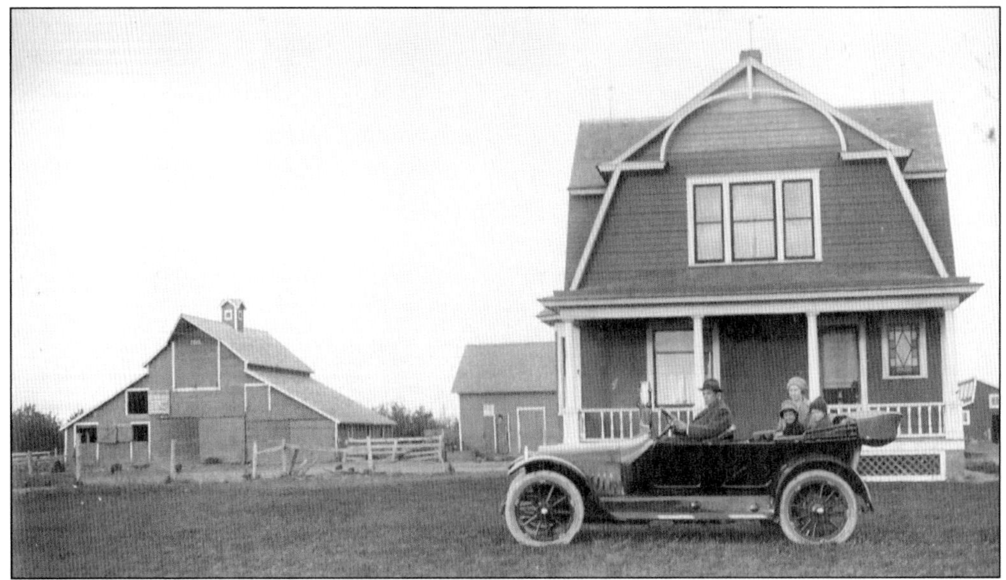

With the passing of years, more and more families switched their primary mode of transportation from horses to cars, even in rural areas. In this farm photograph, James Gardner poses with his family in their automobile. The Gardner farmstead was located on Section 33 in Graham Lakes Township.

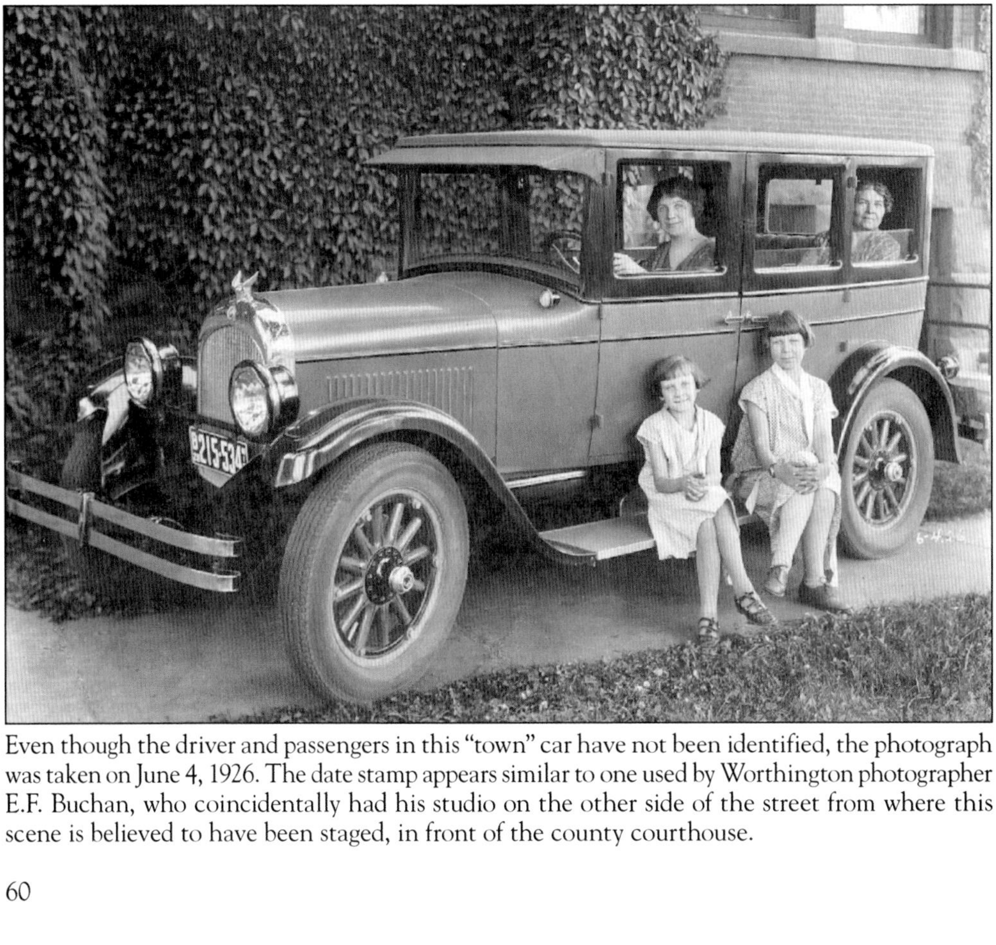

Even though the driver and passengers in this "town" car have not been identified, the photograph was taken on June 4, 1926. The date stamp appears similar to one used by Worthington photographer E.F. Buchan, who coincidentally had his studio on the other side of the street from where this scene is believed to have been staged, in front of the county courthouse.

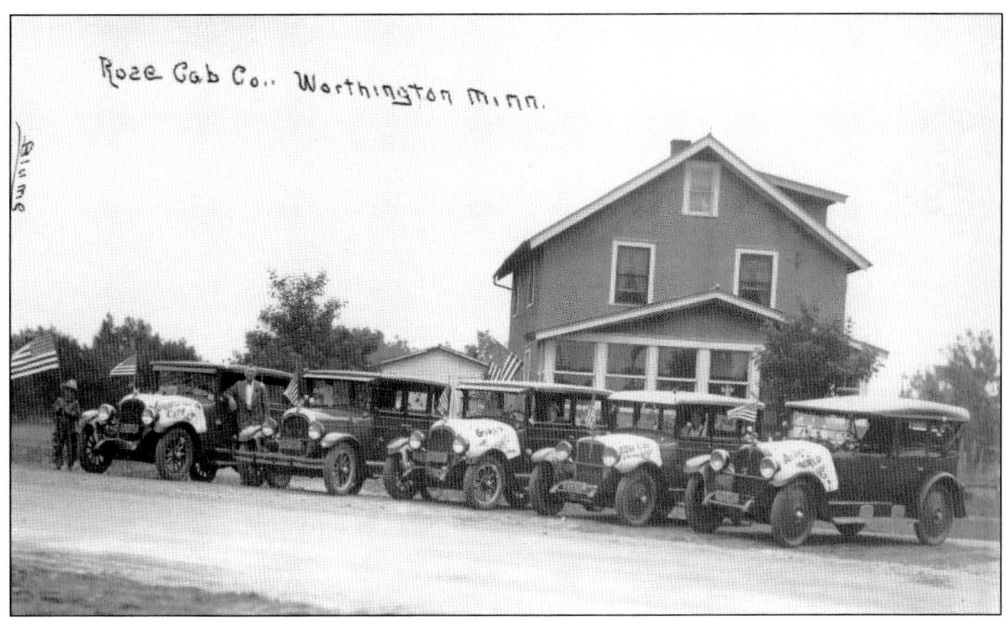

On page 53, Worthington dray line operator Fred Rose is pictured with his horse and wagon. Here, some 20 years later, he is still in the drayage business, but this time his cargo is people. Fred is shown standing among his fleet of five cabs around 1930. His son, Bill Rose, is holding an American flag in a patriotic gesture. In the background is the Rose family home at 1301 Sherwood Street.

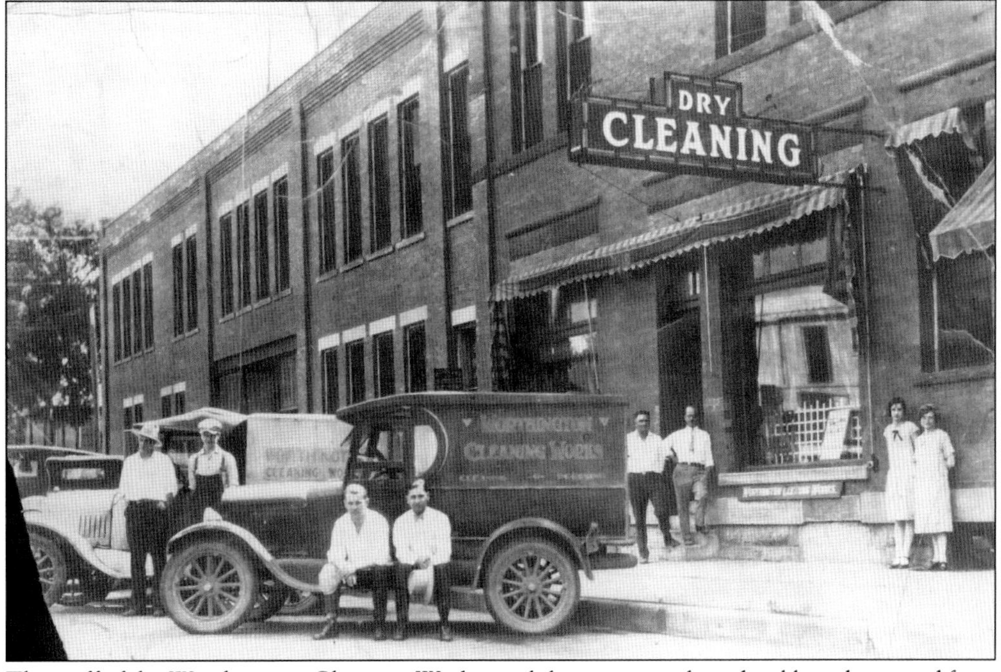

The staff of the Worthington Cleaning Works used these two trucks to haul laundry to and from their cleaning business. The shop was located in the back of the old Citizens National Bank building on Fourth Avenue, where the side entrance to the Buffalo Billfold Company store is now. Among those pictured are Leverett White (far left), Fred White (second from left), and Ruth White.

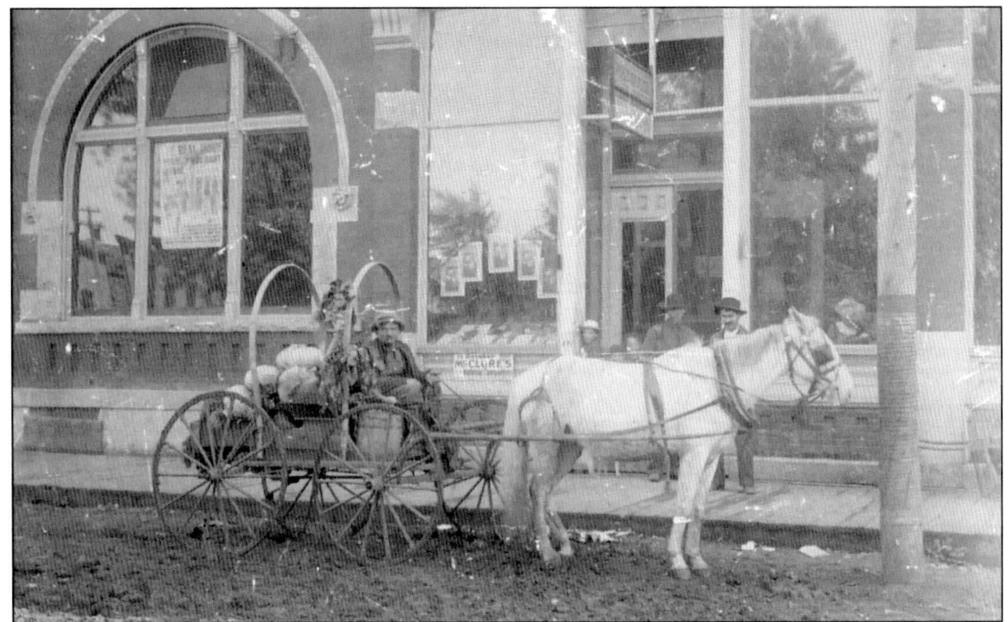

This photograph, dated September 26, 1900, captures Worthington character Erastus Church, parked with his horse-drawn vegetable wagon in front of Worthington's post office. Church was a jack-of-all-trades who was known by everyone in the community. He specialized in peddling vegetables and picking up junk, and even distinguished himself by having the street where he lived renamed Church in his honor.

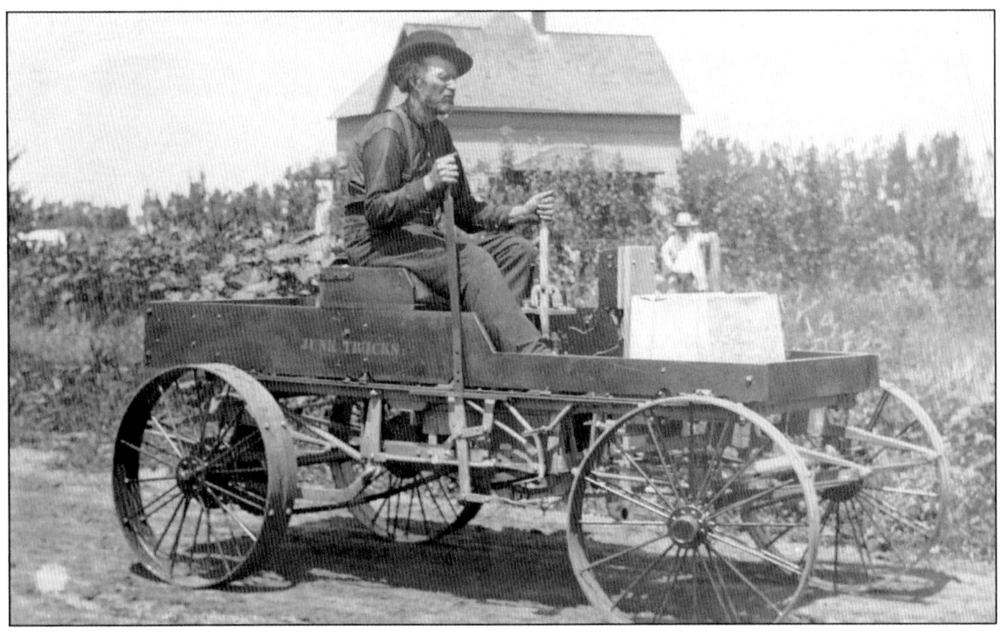

Another Worthington-based character had a countywide reputation. To most people, he was known only as "Old Grubs." He traveled throughout the county, town by town and farm by farm, buying junk. He would assess the value of people's items and then make an offer—take it or leave it. Grubbs (his actual last name) can be seen here around 1912 driving a stick-driven horseless carriage. On the side is a sign reading "Junk Trucks."

At the turn of the 20th century, bicycling had become increasingly popular. The safety bicycle, particularly the style with no top tube, could accommodate female riders dressed in the cumbersome clothing of the time. Susan B. Anthony claimed that bicycling had "done more to emancipate women than anything else in the world." Undoubtedly, it increased their mobility. Supposedly, the first woman's bicycle in Nobles County was owned by Worthington's Carrie Ferrin, pictured here.

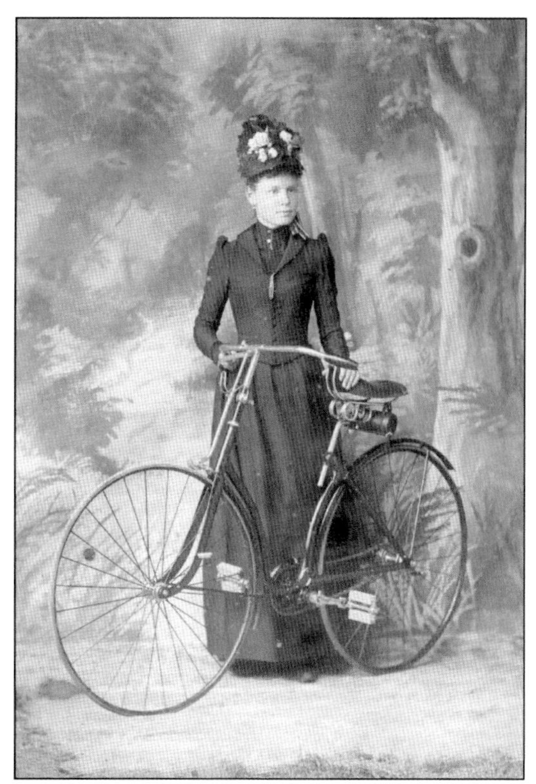

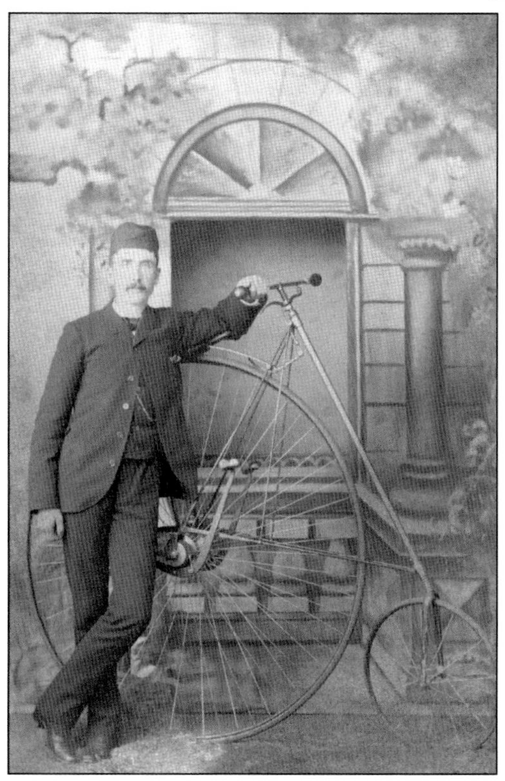

The high-wheel bicycle appeared a little earlier and became stylish in the 1870s while Nobles County was first being settled. Unfortunately, they did have some drawbacks. Encountering bumps or obstacles in the road sometimes caused riders to "take a header" over the handlebars, potentially resulting in serious injuries. Other than this posed studio photograph of an unidentified Worthington man, there is no other evidence of this style of bicycle being used in Nobles County.

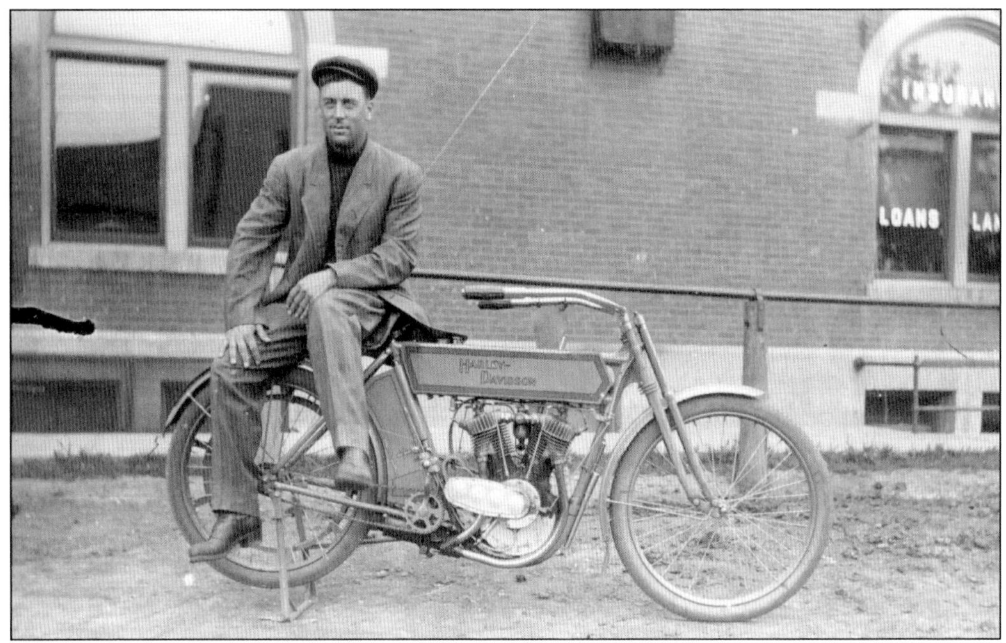

There is no denying today's popularity of the Harley-Davidson motorcycle, but the interest and enthusiasm for this street machine began more than a century ago. In this c. 1910 photograph, John McCord can be seen posing on his Harley-Davidson in front of a bank building on Worthington's Third Avenue.

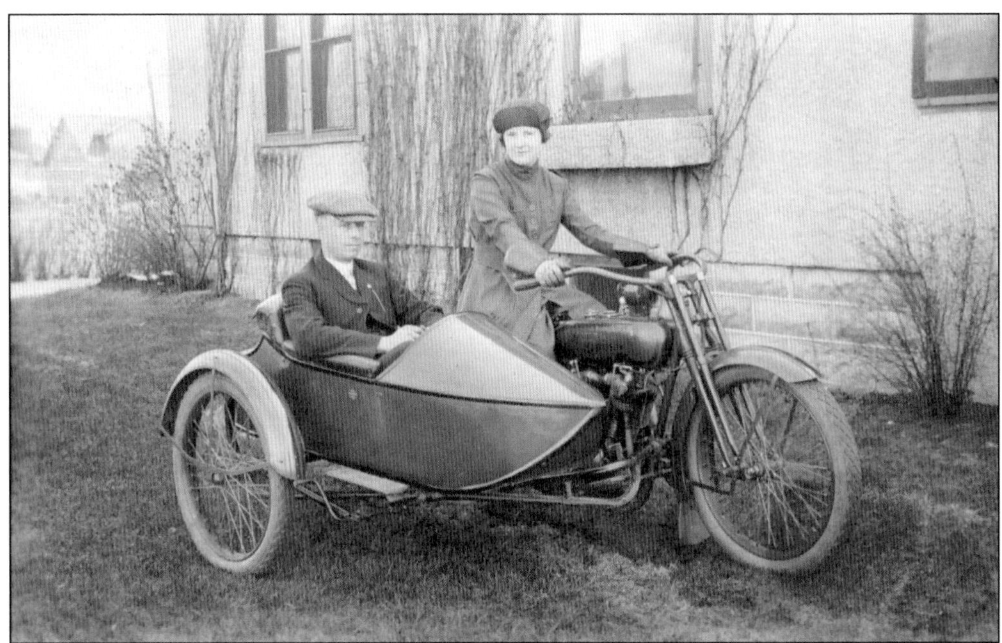

Frank and Ada LaPachek were Worthington residents who had a passion for traveling. Their journeys took them to different locales, many even outside the country. Some of the objects they picked up on these trips were ultimately donated to the historical society. For some of their US excursions they enjoyed traveling by motorcycle, sometimes with a sidecar, as shown here.

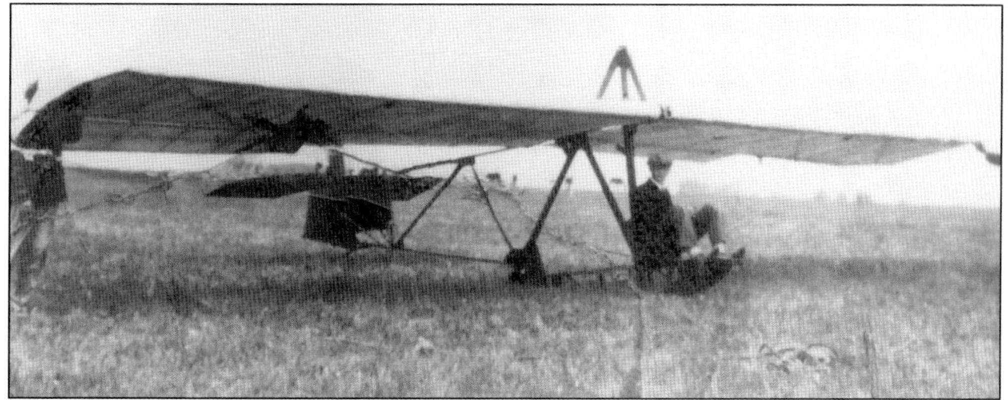

Air transportation in this area was very limited during the first half of the 20th century. No commercial airline service was available, and there was limited use of air delivery service. Nevertheless, there were some airplane enthusiasts who pursued flying as a hobby. One such individual was Worthington resident Howard Sevdy, who built this primitive glider.

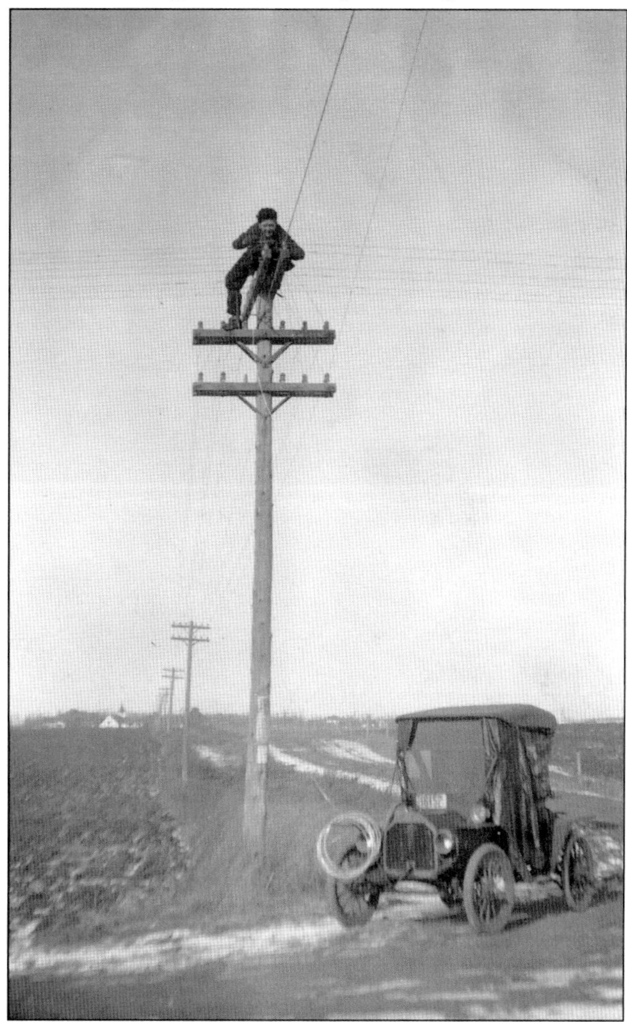

In 1911, a high-wire act came to Dundee. It was not one of the itinerant circuses that occasionally brought wild animals and shows to pioneer towns, but rather it was the hanging of telephone lines to offer service to Dundee's residents. Note the coil of wire hanging on the right front fender and headlight of this lineman's car. (JD.)

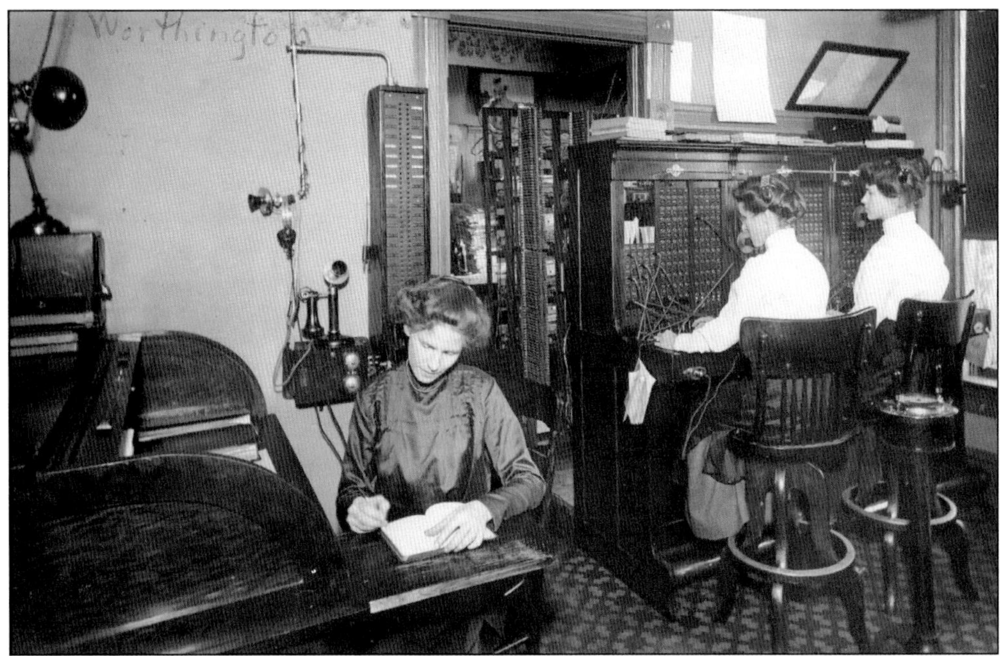

With the establishment of the early telephone systems came the position of telephone operator. Someone was needed to connect the callers to the appropriate telephone line so they could talk to each other. This picture shows three women working in the back office of Worthington's telephone company. Two are plugging telephone lines into the operator boards, while the third appears to be doing book work.

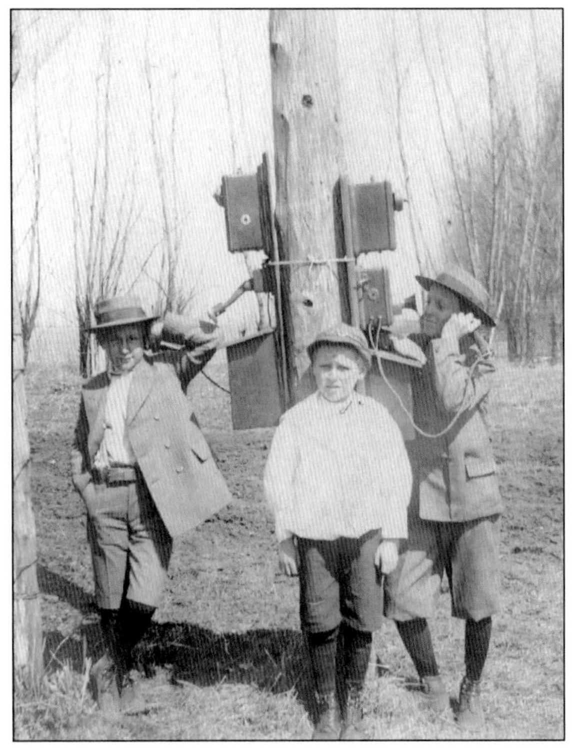

Pictured in Dundee around 1912, this may be the county's first outdoor telephone booth. It shows three young boys dressed in their "Sunday-go-to-meeting" clothes—dress knickers, double-breasted suitcoats, and sporty hats. The crank telephones have been mounted with a rope to a wooden pole. Presumably the phones were located somewhere in town for the convenient use of Dundee residents. It is not known if these phones were actually operational or just props for a scene staged by the photographer. (JD.)

Five

Educating the Children, Keeping the Faith

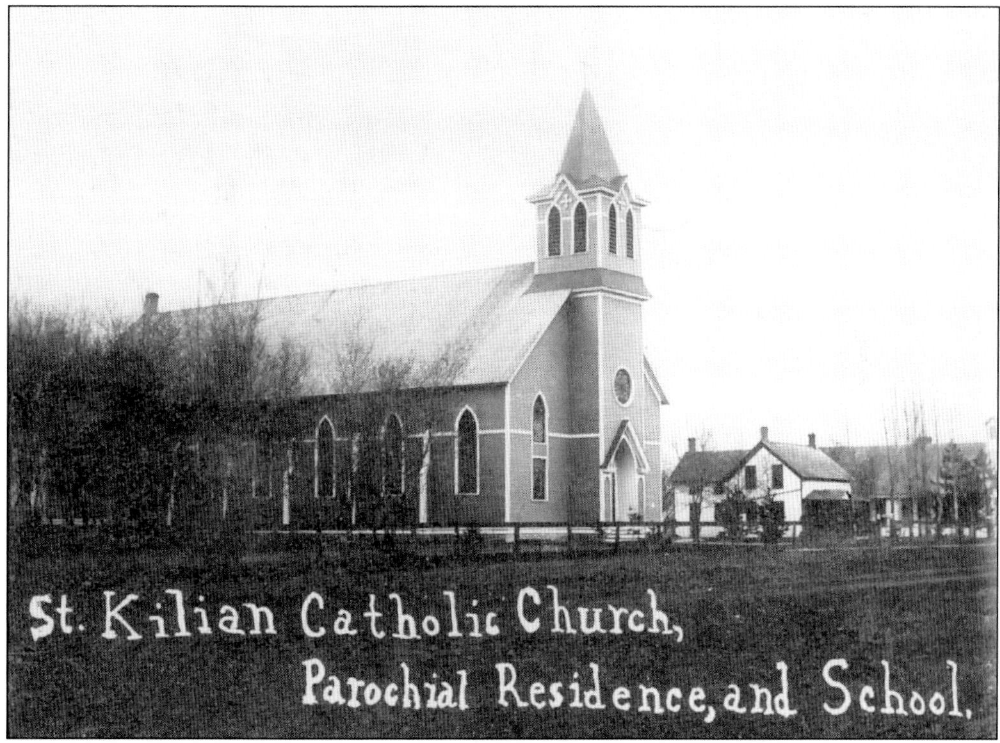

Thirteen of Nobles County's original 15 communities were established due to the development of the railroads. The other two, St. Kilian and Leota, were organized around churches. In St. Kilian, the first St. Kilian Catholic Church building was constructed in 1887 but was destroyed by fire some 10 years later. The congregation then built a Catholic school where church services were held until the second church structure could be erected in 1900. This property was listed in the National Register of Historic Places in 1998. (AB.)

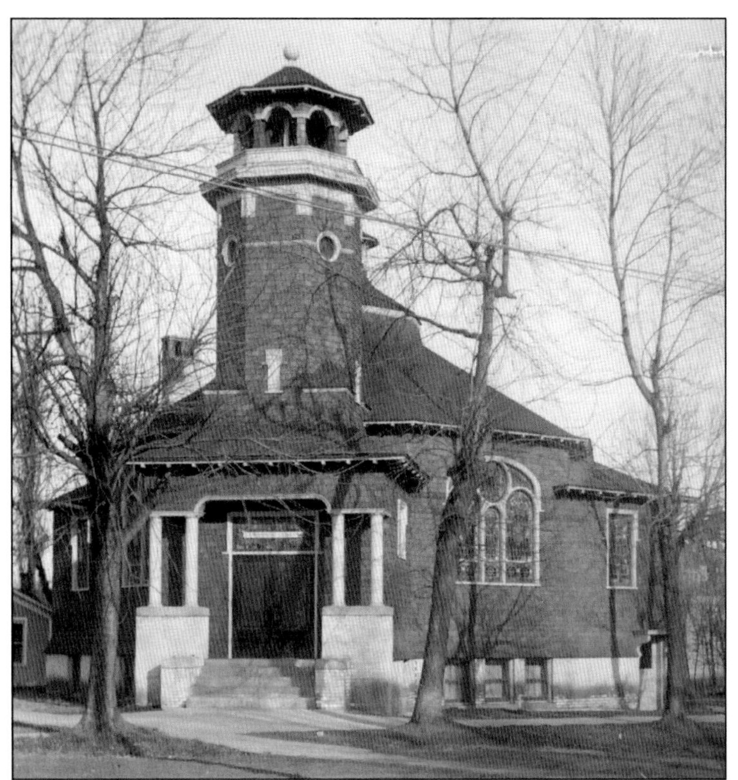

The Union Congregational Church was Worthington's first building to be constructed solely for religious worship purposes. This also qualifies it as the first church built in Nobles County. However, the 1873 structure was ultimately destroyed by fire on January 5, 1905 (see page 85). To replace it, the congregation built the second church, seen here in 1906, for a cost of $7,000.

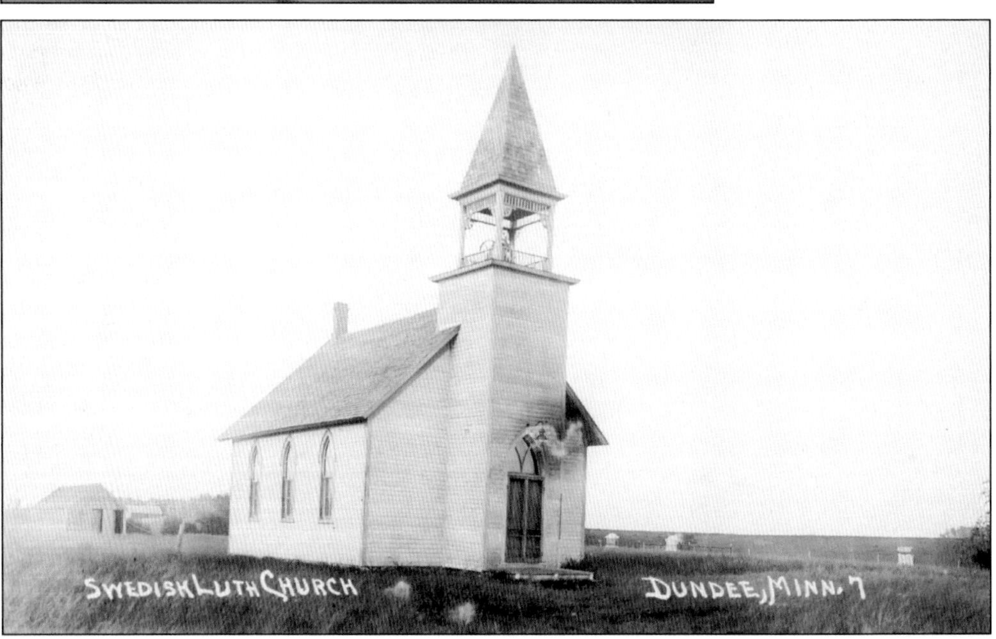

Many of Dundee's early settlers were of Swedish descent. Like other ethnic groups, these immigrants had a strong desire to practice their religion as they had in their home country. In addition, they wanted to preserve their cultural traditions, including their first language. To fulfill these purposes, they established the Swedish Lutheran Church during the summer of 1886. Church services were regularly scheduled, including some in Swedish.

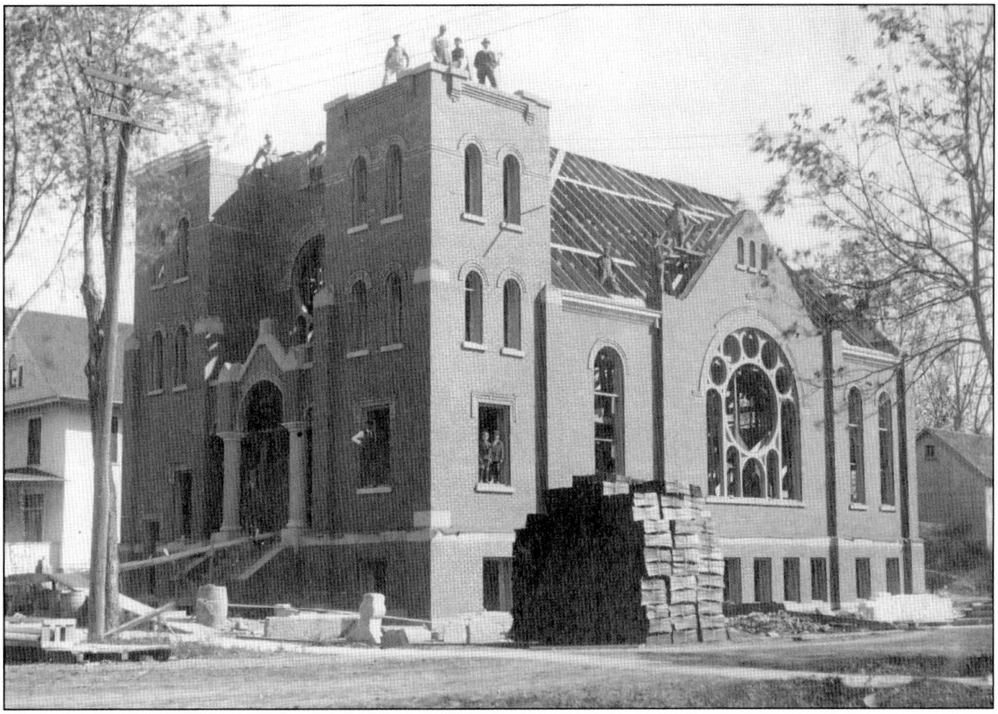

Worthington also had a sizable contingent of Swedish immigrants. Like their fellow countrymen who settled in the Dundee area, they had a desire to establish their own church, which they founded in 1874, the Swedish Evangelical Lutheran Church. Nine years later, they erected a wooden church building on the corner of Fourth Avenue and Twelfth Street. In 1910, they constructed a larger brick structure to replace it. Today, it is Worthington's oldest functioning church building.

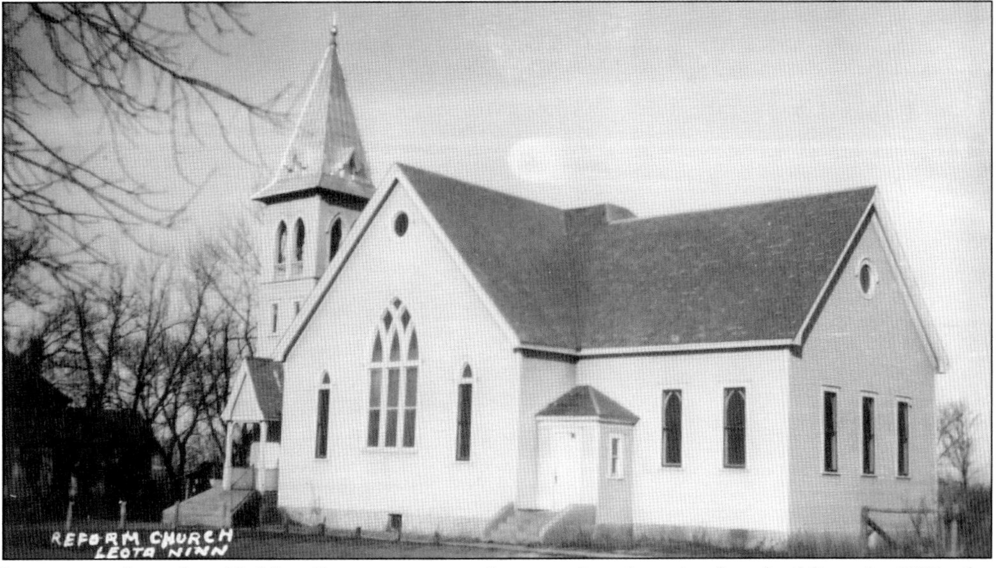

Leota was the other Nobles County town to have a church as its first building. In 1891, the community's initial group of Dutch settlers, many of whom migrated here from northwest Iowa, established and built the Bethel Reformed Church. Due to a need for more space, they decided to construct a larger church in 1911, pictured here. Since then, it has been remodeled twice.

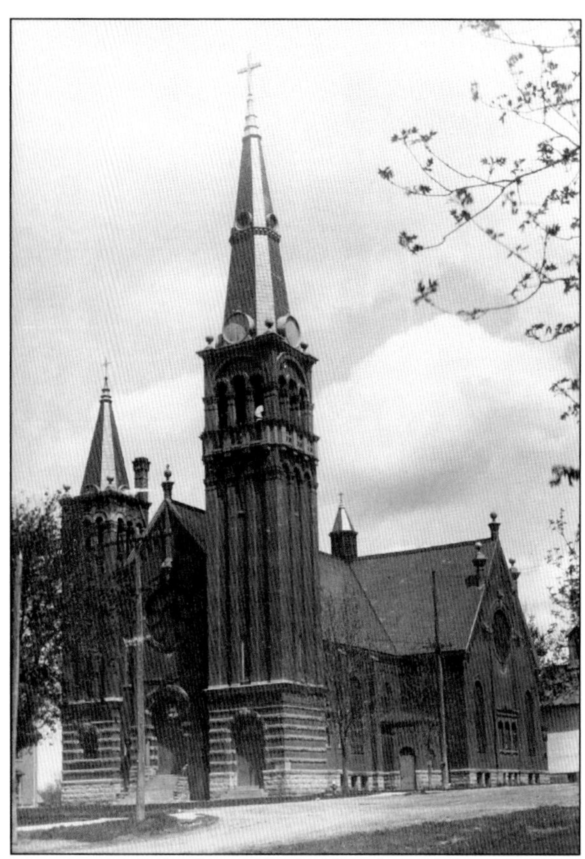

From 1878 through the early 1880s, the Catholic Colony Company was instrumental in relocating hundreds of people, mostly German and Irish Catholics, to western Nobles County. Because of this burgeoning Catholic population, St. Adrian's Catholic Church was organized. After the parish's second church building burned down on Christmas Eve 1899, this larger replacement was constructed within six months at a cost of $30,000. It can seat up to 800 churchgoers. This property was listed in the National Register of Historic Places in 1980.

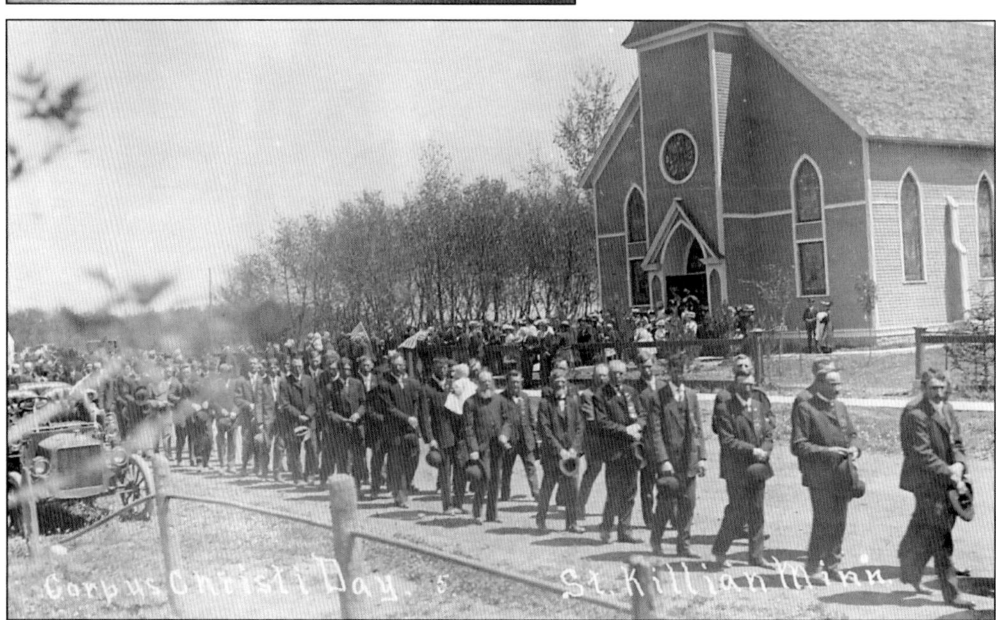

The Feast of Corpus Christi is observed by the Catholic Church approximately 60 days after Easter. Seen in this 1915 picture of St. Kilian's festivities is the traditional procession that takes place in the neighborhood of the church. It is typically followed by prayer and singing. (AB.)

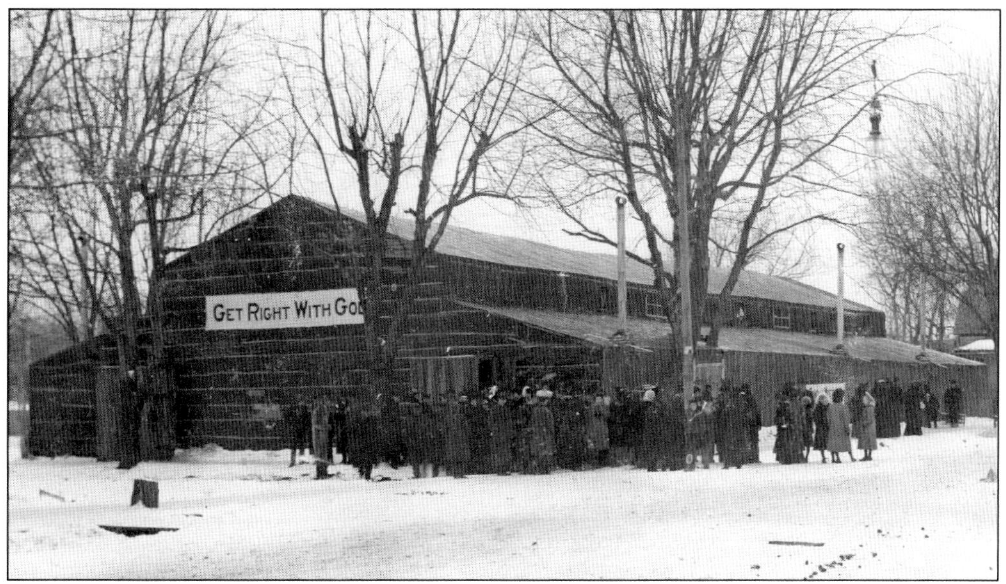

It is believed this religious revival meeting took place somewhere in Worthington around 1910. On the building is a sign proclaiming "Get Right with God." No other details are known about this event, including what church might have sponsored it. The lack of any recognizable landmarks also makes it difficult to identify where this building may have been located. (TG.)

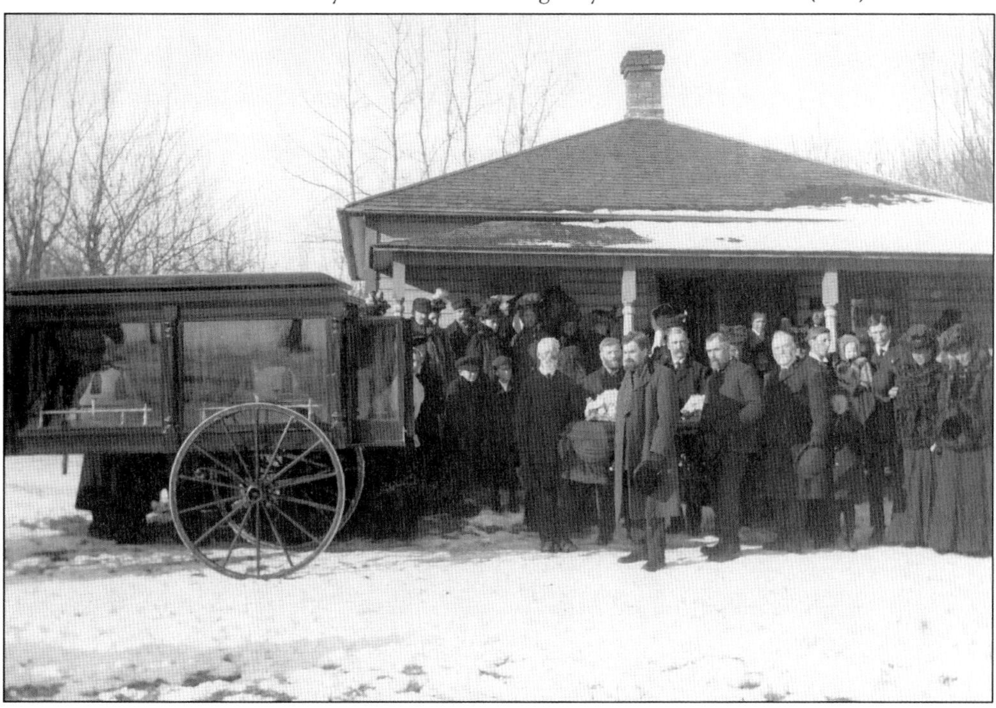

This 1908 scene is of the funeral for Mrs. Jonas Moberg of Bigelow Township. Her casket is being transported in a horse-drawn hearse. Relatives and friends who attended her funeral service included Ruben Nystrom, Linden Moberg, Oliver Thompson, August Anderson, Hans Nystrom, Edwin Moberg, Hilda Moberg, Mrs. Nels Moberg, Kristine Moberg, Kristine Nystrom, Mrs. Ola Nystrom, John Blixt, Nels Moberg, and Mildred Moberg.

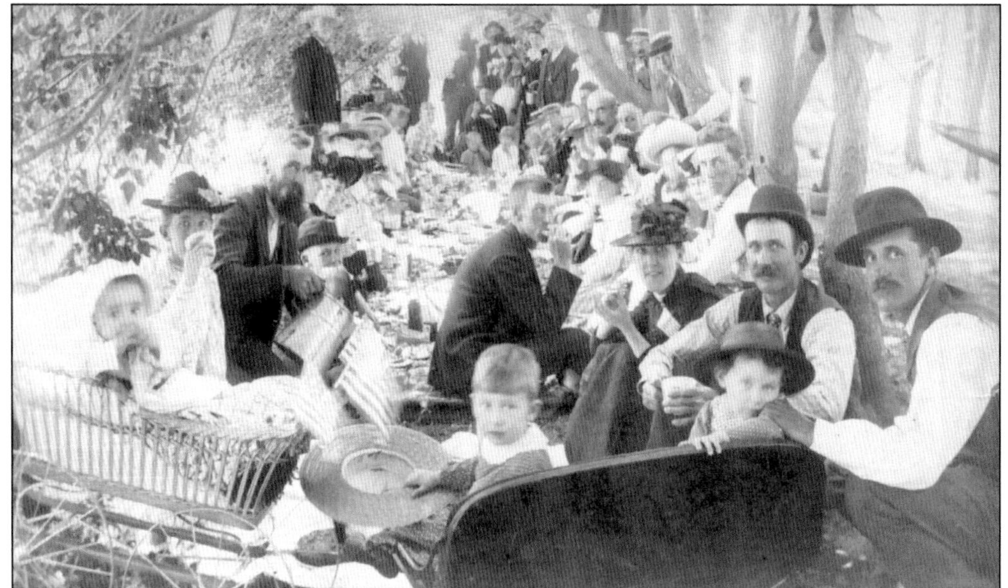

In addition to worship services, church functions included social activities that brought parishioners together to create a more cohesive congregation. This photograph shows a Presbyterian picnic party at Round Lake on July 4, 1890. Unfortunately, it is unclear if the attendees are from nearby Worthington's Presbyterian church or if the people were actually from Round Lake, where the Presbyterian church was the only established church in town at that time.

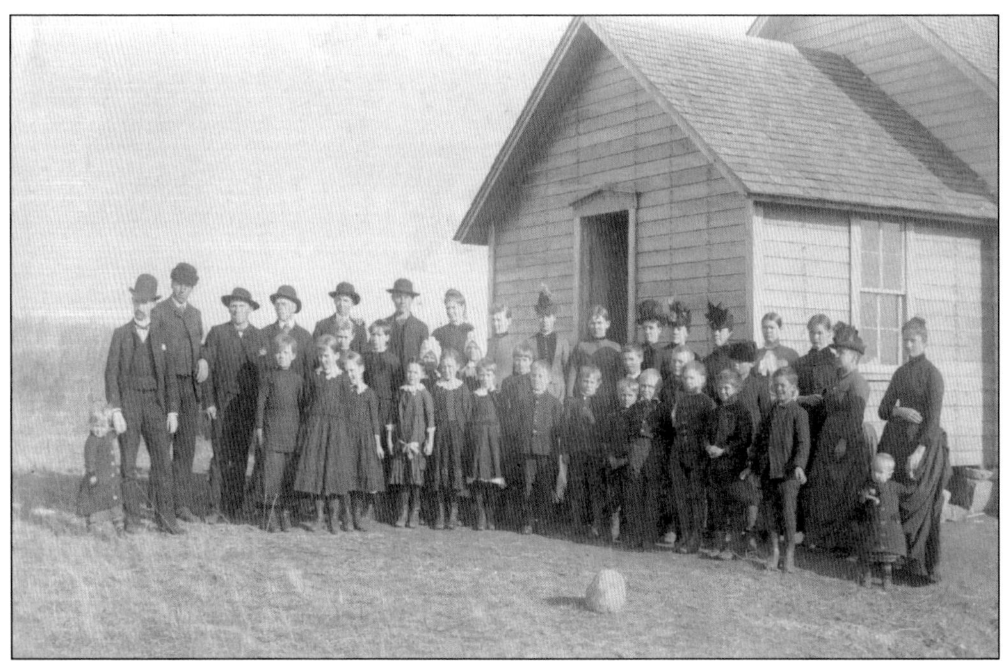

Pictured here is a group of church members, children as well as adults, attending Sunday school activities in their nearby public rural school. From pictorial records, the schoolhouse has been identified as District No. 1 in Indian Lake Township, which was the first school district established in the county. This photograph was taken by E.F. Buchan around 1890.

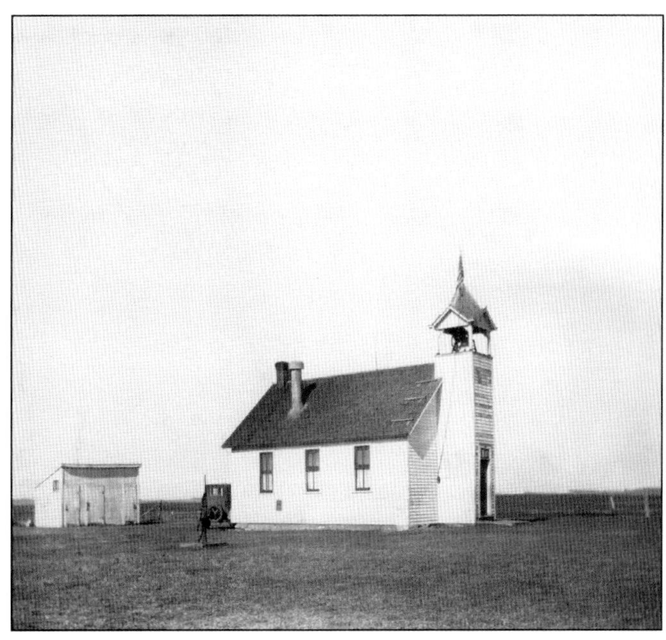

From the 1870s through the 1960s, there were more than 100 rural education districts spread throughout the county. Schoolhouses were situated every two to three miles to ensure that all children could attend school. Typically, classes were offered September through May, although in earlier years, some schools were open only six months a year. The rural school teachers provided instruction for students in grades one through eight. This country school, District No. 109 Bloom Center School (Bloom Township), was open from 1906 through 1943. (LFe.)

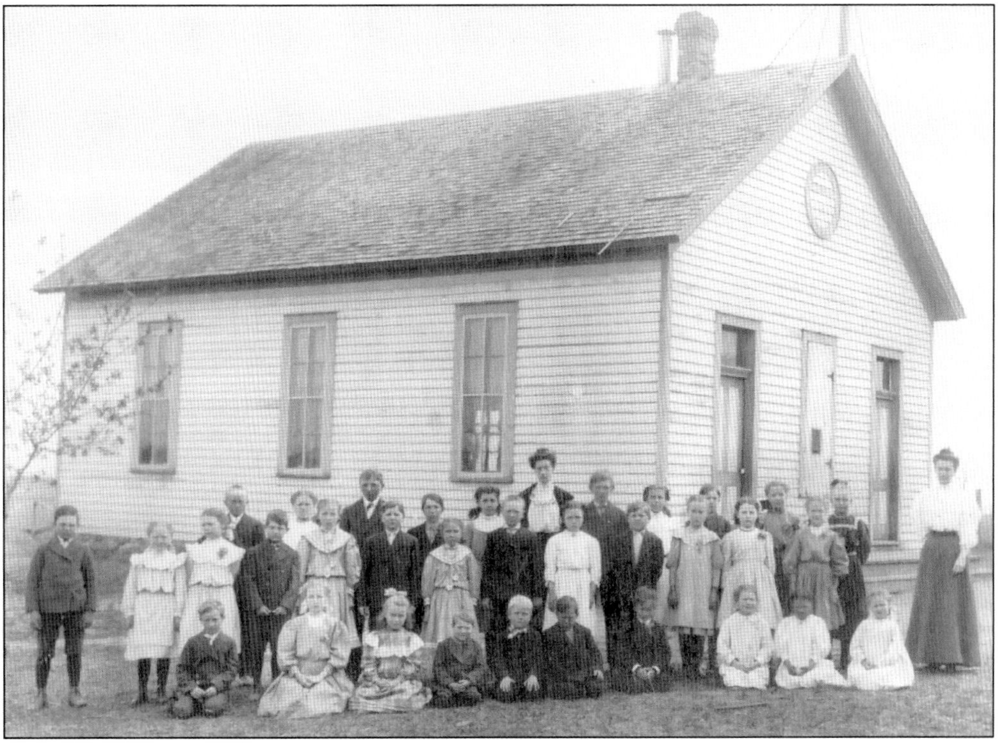

Country schools were classified as ungraded. Students were not separated into different classrooms by grade but rather attended a one-room school that included children from ages five through sixteen. In some instances, especially in the early years before many high schools had been established, a few students were as old as 21. This photograph of District No. 48 Okabena School (Worthington Township), taken on May 29, 1907, shows the teacher, Stella Mosher, with 34 of her 36 students.

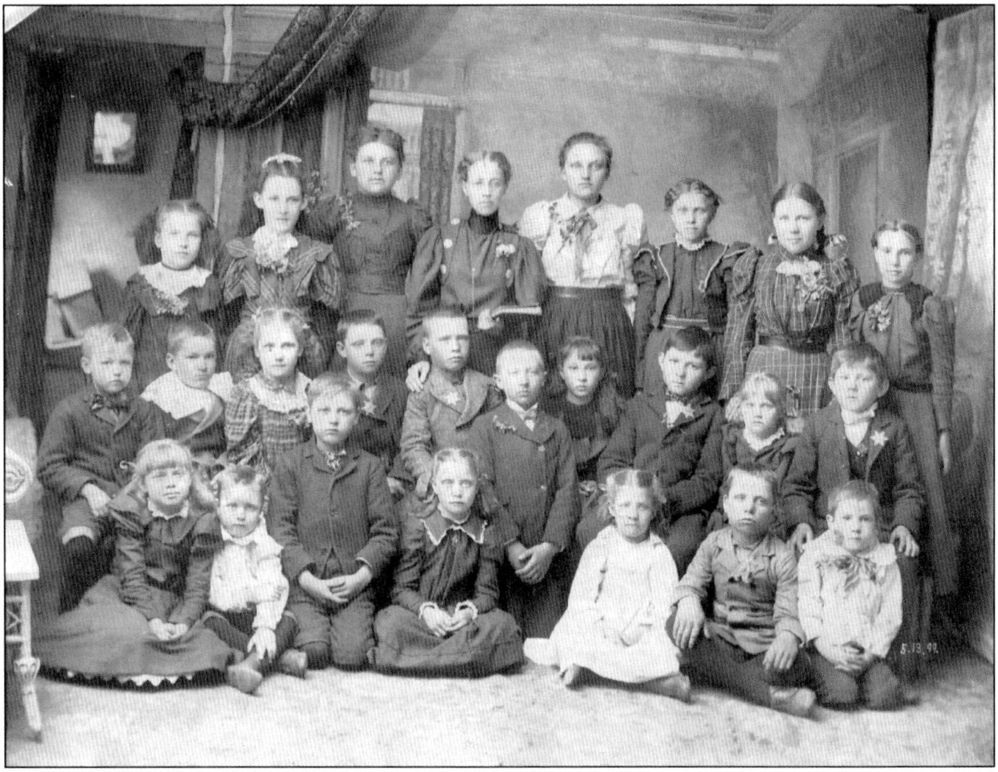

This is the District No. 29 Prairie Hill School (Elk Township) class of 1899. Note the age and physical disparities between the older and younger students. One of the unique challenges facing country school teachers was the number of different lessons they needed to prepare on a daily basis. They would offer each age group (eight different grades) the appropriate grade-level instruction in all subject areas (reading, language, spelling, arithmetic, history, geography, and science).

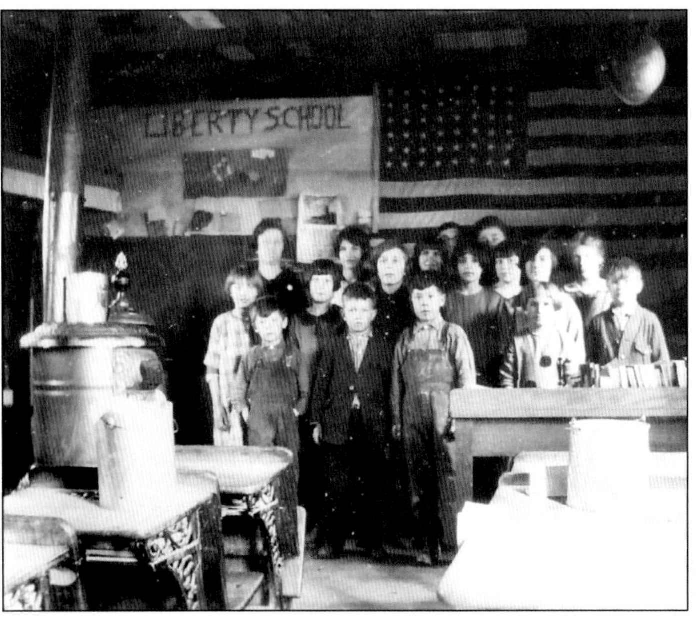

The distinguishing feature in this image of the interior of District No. 112 Liberty School (Hersey Township) is the potbelly stove. Most rural schoolhouses had a comparable stove or furnace that provided heat during the cold winter months. They ran on wood, coal, or fuel oil. Students fondly recalled how these stoves also were instrumental in preparing hot lunches—a can of soup or a baked potato. Occasionally, one of these spuds would overheat and explode.

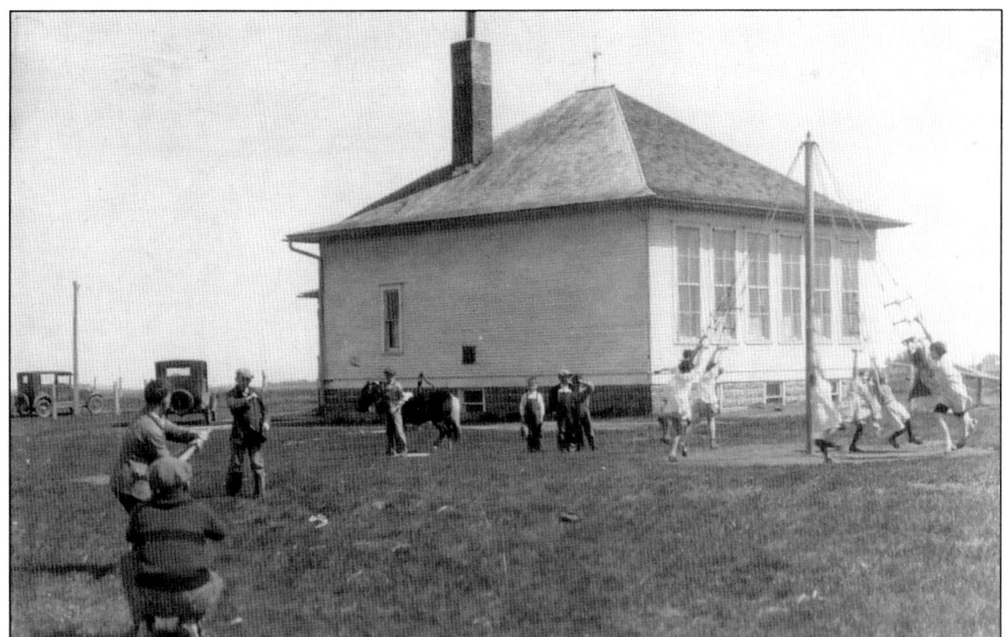

Like their town counterparts, country school students also enjoyed recess activities. Rural schools had playground equipment for their children to play on when classes were not in session: teeter-totters, swings, monkey bars, slides, or merry-go-rounds. Here, the students of District No. 76 Fairview School (Lorain Township) are playing on a maypole-type swing known as Giant Strides, while others are playing baseball.

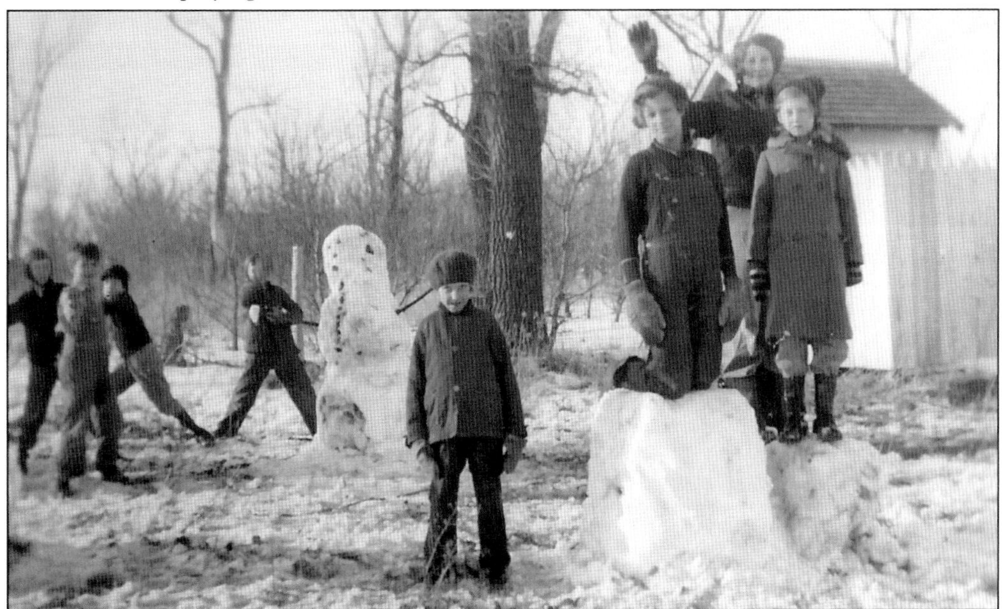

Playing outside during the winter months had advantages and disadvantages. On the negative side, brutally cold temperatures or deep snow could significantly limit the games children could play. Nevertheless, they could build snow forts, dig tunnels, make snow angels, or build snowmen. Here, the students of District No. 35 Shady Cove School (Seward Township) enjoy their winter outdoor recess time around 1935.

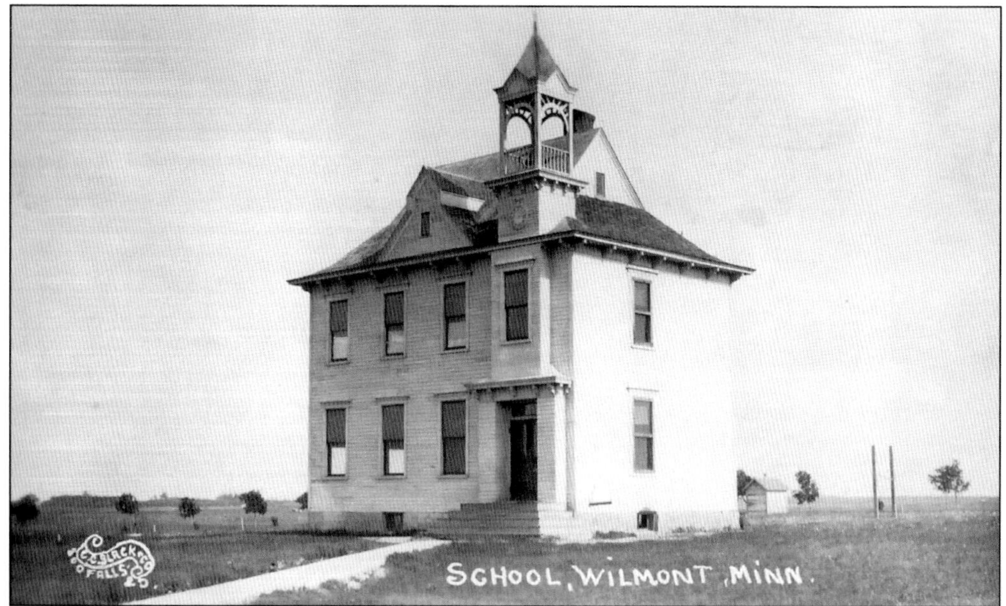

When the townsite of Wilmont was established, it was included within the boundaries of a nearby country school district. However, with Wilmont's increased population, the county was petitioned to create a new school district for the village itself. In 1902, District No. 104 was established and a two-story wooden structure was built for $2,600 to educate approximately 60 to 75 students. There were two ungraded classrooms, each with its own teacher. (AB.)

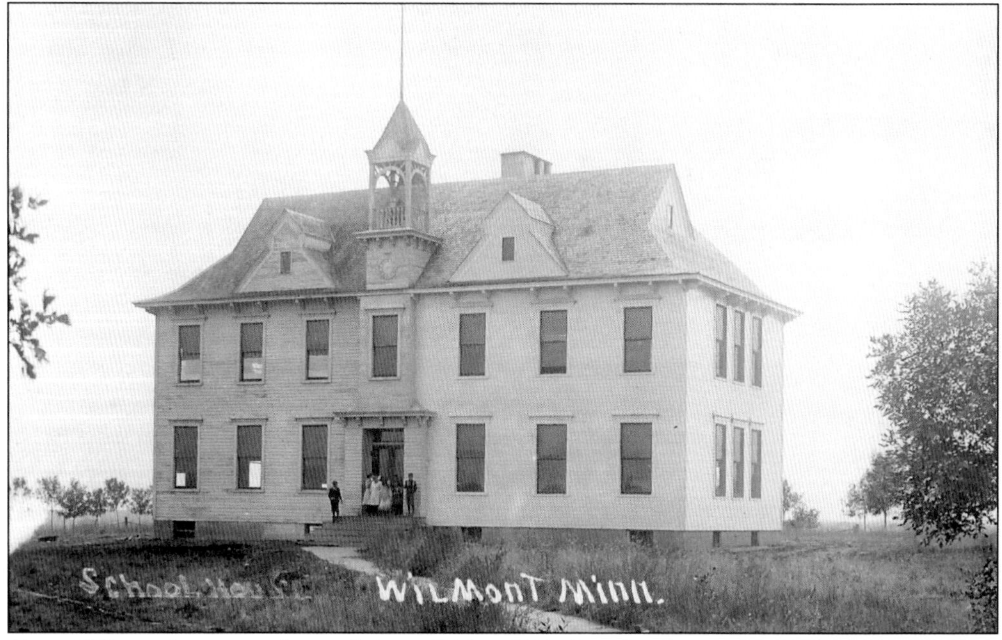

Given Wilmont's continued growth from 1900 to 1910, the school system needed to accommodate more students. Since this could not be done in the existing school building with its limited space, the school board and community decided to construct an addition on the original structure. It was completed in 1913 at a cost of $3,920. District No. 104 became a graded school where the students were now separated by age. (AB.)

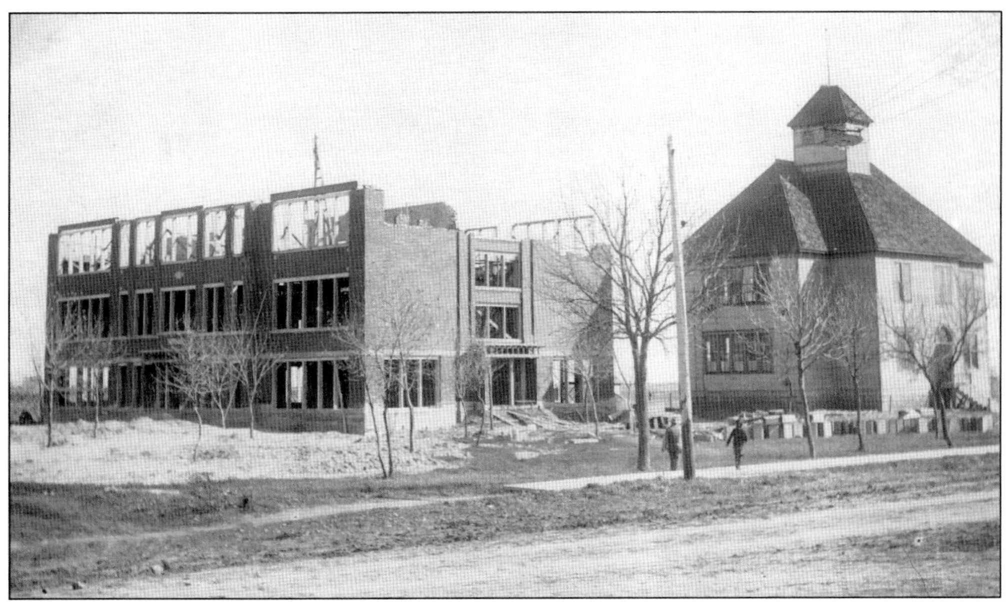

Brewster's first school was a small, one-room building similar to most country schools. As the town grew, a larger, two-story wooden structure was erected in 1898. It had four classrooms on the first floor and a large upstairs auditorium. Here, the construction of the town's third school building in 1914 can be seen alongside the one it was to replace. The new structure included an auditorium with a seating capacity of 300 and scenery sets and curtains for a stage.

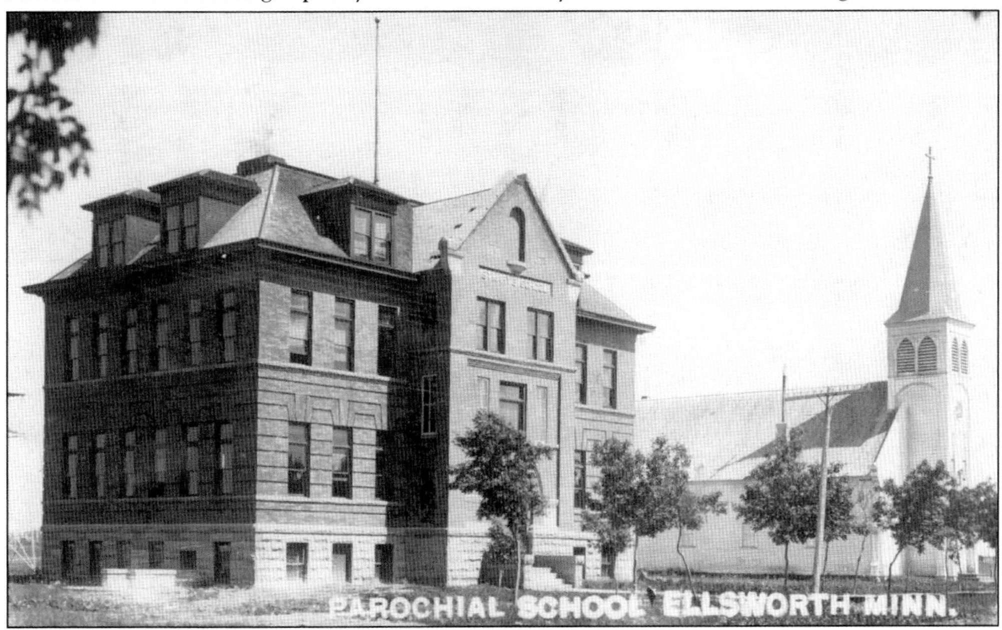

In the county's western half, many residents of predominantly Catholic communities wanted to raise their children in the Catholic faith. They believed having Catholic schools would be the best way to carry on this tradition. Ellsworth's St. Mary's Church built a parish school in 1906 at a cost of $18,000. The classrooms were on the first floor, a kitchen and dining room were in the basement, and dormitory rooms for boarding students and the teaching nuns were on the second floor. There were approximately 120 students enrolled in grades one through 12.

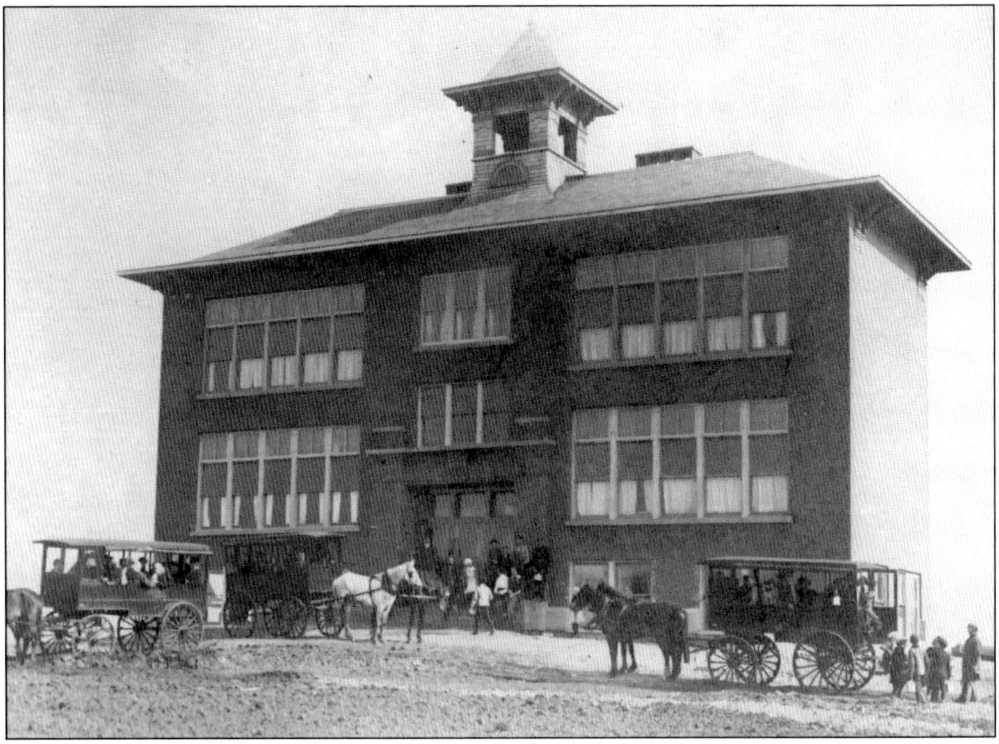

Meanwhile, a few miles southeast of Wilmont, the village of Reading also experienced growth and increased population. In 1913, it spent $22,000 to erect and furnish a new two-story brick school building. To ensure the area's farm children could get to school, a transportation service was instituted using three horse-drawn buses, as pictured here.

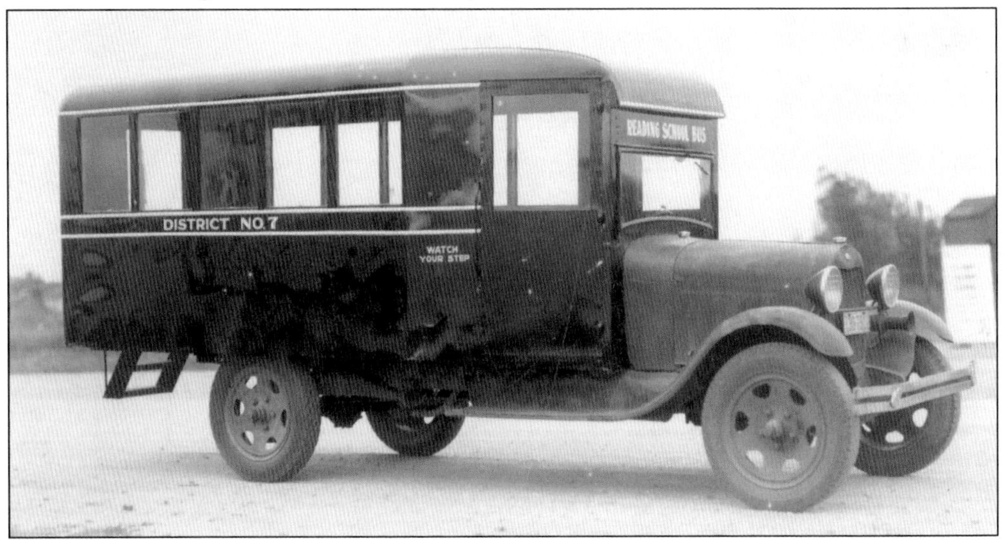

In 1916, the horse-drawn buses were replaced by gasoline-powered models. The first motorized vehicle was a Maxwell, and a little later two more were purchased: a Ford Model T and a Buick. However, when confronted with muddy or snow-covered roads, the school would revert to using horses and wagons equipped with wooden runners rather than wheels. This bus is a model that was used slightly later, a 1930 Ford.

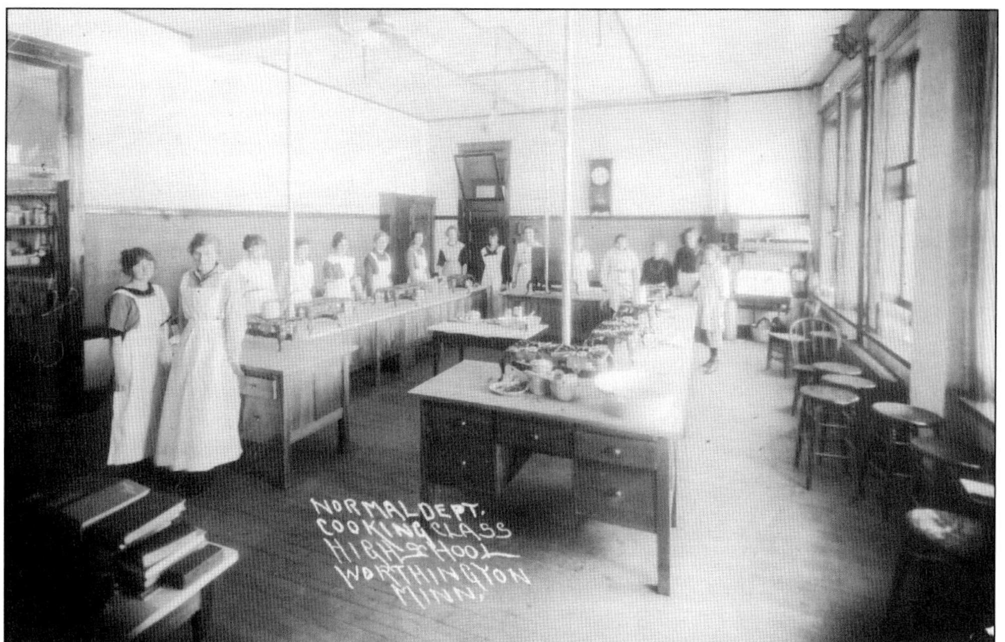

Many early teachers had limited schooling. In 1916, half of the county's country school teachers had only a high school education. To improve teaching standards, the normal school training system was adopted. It was based on the concept of showing student teachers how to use effective teaching practices by modeling these skills in a laboratory classroom. There was a normal school training program in Worthington High School. Shown here are prospective teachers in a model classroom.

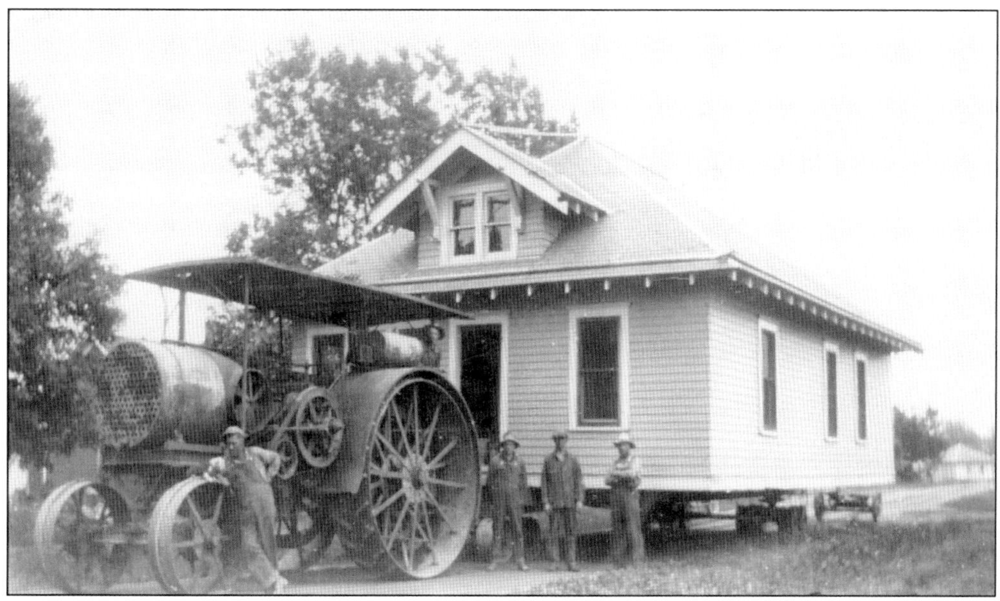

As declining enrollments forced the closure of country schools, the schoolhouses became obsolete. Some townships converted the buildings into township halls, while others sold them off, even the outhouses, at public auction. This school from the Bigelow area in Little Rock Township is being moved to another site.

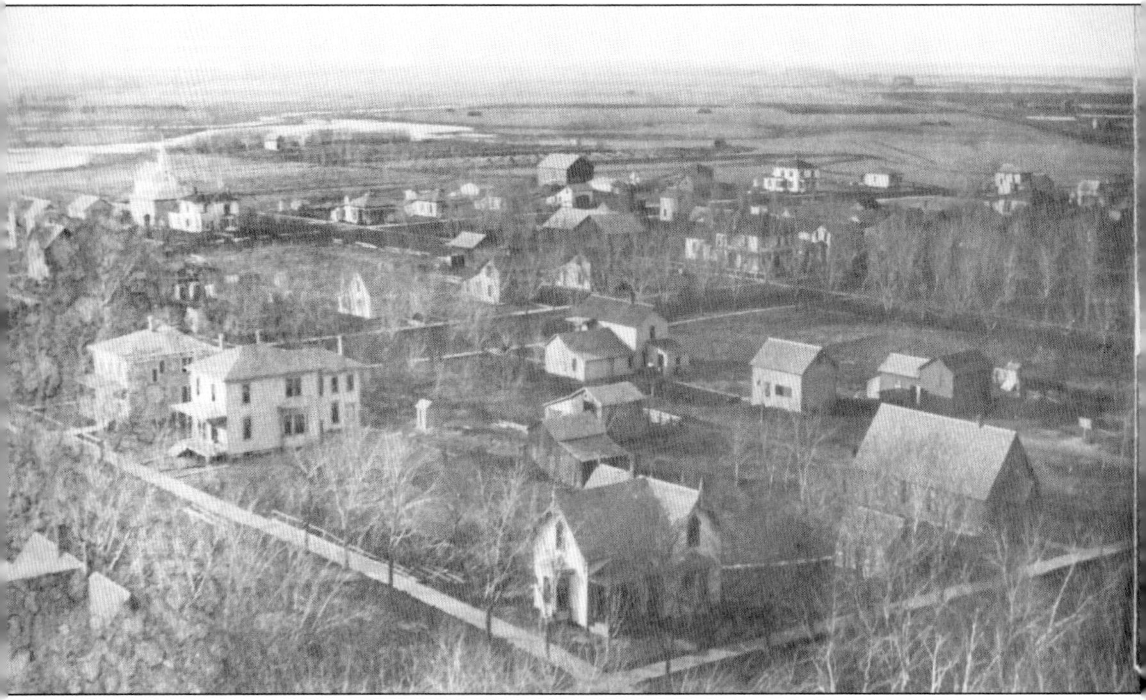

This panoramic view of Worthington from the top of the water tower in May 1893 shows the town's schools as well as some other buildings. At right center is the first school building, the Hexagonal School, which was built in 1875. In 1889, it was replaced by the larger brick structure

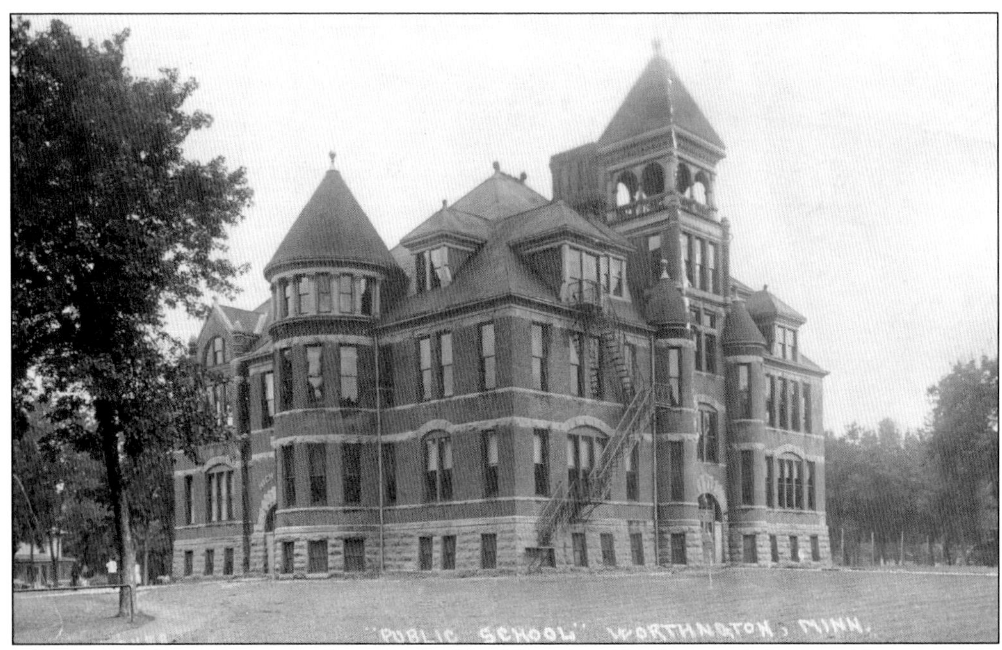

This is one of the two most photographed buildings in Worthington's history. Known as the Castle School, it was designed by Minneapolis architect T.D. Allen and was constructed in 1889 at a cost of $29,000. It was razed in 1929 so that a larger school could be built.

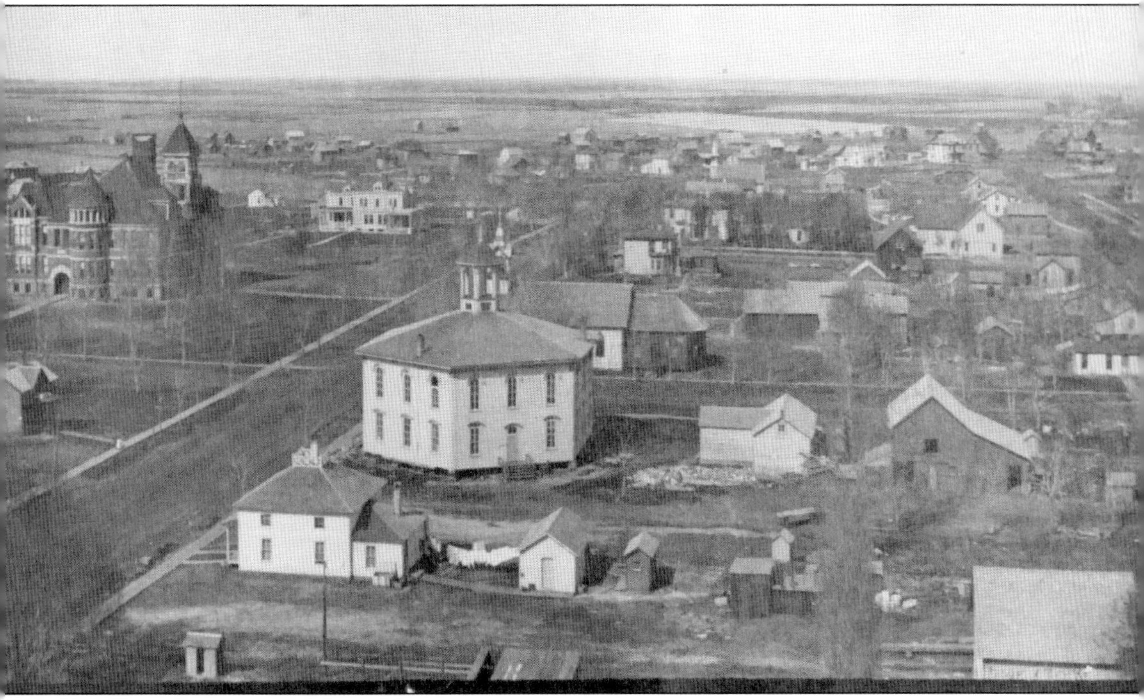

just to the left. To the right of the new school is the George Dayton house, constructed in 1890. Immediately behind the older Hexagonal School is the Swedish Evangelical Lutheran Church (now First Lutheran).

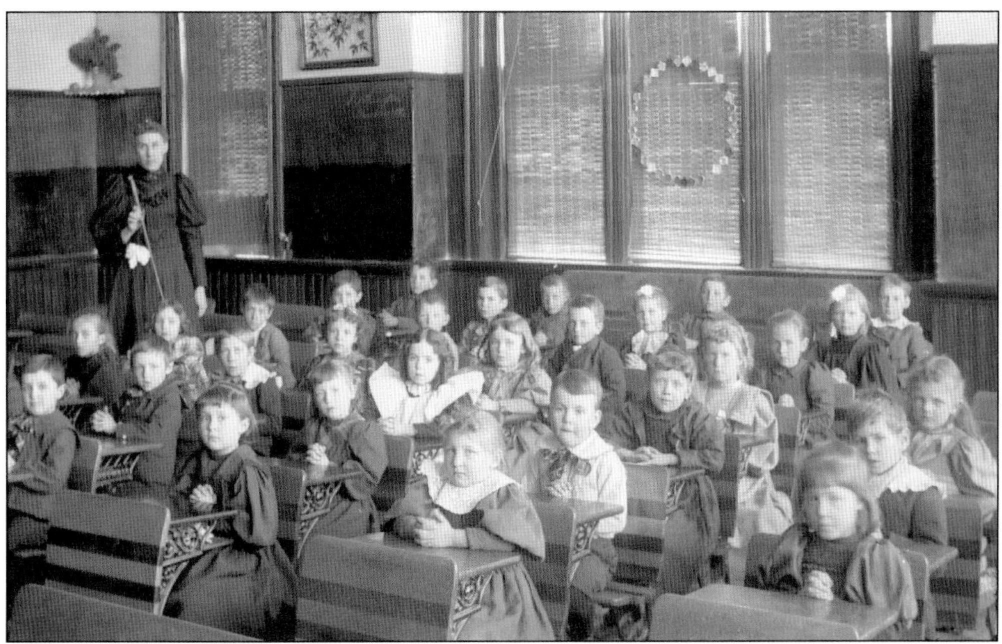

Dated March 10, 1896, this photograph shows an elementary classroom in Worthington's relatively new Castle School. The teacher stands in the background holding her pointer while her 30 students look attentively toward the front of the room. (HDH.)

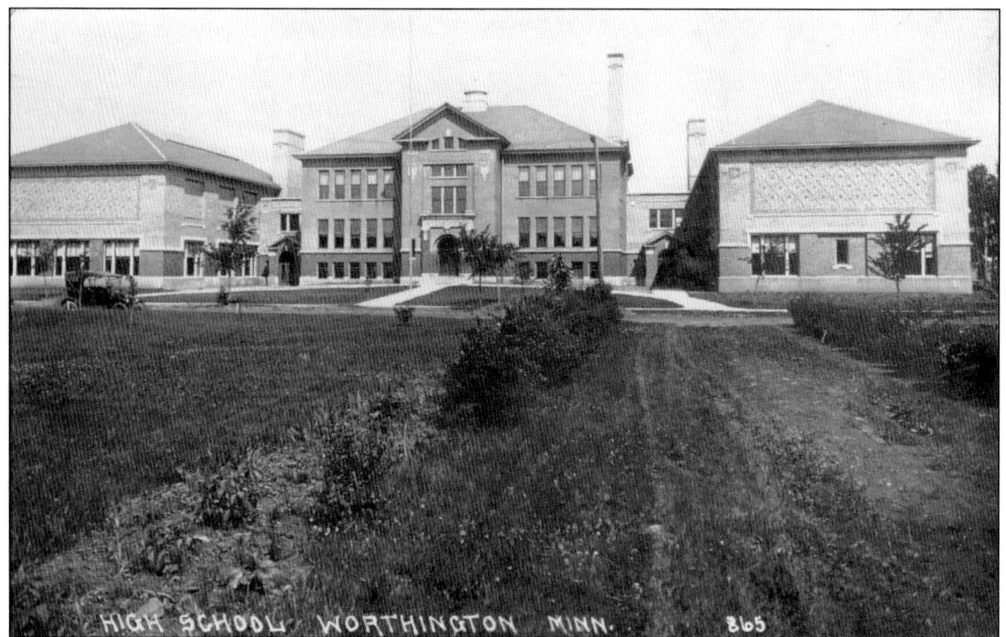

In 1907, Worthington residents decided they needed more school space. They passed a bond referendum approving plans for the construction of a new high school, which was erected in 1909 for $35,000. The building was located in the 1300 block of Seventh Avenue. The original high school is the center section seen here. Within just eight years, a school expansion was completed when the building wings were added on each side of the original structure.

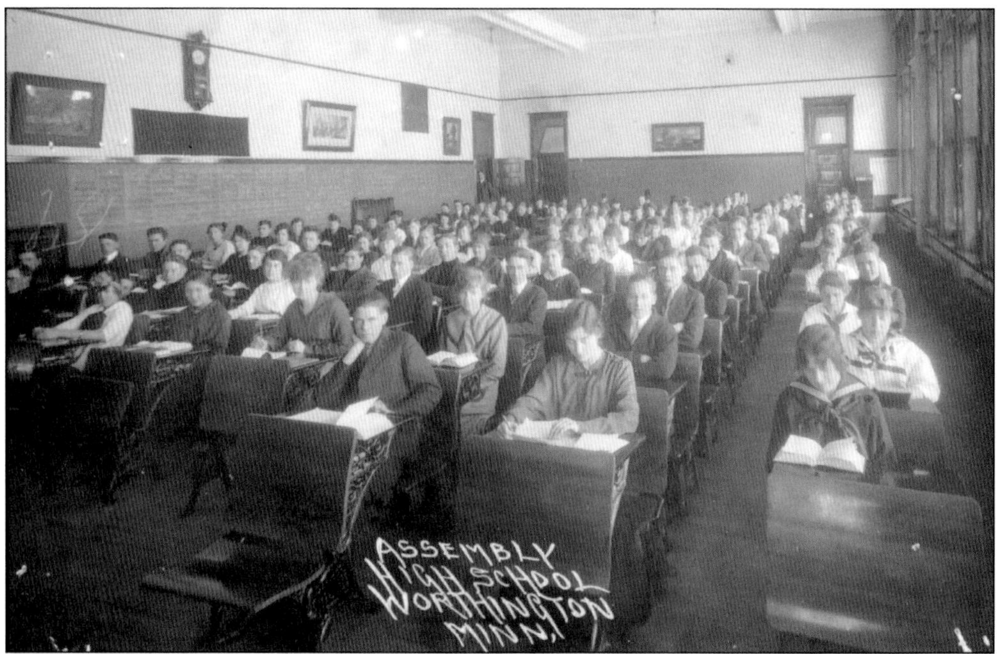

This is one of a series of photographs taken for Worthington High School's yearbook in 1916. They portray students actively participating in different high school classes. This one shows students sitting at their desks during an assembly, which appears to be a version of today's study hall.

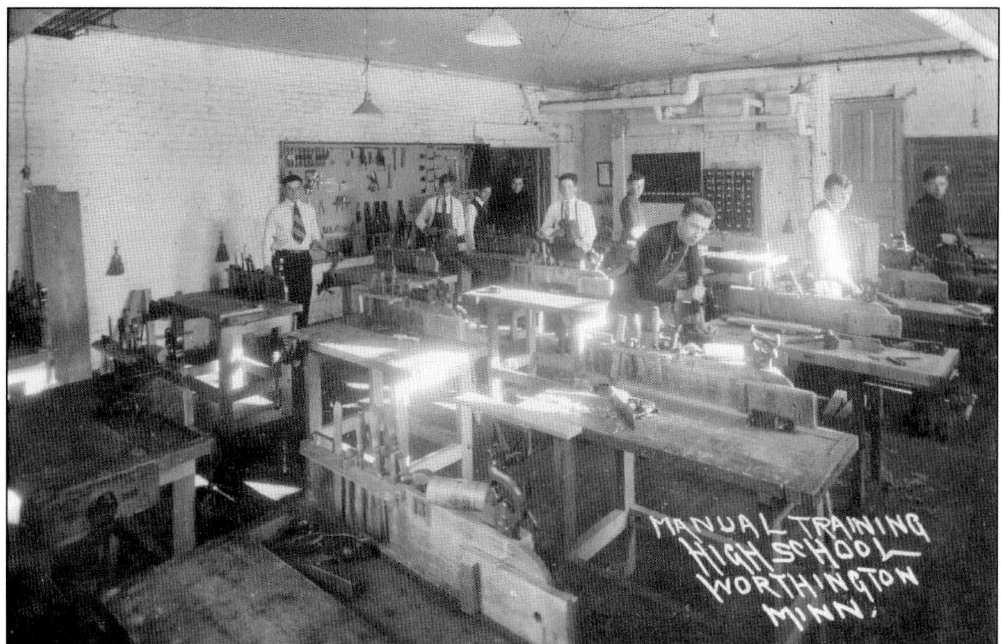

This is another image that appeared in the Worthington High School yearbook of 1916. This picture shows several high school boys taking part in a manual training class, equivalent to today's shop class.

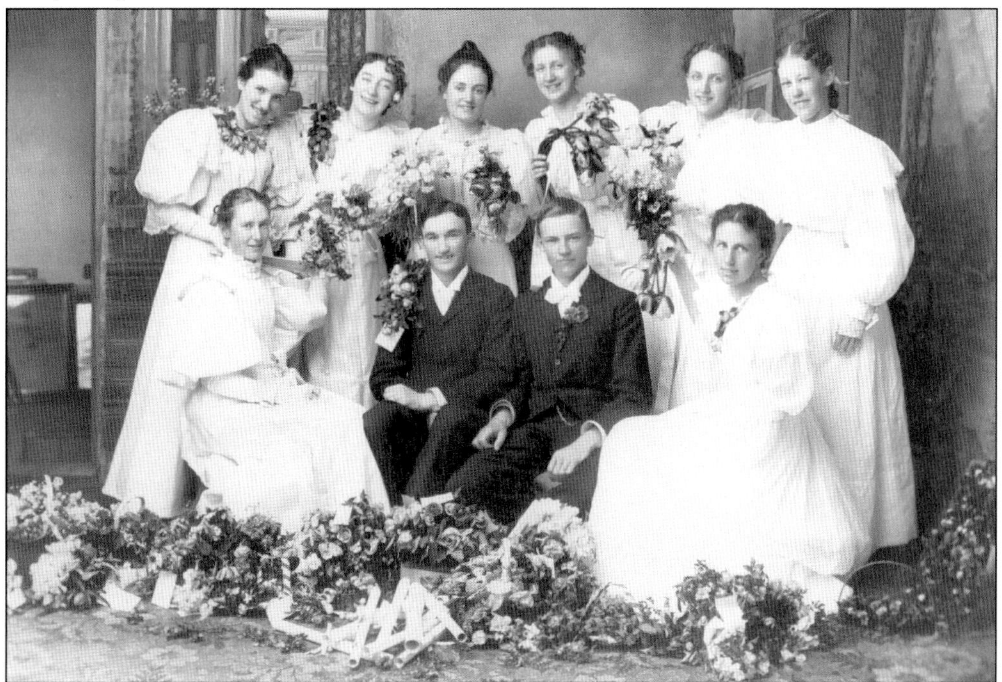

These are the Worthington High School graduates for 1896. This graduation photograph was taken by E.F. Buchan in his photography studio on June 13 of that year. Students pictured include Lulu Putnam, M. Edgar Barnes, Jennie Beckly Boddy, Mary Blair, Cora Covey, Susan Gibson Schekter, Sadie Lewis Tibbets, Laura Hoberly, Mary Moffet, William Stoutemeyer, and Jennie Torrance.

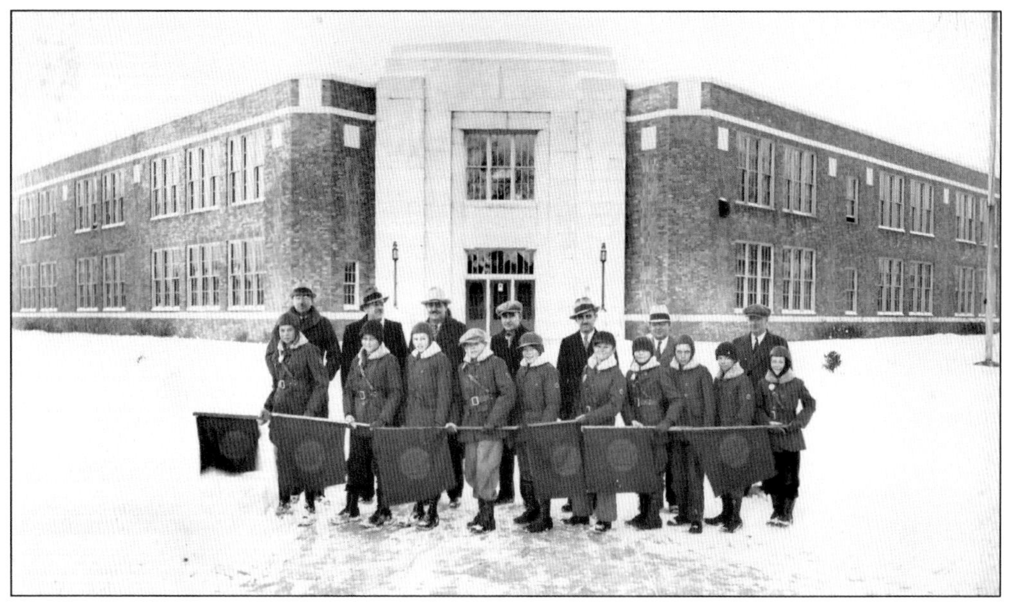

In 1930, Worthington's iconic Castle School was replaced by the Art Deco–style Central Elementary School. The two-story building with its accompanying playground covered an entire block. Taken during the winter, this c. 1935 photograph shows 10 of the school's sixth-grade patrol boys holding their street-crossing flags. Only one of the patrol boys has been identified: Ralph Gruye, third from left. Behind them are seven community leaders; from left to right are Arnold Brecht, Ray Lowry Sr., Eldon Rowe, unidentified, V.M. Vance, Roy Martin, and unidentified.

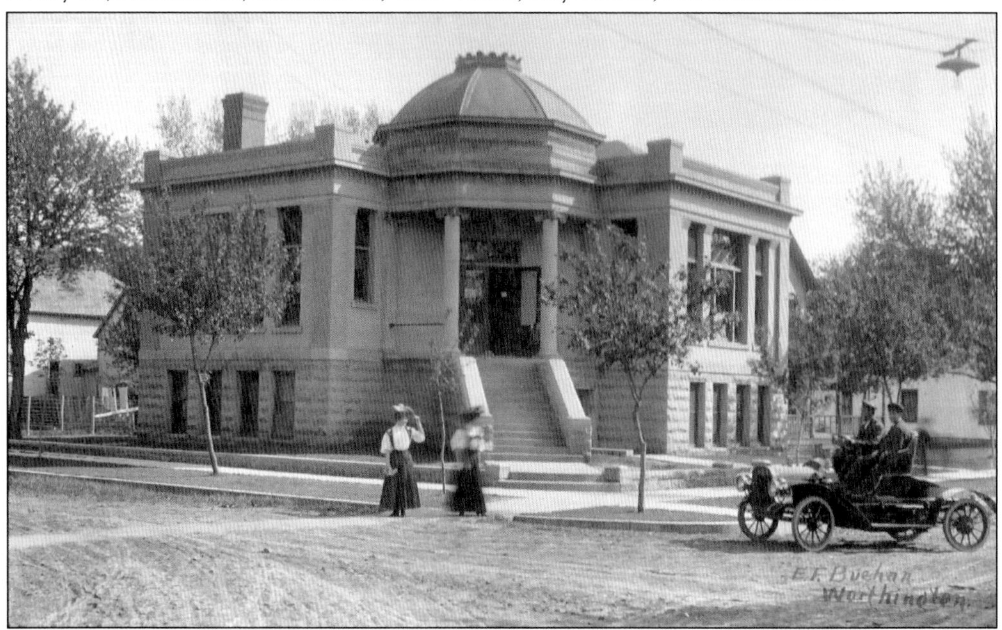

In the late 19th and early 20th centuries, industrialist and philanthropist Andrew Carnegie helped to found 1,679 public libraries across the United States, including one in Nobles County. Carnegie contributed $10,000 towards the cost of establishing a library in Worthington. Completed in 1904, the Carnegie Library was located on the corner of Fourth Avenue and Eleventh Street, across the street from the First Lutheran Church. The building was razed in 1966.

Six

Events and Disasters

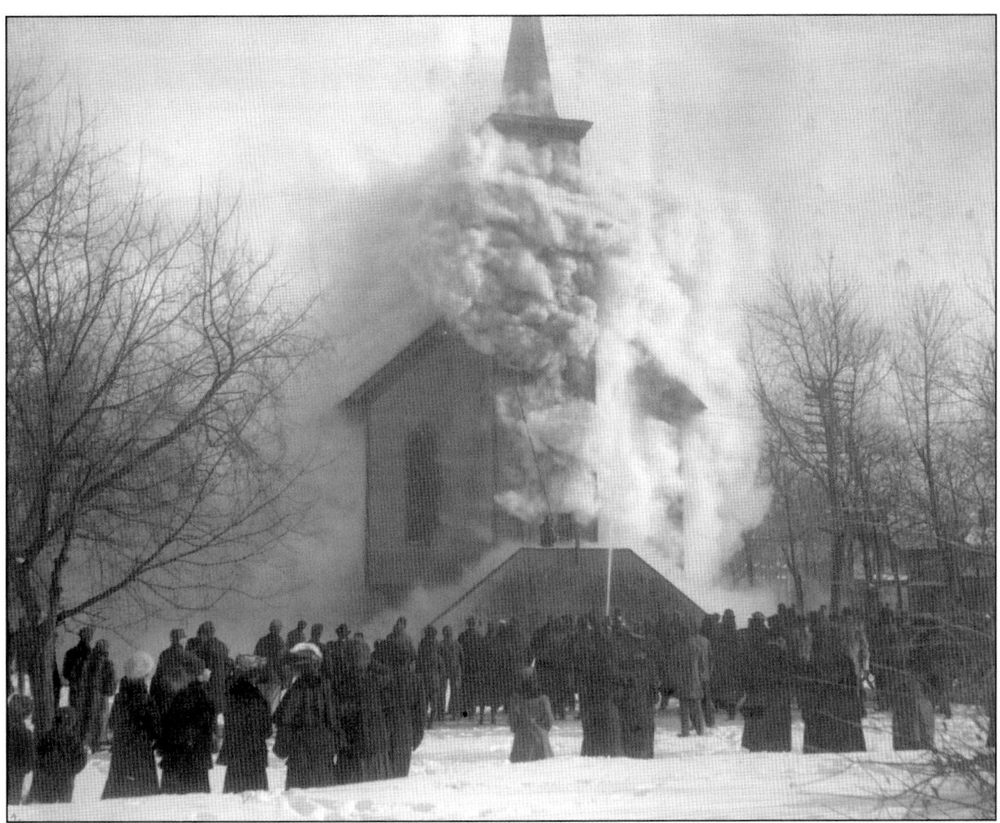

Worthington's first settlers wanted to establish an interdenominational church known as the Colony Christian Union. However, when the different church groups could not agree, they split up. The Congregationalists were the first group to build their own church, the Union Congregational Church, which they dedicated in December 1878. It was the first church building to be constructed in Nobles County. This image captures some parishioners on January 5, 1905, as they watch the original church structure be destroyed in a morning fire.

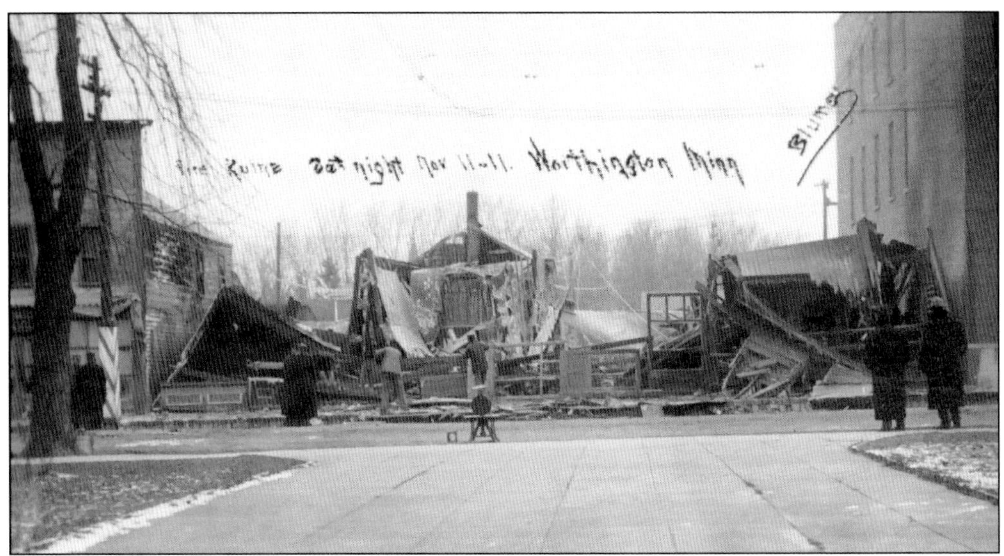

Fire was an ever-present danger in the early years. Wood structures and a small fire fueled by strong prairie winds could destroy several buildings in one fell swoop. This fear became reality in Worthington on the night of November 11, 1911, when an overheated stove in the T.A. Palmer Music Store ignited the wallpaper. Before the night was over, four other businesses were destroyed: Brammer-Thomson Meat Market, D.W. Anthony Barbershop, F.C. Brace Jewelry Store, and J.A. Snyder Harness Shop.

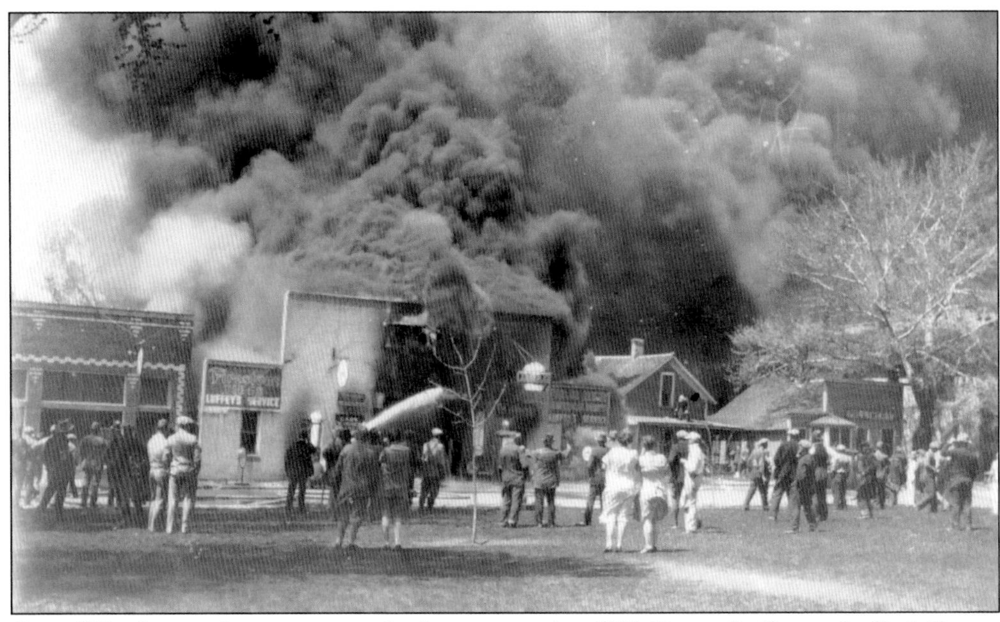

One of Worthington's more spectacular fires occurred in 1929. George Luffey ran Luffey's Garage across from the courthouse. Scattered about inside the building were large basins of used oil, lubesters with new oil, new and used tires, and tubs of grease. When a small fire started in the middle of the garage, it quickly grew out of control, resulting in a roaring blaze with clouds of billowing gray and black smoke.

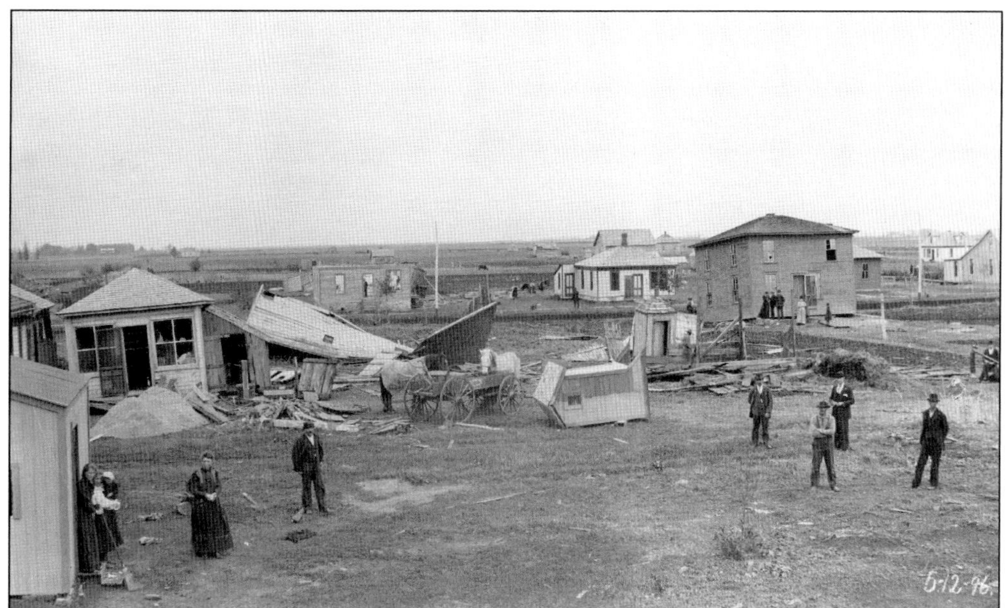

As can be seen in this picture, the primitive wooden buildings of the early prairie towns were certainly no match for a tornado. Not much is known about the actual strength of the twister that blew through Worthington on May 12, 1896, but its force is evident in how it blew over some buildings and shifted the larger house off its foundation.

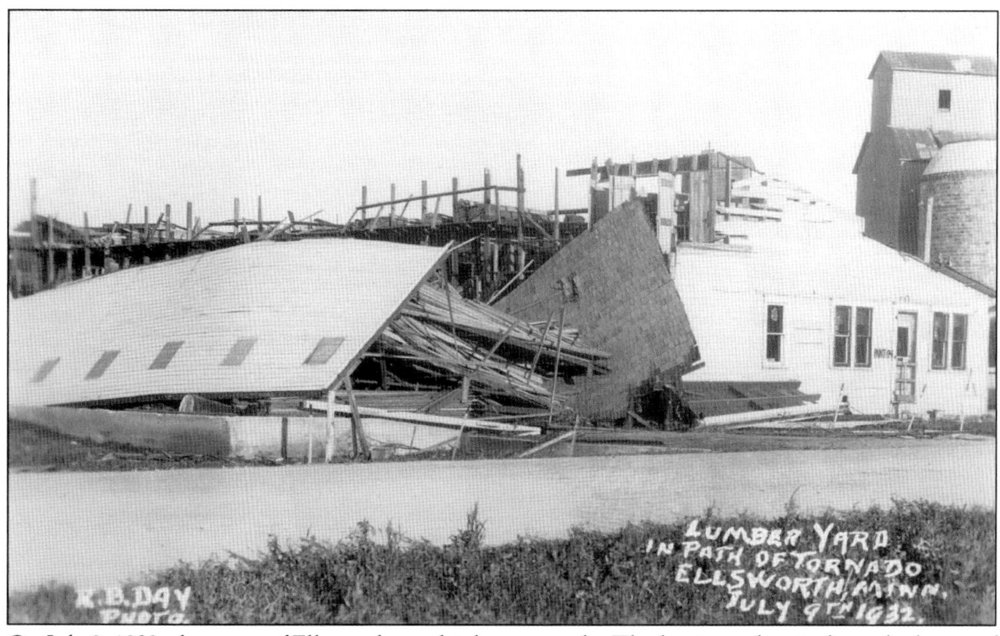

On July 9, 1932, the town of Ellsworth was hit by a tornado. The business district bore the brunt of the storm. This photograph shows the extensive damage that was done to the lumberyard, which had its roof blown off and one of its walls collapsed. Other businesses that suffered significant damages include the Koplow Brothers Store in the Crowley Building, the Rock Island Depot, the Barney Richter grocery store, and Dan McArron's pool hall.

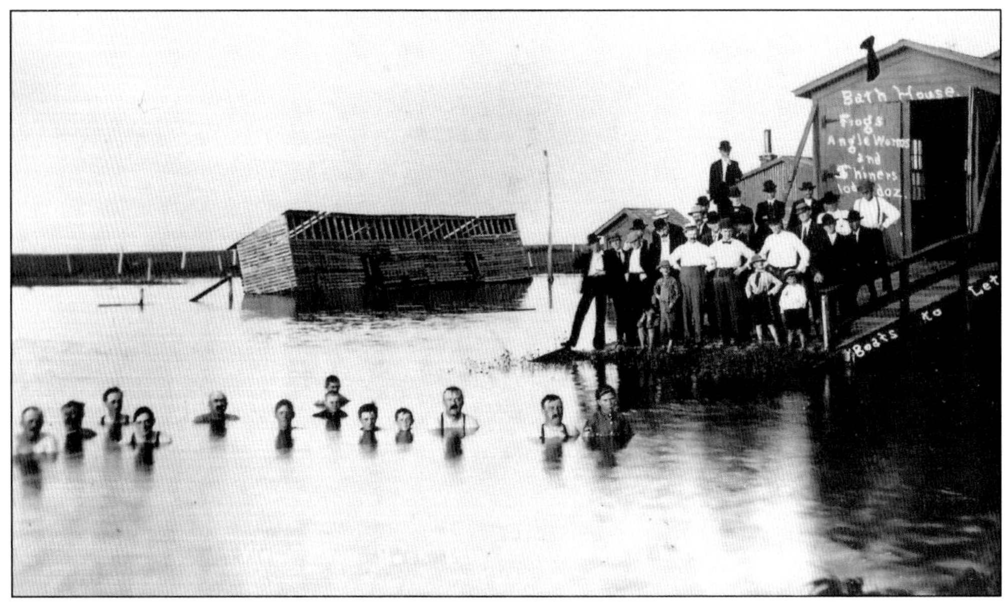

Occasionally, a photographer would use an actual image to create his own version of reality. In this c. 1908 picture of a flooded street in Wilmont, the photographer depicted a community beach setting. Individuals sat in the water puddles to give the appearance they were swimming. Fake signs on the nearby elevator buildings promoted the availability of boat rentals and fishing bait. (AB.)

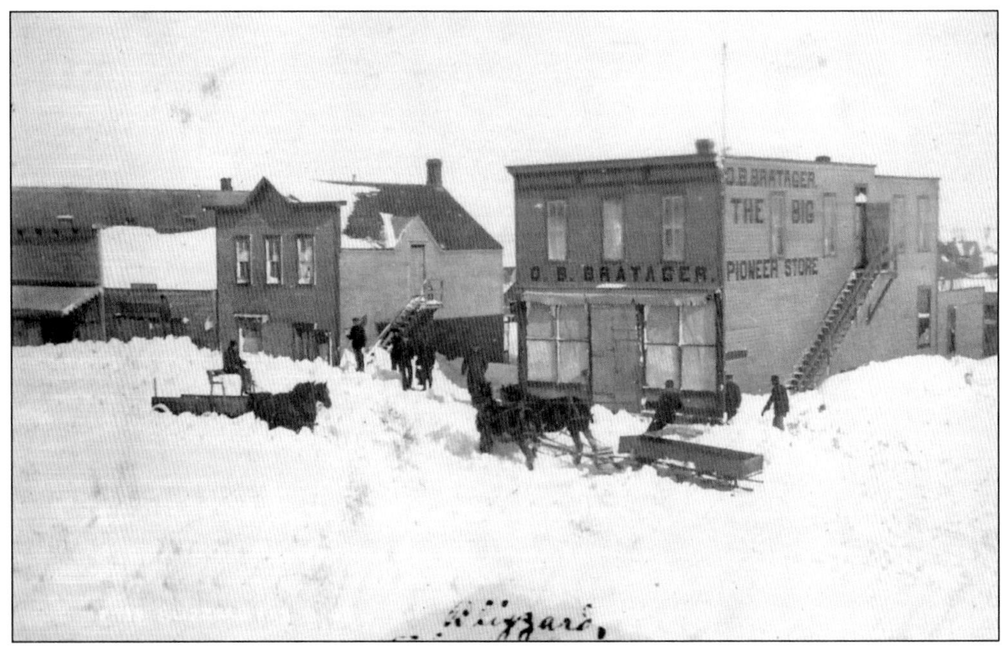

Early residents had to dig out from blizzard-level snows without the help of graders, plows, and front-end loaders. In February 1909, the streets of Lismore were covered by several inches of snow that had blown into huge drifts. Using horse-drawn wagons equipped with wooden runners, the townspeople scooped the snow by hand into the back of wagons.

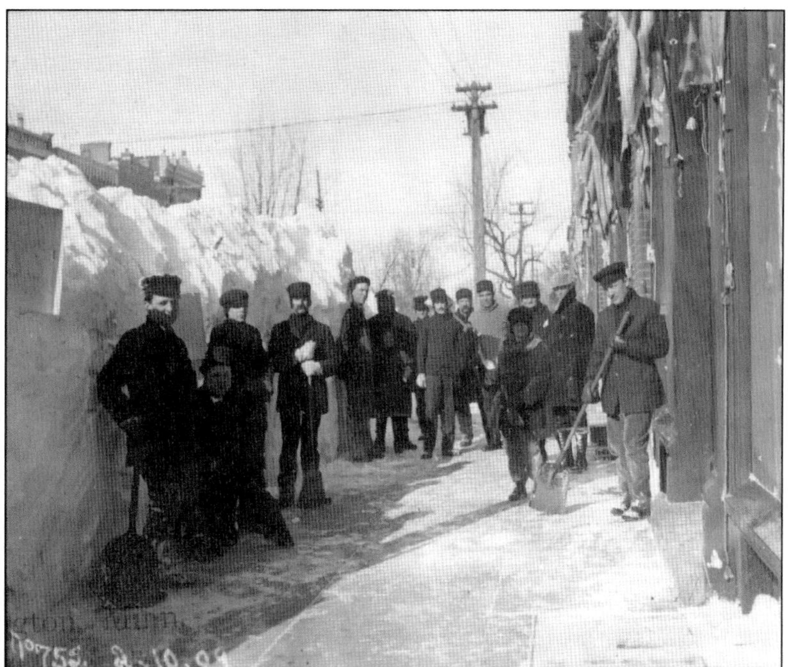

Taken in Worthington on February 10, 1909, this picture appears to show the impact of the same blizzard that befell Lismore in the previous photograph. Here, an army of shovelers has been busy clearing the sidewalks in front of several downtown stores. It appears they piled the snow on top of the high drifts in the street.

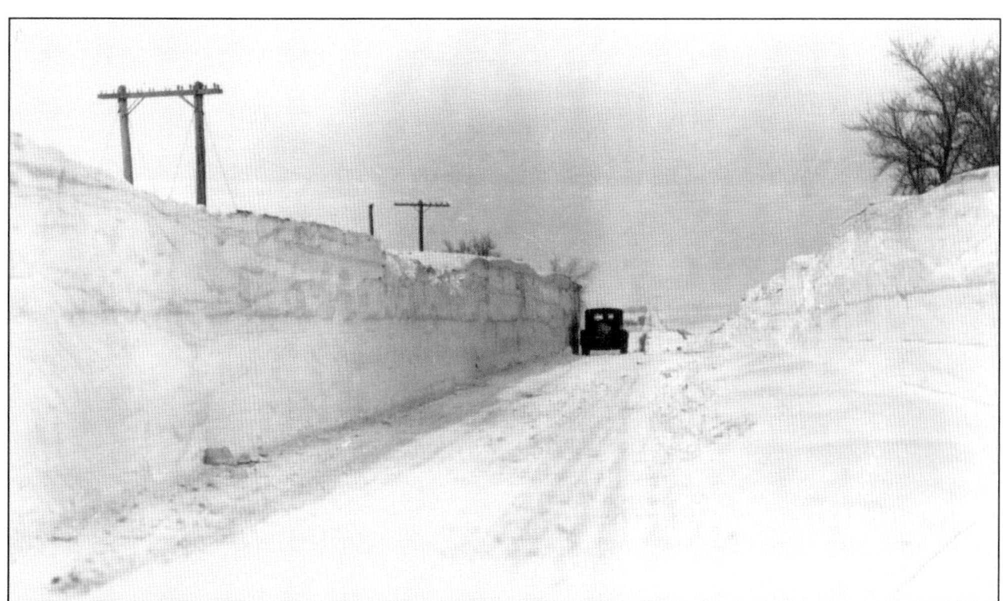

Given the presence of the automobile at the end of this snow-engulfed road, this winter storm happened several years later, probably in the 1930s. It appears that a grader or plow was used to cut a path through these huge snow embankments to allow vehicle traffic to get through. Notice the height of the snow bank against the trees and the telephone poles.

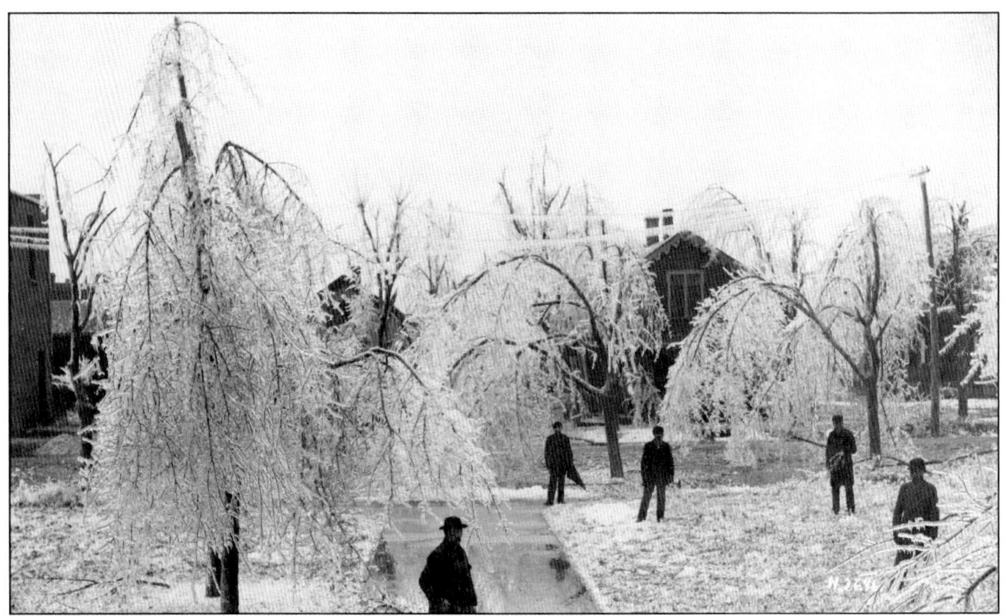

Storms can come in many different forms—rain, wind, or snow. Though ice storms probably do not carry as much total damage potential as some of the others, they certainly can wreak havoc with trees and powerlines. This E.F. Buchan photograph captures the effects of Worthington's November 26, 1896, ice storm on the town's trees.

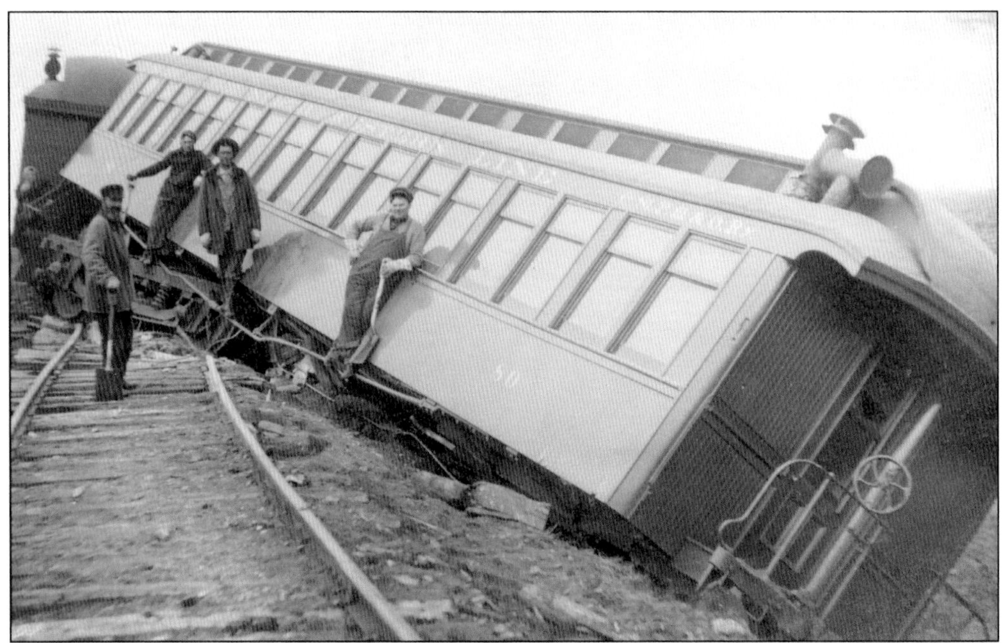

As railroad lines were expanded across Nobles County, there was increased freight and passenger traffic. Train service to the Dundee area started as early as 1880. This derailed passenger train car, pictured around 1910, was the first train wreck in Dundee's history.

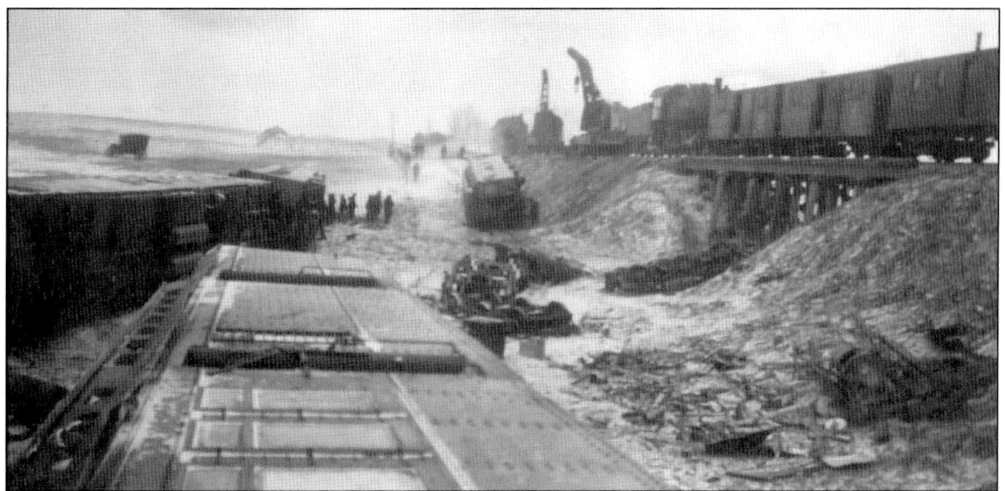

On February 9, 1914, the *Twin City–Omaha Limited*'s Train No. 1 derailed three miles north of Bigelow. It had been bound for Minneapolis when supposedly a faulty rail shattered due to cold weather, causing the train to leave the track. Two people were killed and 16 were hospitalized. Some of the injured had to be removed from the wreckage through the train car windows. A freight conductor who was on the train ran back to Bigelow for help.

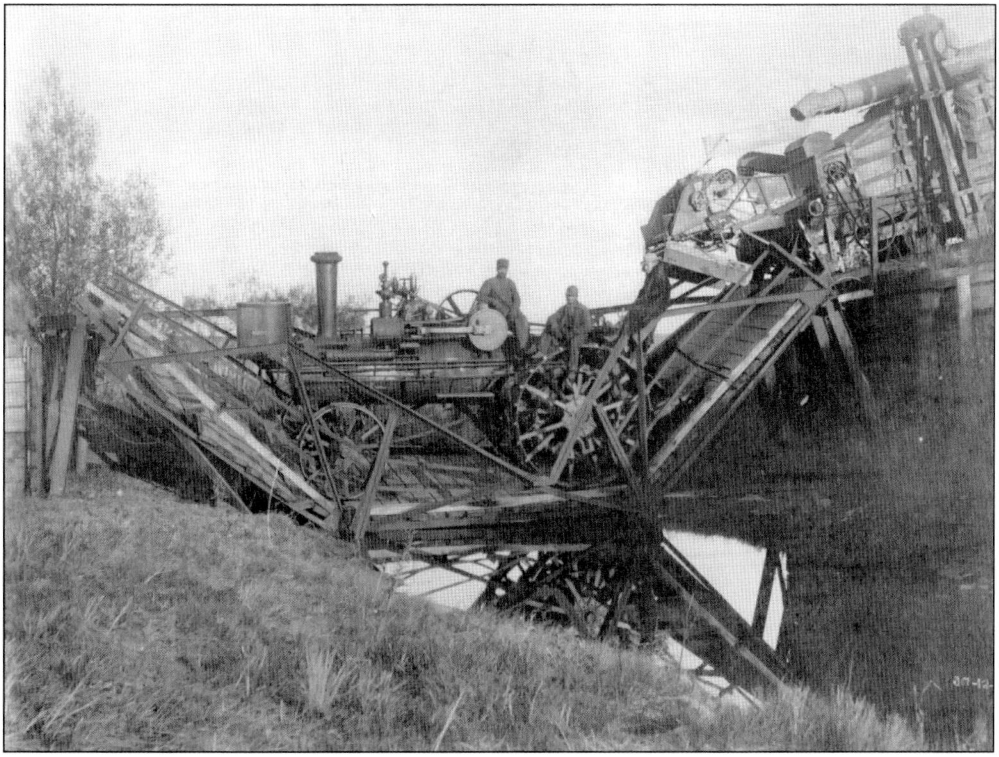

Early in the 20th century, more modern steam- and gasoline-powered tractors began to replace horses for pulling farm equipment. Their increased size and weight sometimes exceeded the capacity of the existing infrastructure, as can be seen in this photograph taken in Seward Township. After succumbing to the equipment's weight, the bridge and steam engine both ended up in the bottom of Jack Creek.

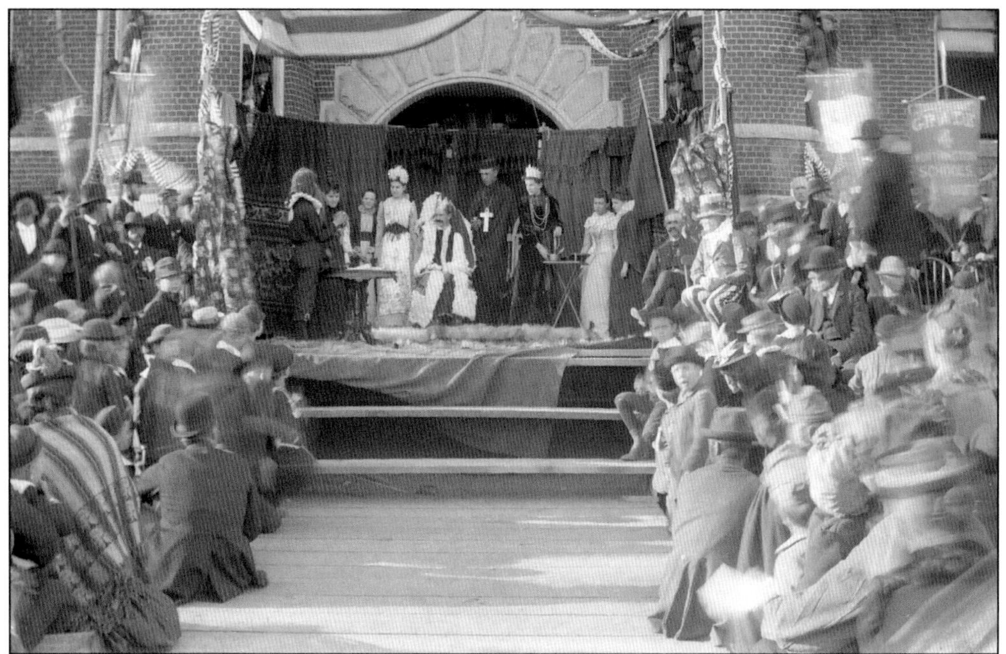

Worthington residents put on a pageant during the summer of 1892 to mark the 400th anniversary of Christopher Columbus's discovery of America. The Columbus play was staged on a platform erected in front of the Castle School's main entrance. The actors wore elaborate costumes to lend authenticity to the performance.

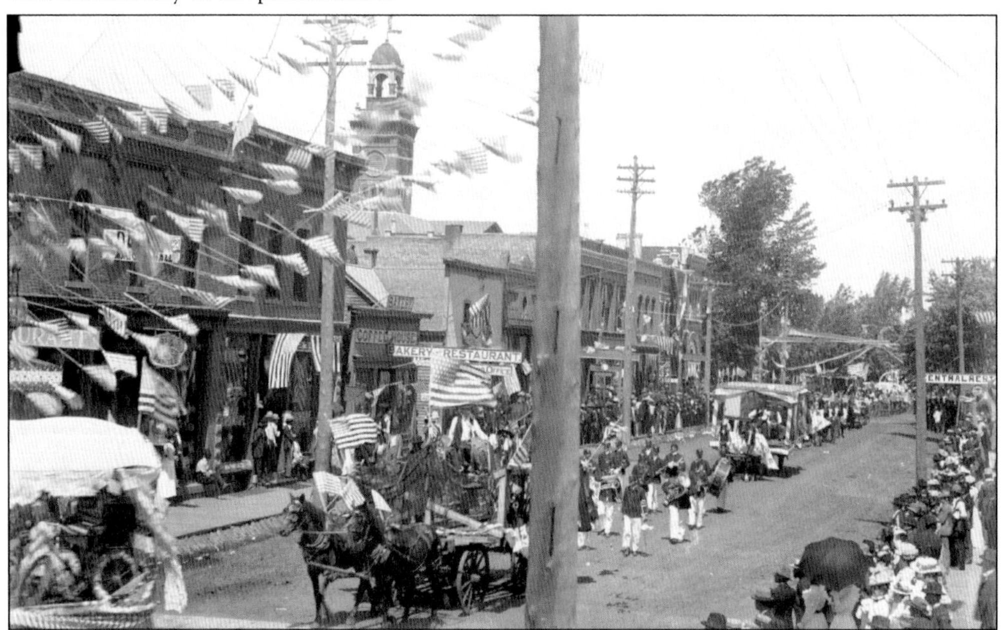

The tradition of community festivals began early in Nobles County. Perhaps one of the earliest was also one of its largest—the first Fourth of July in the 20th century. Held in Worthington, the 1900 celebration was a two-day event featuring music, fireworks, baseball games, horse and bicycle races, awards for best-decorated homes and businesses, and parades like this one. According to newspaper accounts, more than 6,000 people took part. (HDH.)

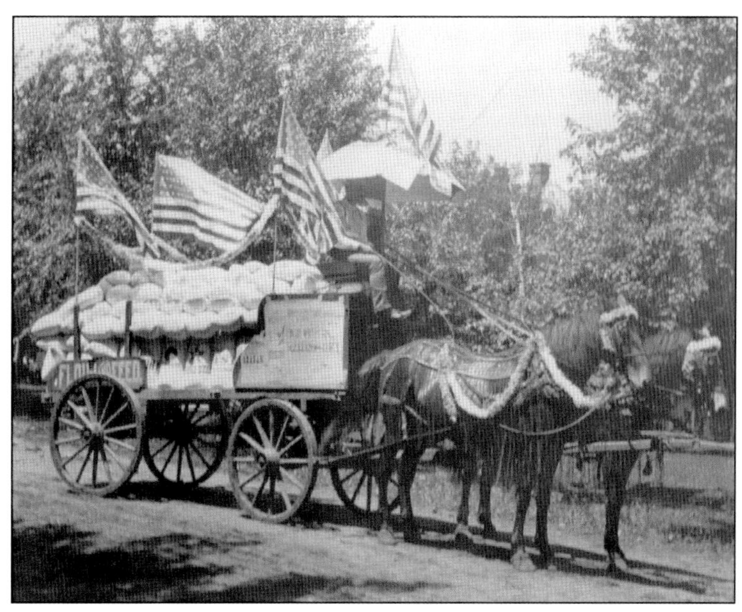

Twenty years earlier, in 1880, this float was part of Worthington's Fourth of July parade. The team of horses is pulling a wagon decorated with US flags and filled with bags of Real White Flour produced by the Worthington Mill Company. The wagon is standing in front of the courthouse, which is obstructed by the trees. The wagon driver, shaded by the umbrella, is J.D. Matteson, the mill's owner and operator.

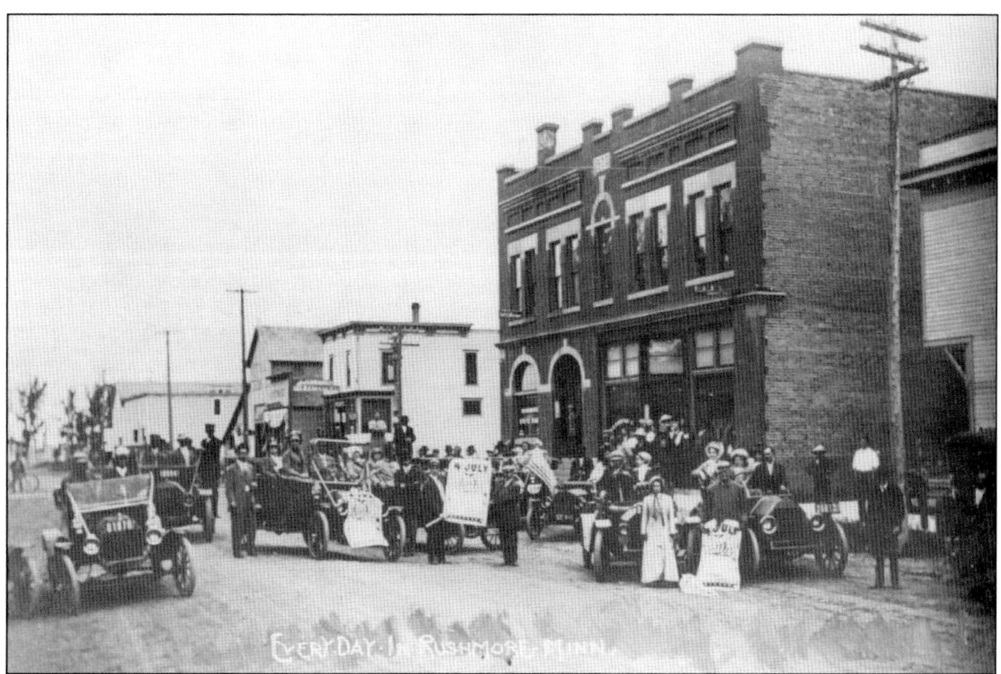

Though the photographer who took this picture labeled it *Everyday in Rushmore Minn*, it appears to be another Fourth of July parade. It is being staged on Rushmore's Main Street, directly in front of the State Bank of Rushmore. It appears as though the parade floats consisted mainly of cars filled with people dressed in their fancy clothes.

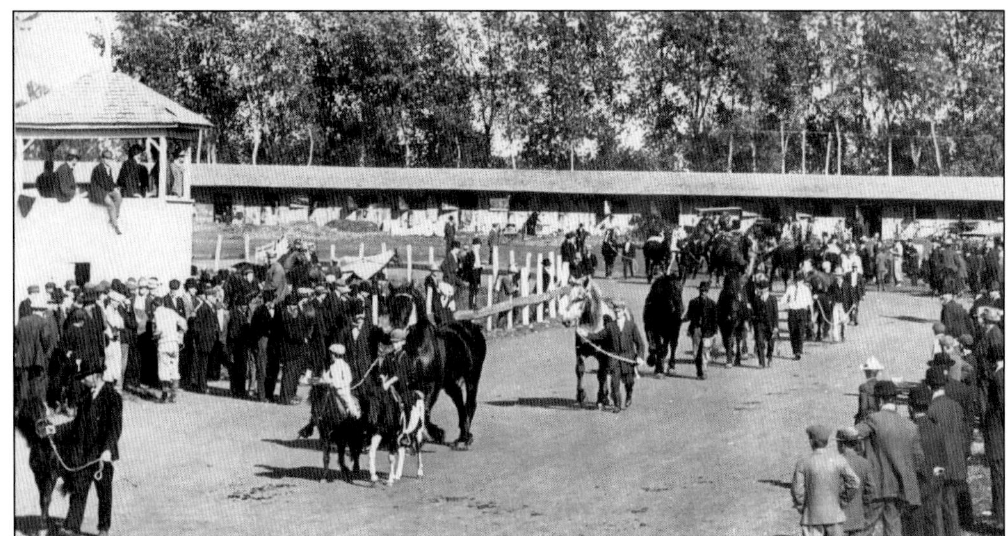

The history of the Nobles County Fair goes back to October 10–11, 1879, when it was first held in Worthington in an open field on the south side of Lake Okabena. Eventually, buildings were erected, and the annual fair continued at this site until 1902. After that, the fair's complex was moved to the town's north side, where the high school is currently situated. This 1909 photograph was taken at that location. In 1955, the fairgrounds were moved to their present location.

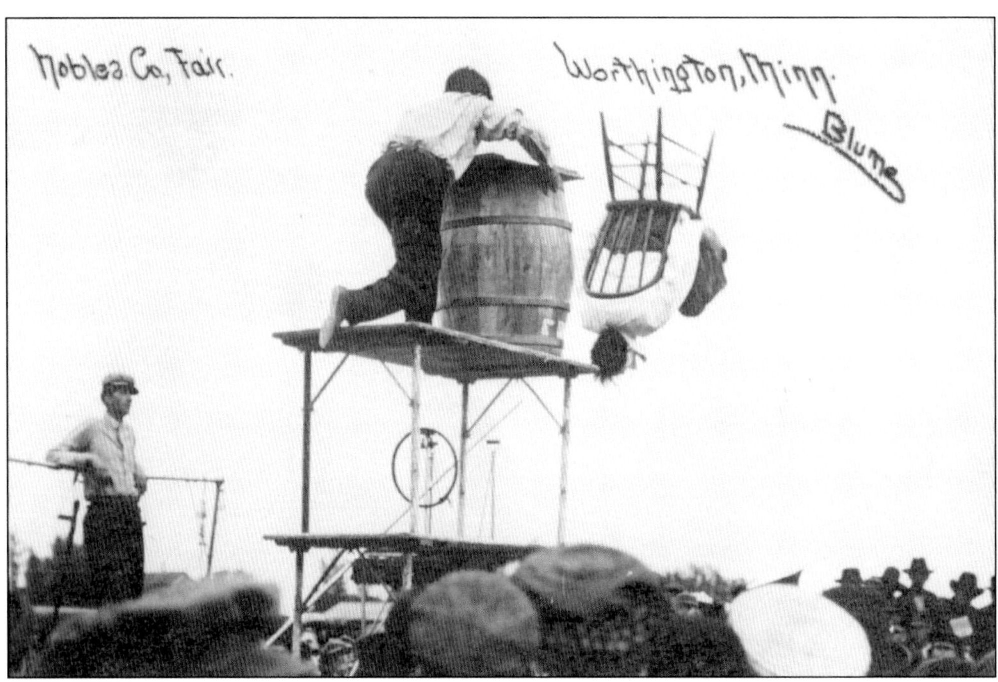

According to historical records, the fair sponsored different activities as part of its multiday schedule. As could be expected, many featured various livestock raised on residents' farms. There were exhibits and competitions centered around the crops, fruits, vegetables, and flowers grown by townsfolk as well as farmers. Horse cart races were run on the fair's oval track, and sideshows like this one were on display.

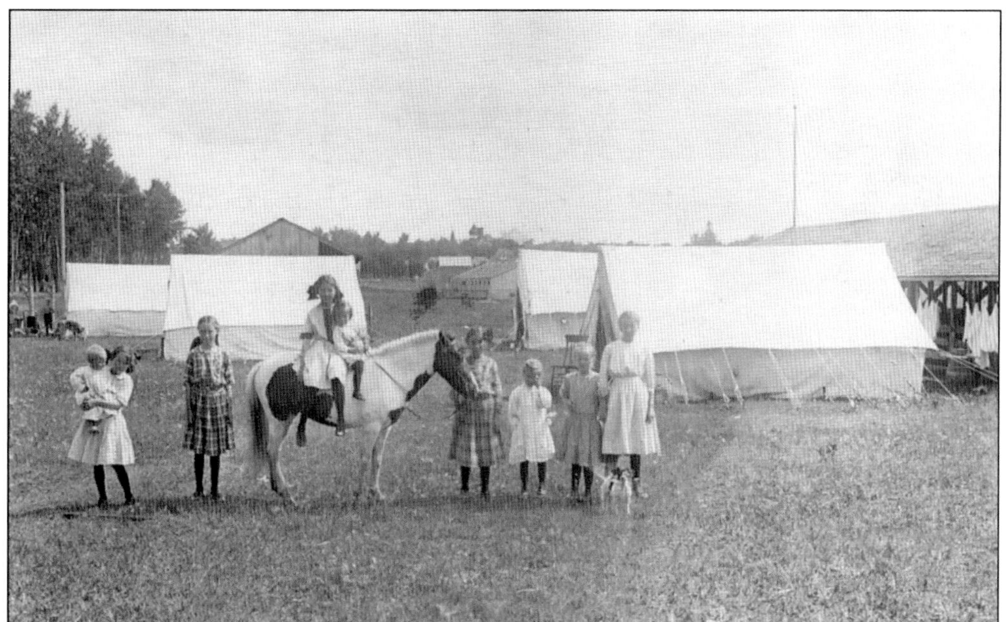

Based on the different steeples in the background, it is believed this picture shows the county fairgrounds when it was at the Clary Street location, where Worthington High School currently is. These young girls are posing with their pony and a small pet dog. Given the pitched tents, it appears some visitors to the fair may have stayed onsite for the duration of the events.

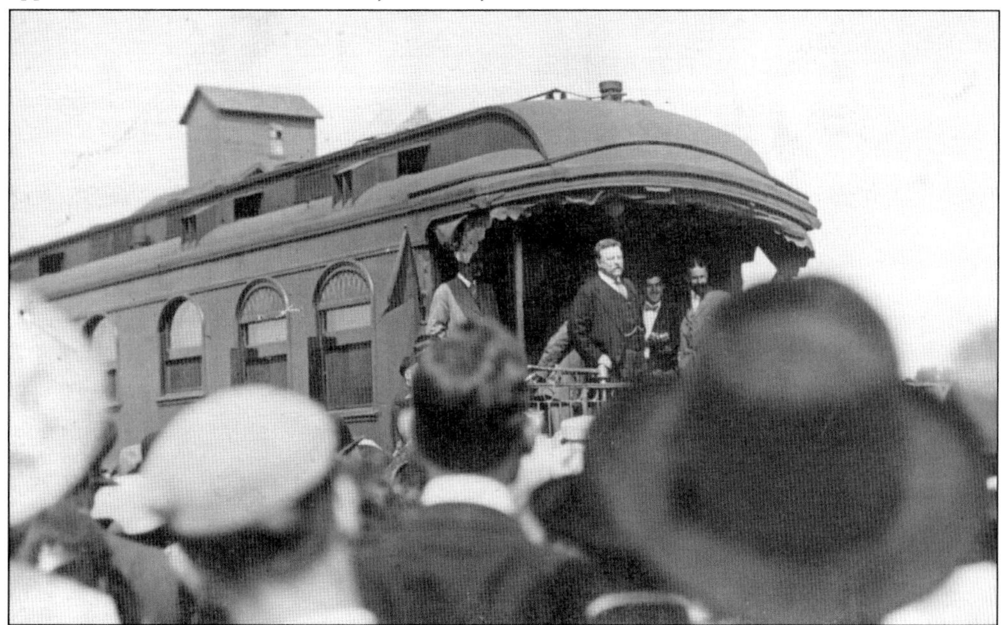

Ray Crippen, a longtime columnist for the *Worthington Daily Globe*, once asked, "Which, for the local region, was the greatest day of all?" His response was the September 3, 1910, appearance of former US president Theodore Roosevelt. Roosevelt is shown speaking from the back of a train car in Org with the town's elevator in the background. As Crippen wrote, there was a large crowd in Org, a place "where hundreds of people never had gathered before and never have gathered since." Roosevelt's train also stopped in Rushmore.

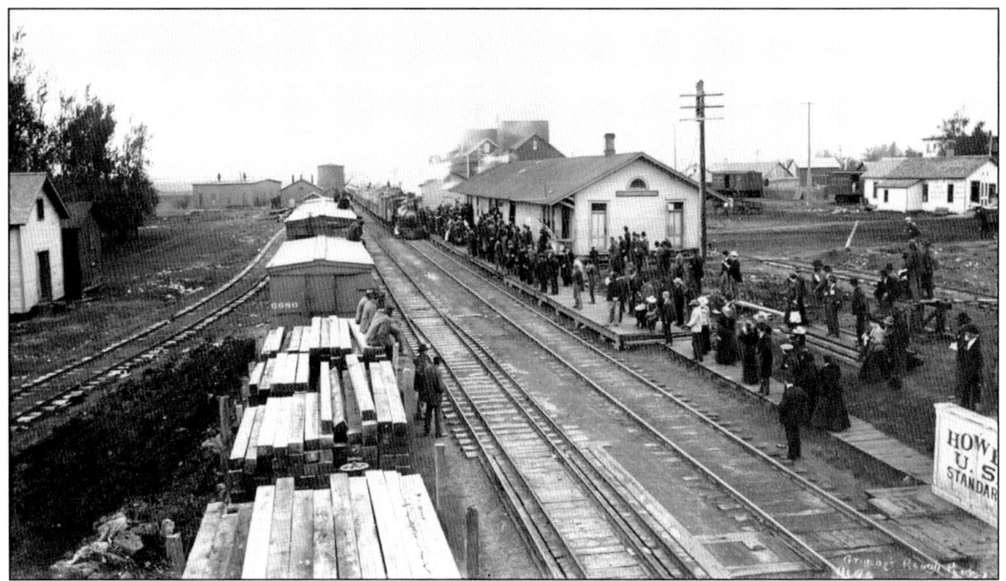

On May 20, 1898, Col. Melvin Grigsby's Rough Riders, a regiment of "cowboy" cavalry, passed through Worthington on their way to serve in the Spanish-American War. Here is the *Worthington Herald*'s account of the soldier train visit: "The boys were a hardy, rugged lot, and if the songs which were distributed among the spectators at the depot are any indication of the fighting qualities of the cowboys, they could lick a whole regiment of Spaniards. About 1,000 people were at the depot to bid the boys God speed. Fifteen boxes of cigars were collected by Landlord Oakes, of the Western, and distributed among the soldiers." (HDH.)

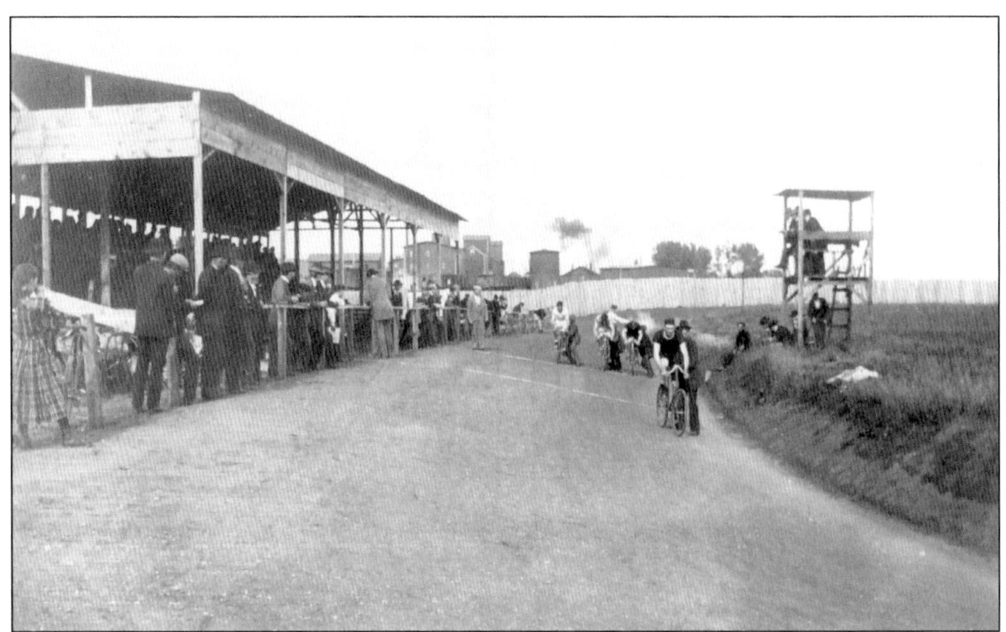

Two images of early bicycles were featured on page 63. In addition to being an important means of transportation, they were also an increasingly popular form of recreation and sport. This c. 1895 photograph shows a bicycle race held on the county fairground's oval track. During this period, the fairground was located on the south side of Lake Okabena.

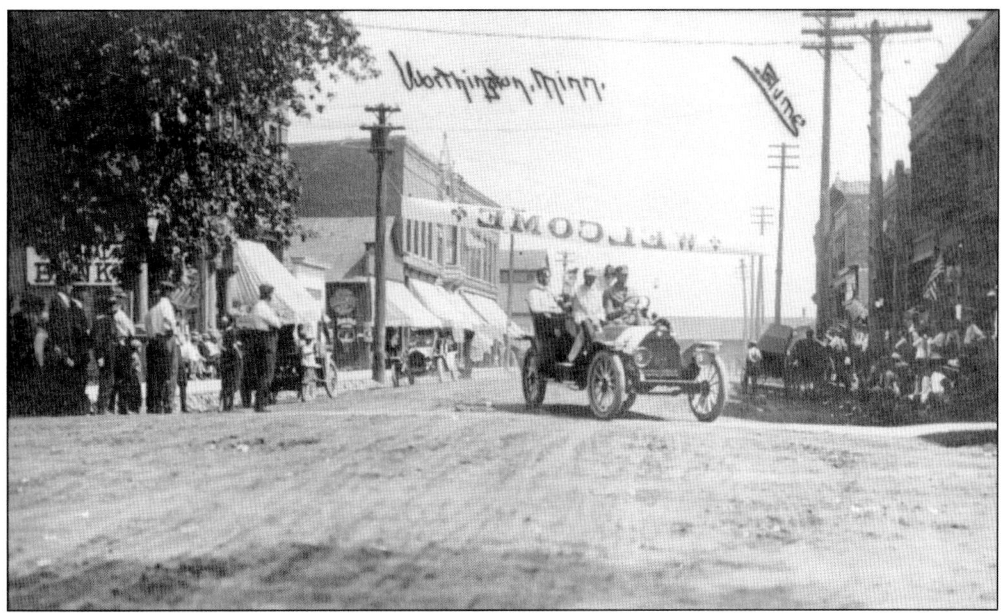

Judging from the "Welcome" banner strung across Tenth Street, this looks like it could have been a car rally or race or possibly even a parade. Some of the people in the car appear to be wearing special clothing for driving. Spectators are observing from both sides of the street.

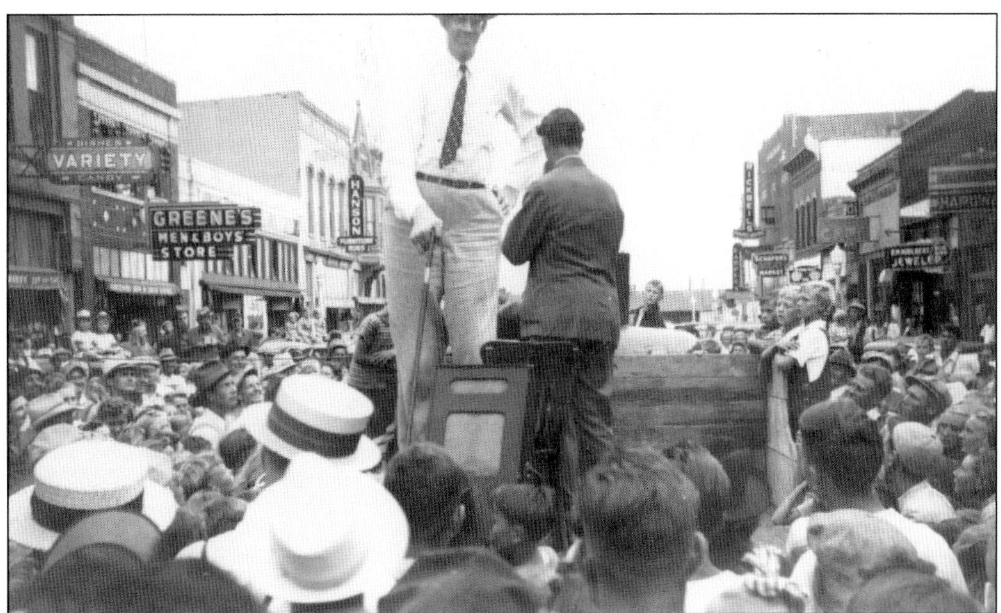

Another event that brought a flock of spectators to downtown Worthington was the appearance of the world's tallest man, Robert Wadlow. He is seen here around 1938 standing on a platform in the middle of Tenth Street by the corner of Third Avenue. By the time of his death four years later, at the age of 22, he had reached a height of 8 feet, 11 inches; he wore a size 37 shoe.

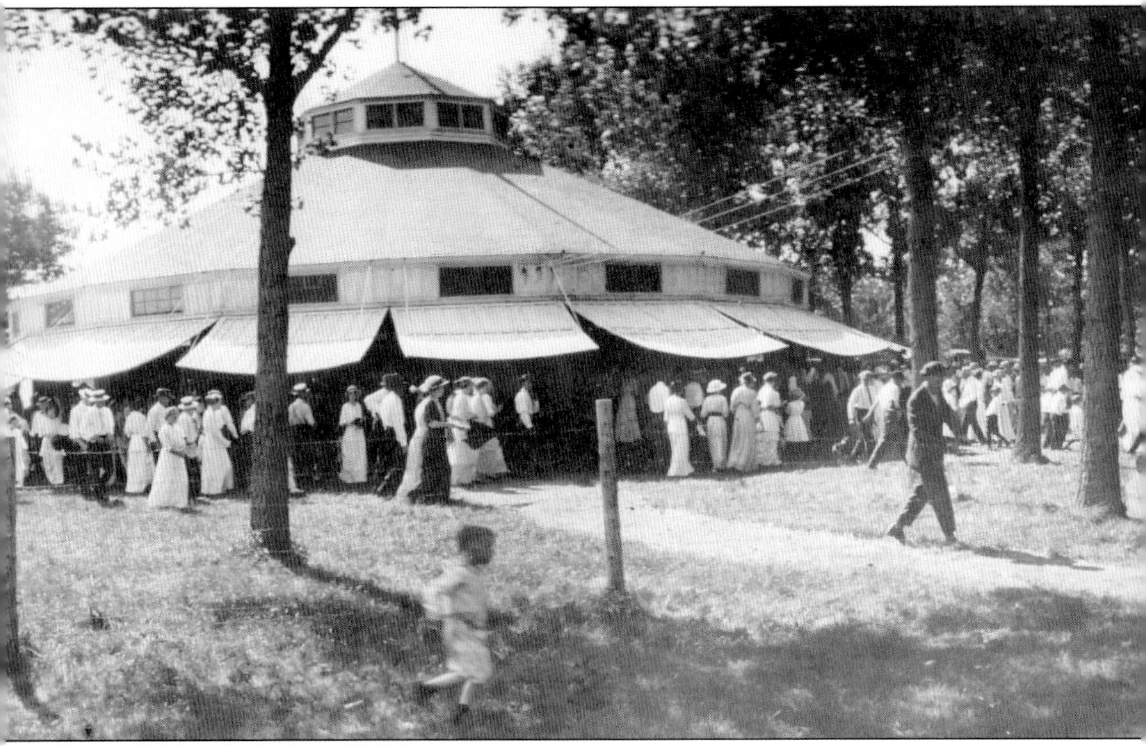

To offer Worthington residents more culturally enriching activities, a group of community leaders decided to form a Chautauqua organization. Its first event was held in 1906. For its location, the organizers chose the city park on the north shore of Lake Okabena. They believed it was an ideal site: it was close to downtown, had access to city water, the grounds were lighted, and there were ample opportunities for camping, bathing, boating, and fishing. This is a panoramic view of the

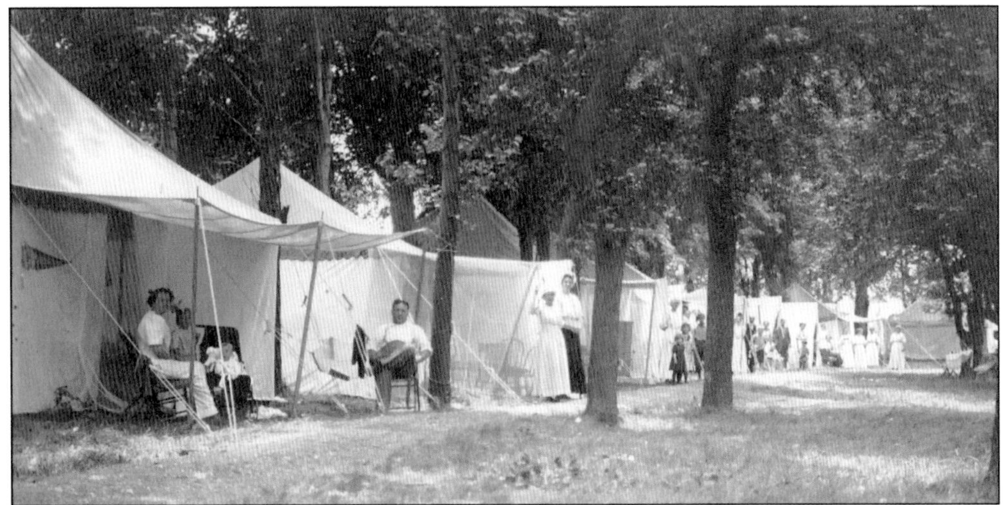

Worthington's Chautauqua festivals were held from 1906 through 1932, featuring a succession of speakers, dramatic plays, and musical entertainment. Programs were scheduled over 7 to 10 days in July or August and included evening as well as afternoon activities. Some of the most famous speakers to appear in Worthington were former US president William Howard Taft, William Jennings Bryan, and Rev. Billy Sunday. Many people opted to rent tents so they could stay on site.

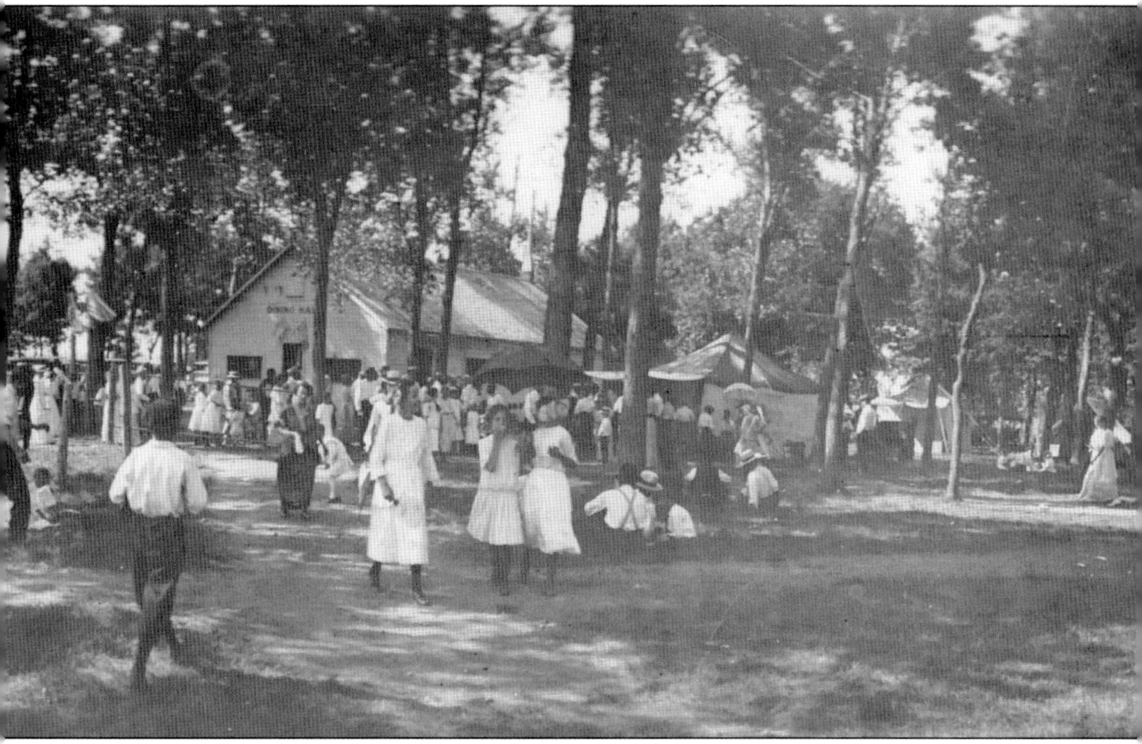

Chautauqua grounds. The large building to the left is the assembly hall, which was constructed in 1907 for $2,500. This is where the presentations were held. Note the side shutters, which could be opened to allow for the lake's cool breeze on a hot summer day. The smaller building is the dining hall, which was built a few years later.

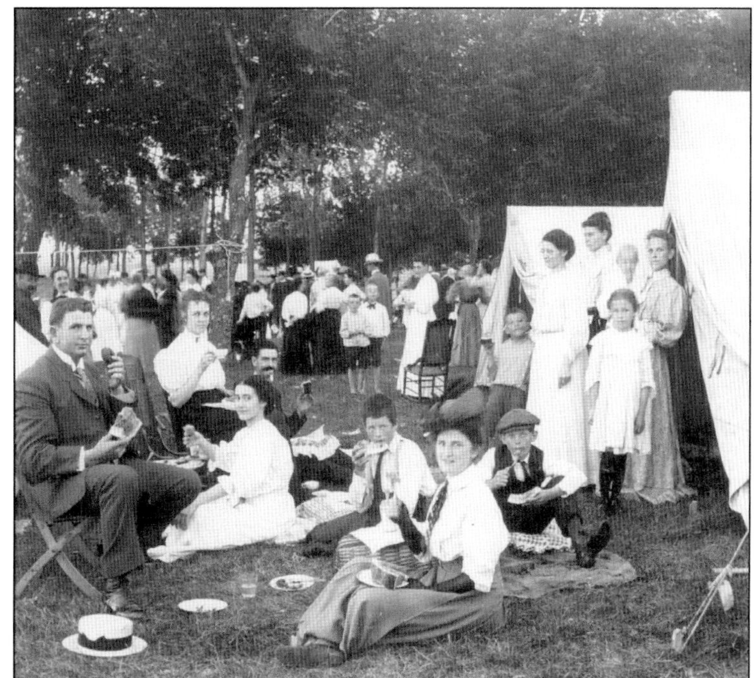

Renting tents was a popular option, especially for out-of-town attendees. Some communities reserved a row of tents so their residents could congregate together. To accommodate travel to and from Worthington's festival, the railroads scheduled special excursion trains. These individuals enjoying a picnic lunch include Anna Hebberg, Loren and Nancy Clark, Mrs. Webster, and Belle Webster.

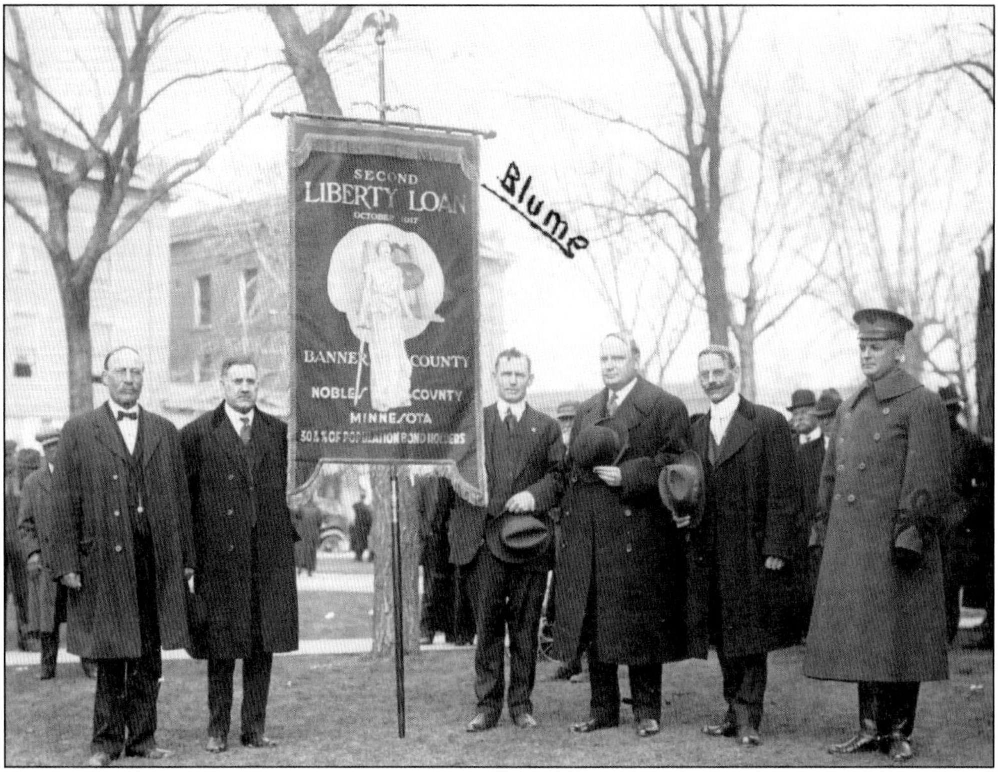

During World War I, the Liberty Loan program was established to help finance the war. Individuals could purchase bonds that were redeemable after the war for the original cost plus interest. Pictured here are officials promoting the local effort to sell bonds, including J. Burr Ludlow of Rushmore, standing to the right of the banner. According to its inscription, Nobles County was recognized as a "Banner County," with 30.5 percent of its population known to be bondholders.

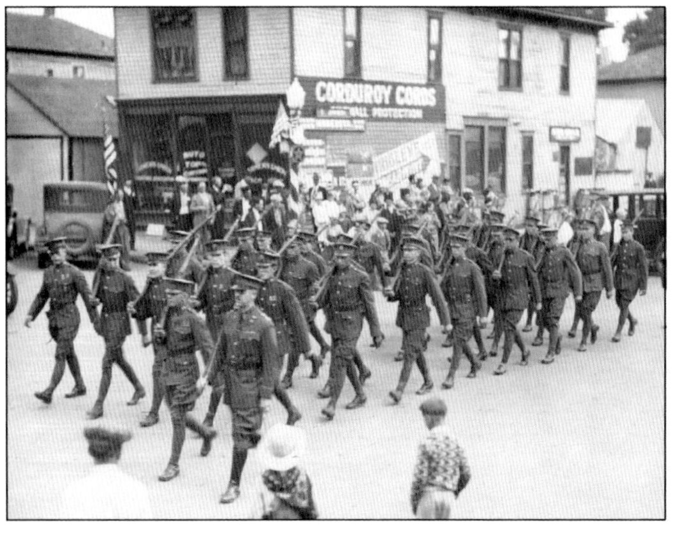

The soldiers of Worthington National Guard's Company F are marching down Fourth Avenue toward Lake Okabena. They are believed to be parading as part of a c. 1927 community celebration, most likely Memorial Day. The captain, at the left, is Dr. Ray W. Lowry Sr., a local optometrist. In the front line of the troops, third from the left, is Hardy Rickbeil, who eventually owned several downtown retail stores.

Seven

For the Fun of It

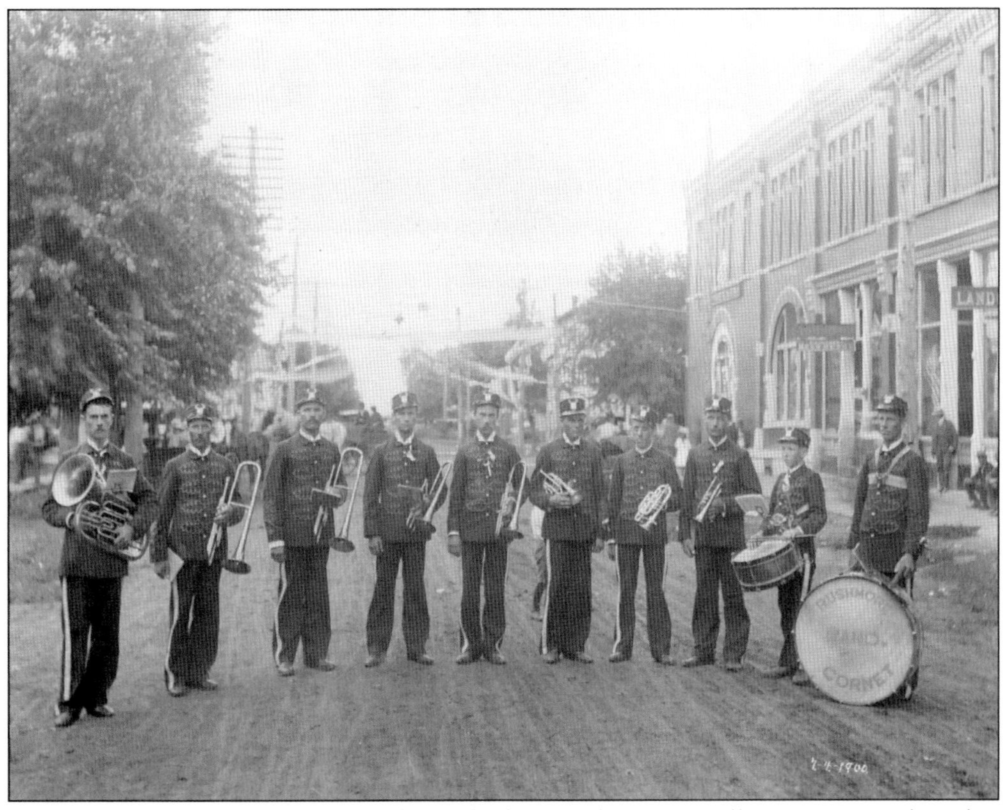

From the number of band photographs in the historical society's collection, it is evident that making music was an important aspect of community life. It seems as though almost every town had its own community band. Here, the Rushmore Cornet Band is posing on a Worthington downtown street after marching in a parade on July 4, 1900. Band members are E.G. Edwards, Chris Fagerness, Steven Fagerness, Charles Morton, Alberg Dahlberg, Henry Thompson, Clayton Bedford, and George Thompson.

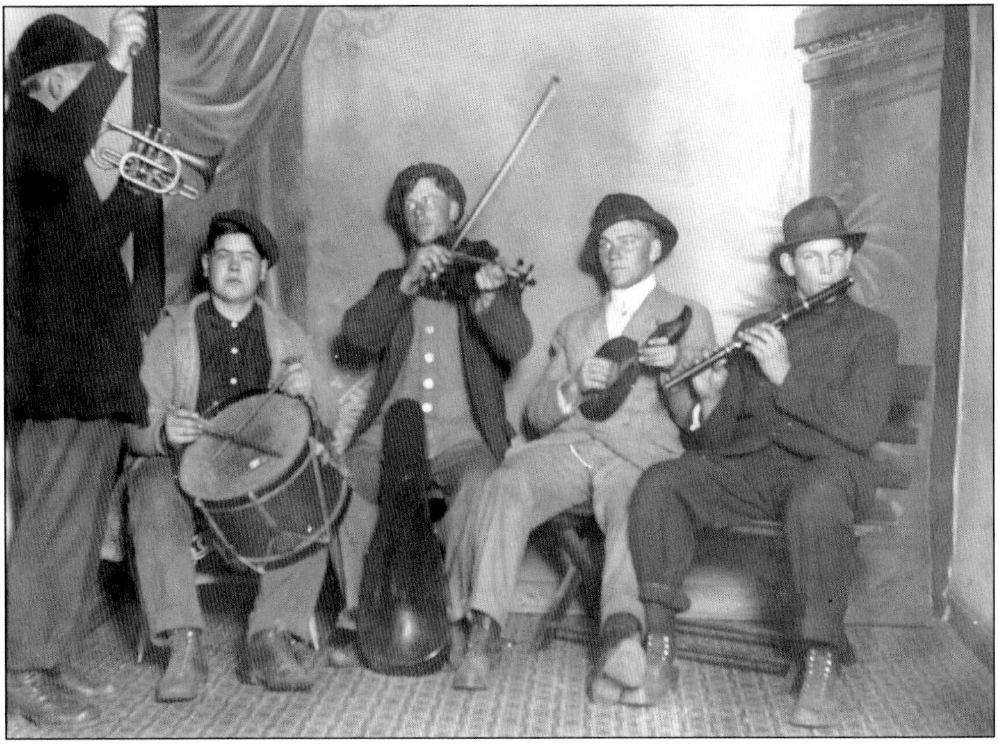

Some bands were well established. Their members wore matching uniforms whenever they performed. However, there were also less formal musical groups like this one from Dundee. They could have simply been friends, relatives, or neighbors who came together to play their instruments for their own musical enjoyment. They may have occasionally played for a church picnic or a wedding dance.

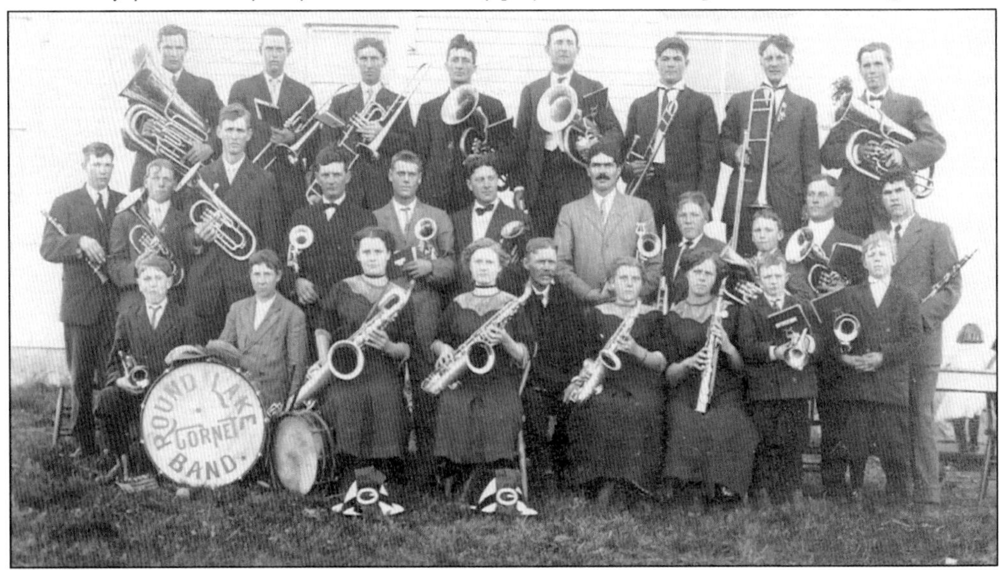

When it was first organized in 1910, the Round Lake Cornet Band consisted of some 20 instruments. For unknown reasons, most of the earlier instrumental groups were called cornet bands, even though there were also trombones, baritones, saxophones, and clarinets. This is the only early band the authors know of that was both multi-gender and intergenerational.

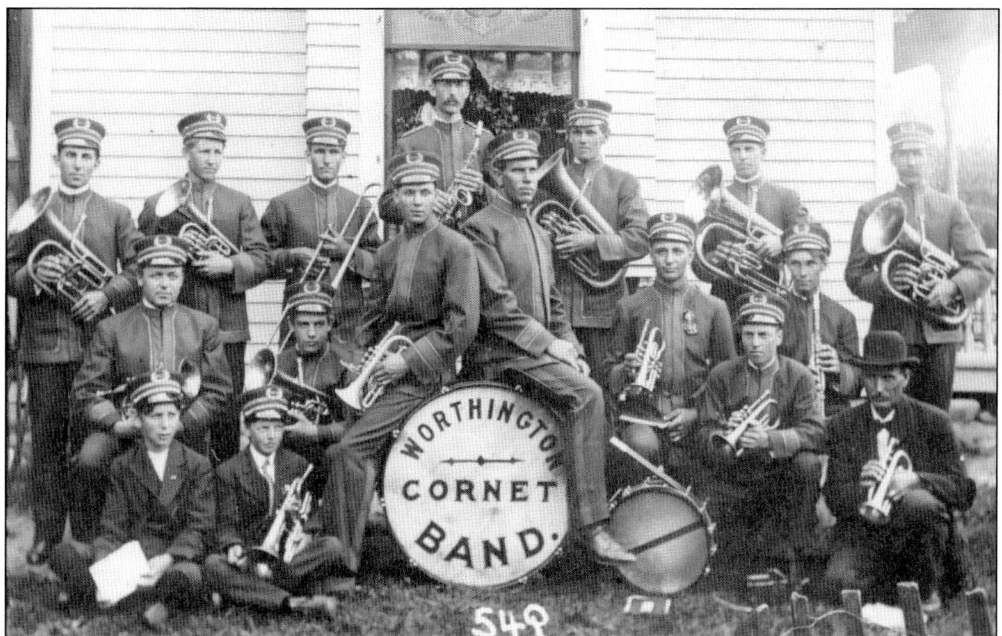

In *An Illustrated History of Nobles County, Minnesota*, A.P. Rose writes that there were two brass bands in Worthington. The first one was organized in 1906 by band leader Prof. Wilson Abbott. Within just a few years, this group consisted of nearly 50 instruments. The other brass band apparently had been around considerably longer and had been "maintained by the Scandinavians of the city." Based on size, the group pictured above is probably the latter. There is no mention of an all-female band in any local historical accounts. There could have been such a group, but it is also possible that the women pictured below were simply posing with instruments and uniform jackets borrowed from the men pictured above. These pictures were taken consecutively by the same photographer. (Below, JF.)

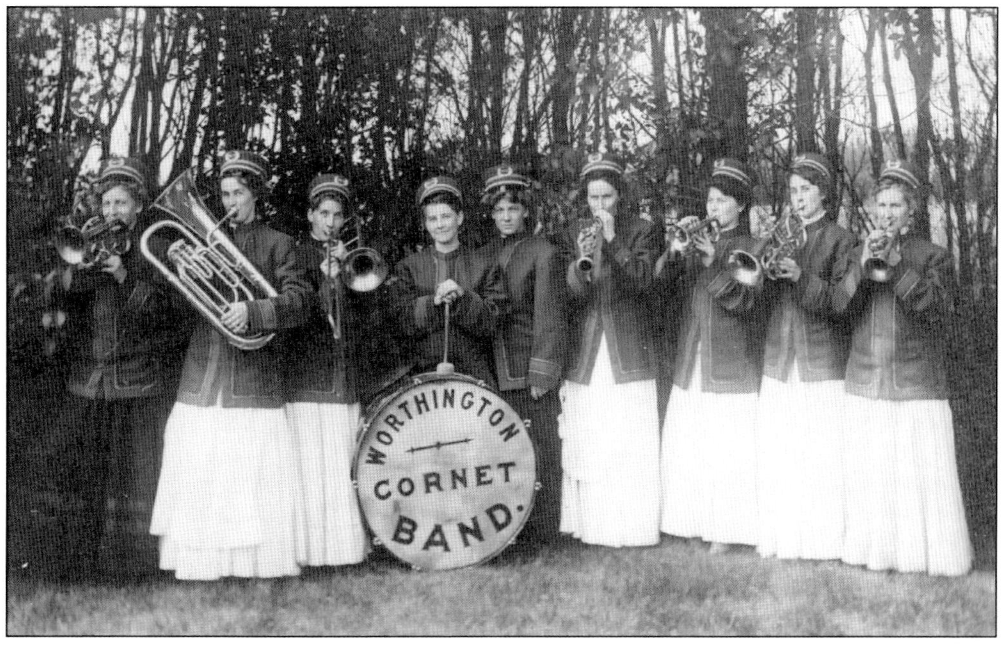

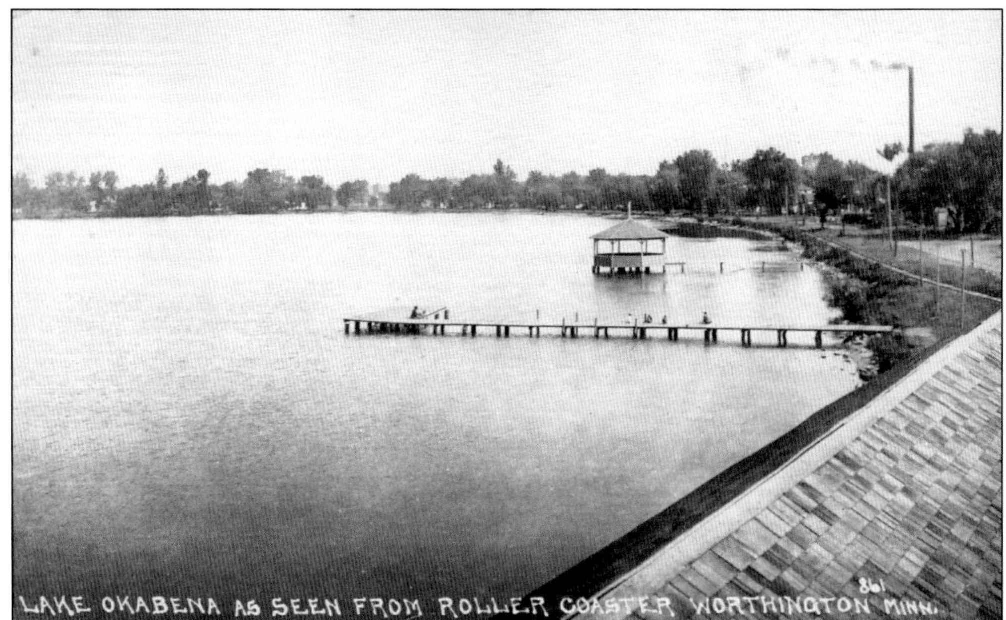

This is the only photograph showing a lake pavilion used to stage early band concerts. It was situated near the southeast corner of Worthington's Lake Okabena, not too far from the current location of the lake's spillway. There appears to be a short dock leading to the band stage, which was surrounded by water. As stated on the photograph itself, it was taken from the top of the tall water slide next to the bathhouse. (TG.)

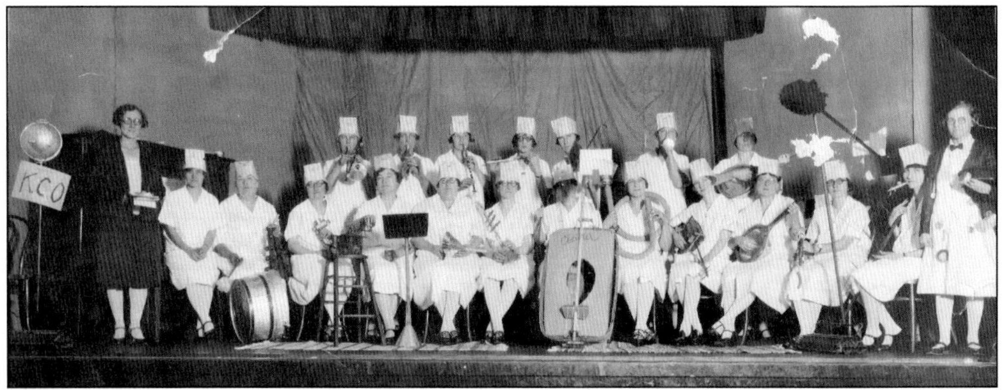

This c. 1929 photograph shows Bigelow's Kitchen Cabinet Orchestra. Though some of the group's members appear to be playing traditional musical instruments, others are performing on more utilitarian household tools. Orchestra members include, from left to right, (first row) Bessie Butcher, Amanda Hubbard, Marion Yeske, Carol Yates, Margaret Russell, Myrt Horstman, Lulu Lane, Clara Foote, Evelyn Lane, Maude Edie, Florence Salstrom, Mrs. Hulme, and Ted Rinkel; (second row) Mrs. O. Johnson, Mary Brever, Hazel Meyer, Dolly Dahlgren, Gladys Stromblad, Agnes Yeske, and Lena Lush.

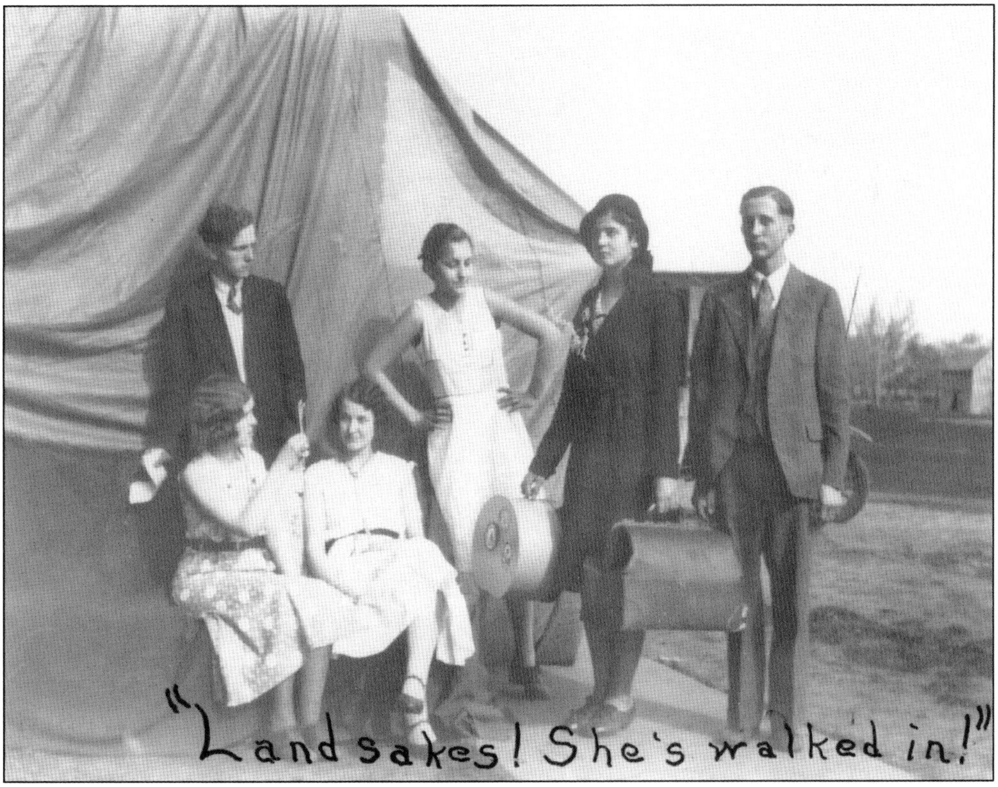

"Landsakes! She's walked in!"

High schools were equipped with stages and curtains to enable dramatic plays to be presented by the school's students. This appears to be a c. 1933 Bigelow High School production of a class play. Based on the picture's inscription, the play may have been entitled, *Landsakes! She's Walked In!* Performers include, from left to right, (seated) Bonnalyn Butcher and Lynn Edwards; (standing) Ronald Yates, Dorothy Kramer, Gertrude Fenske, and Marvin Horstman.

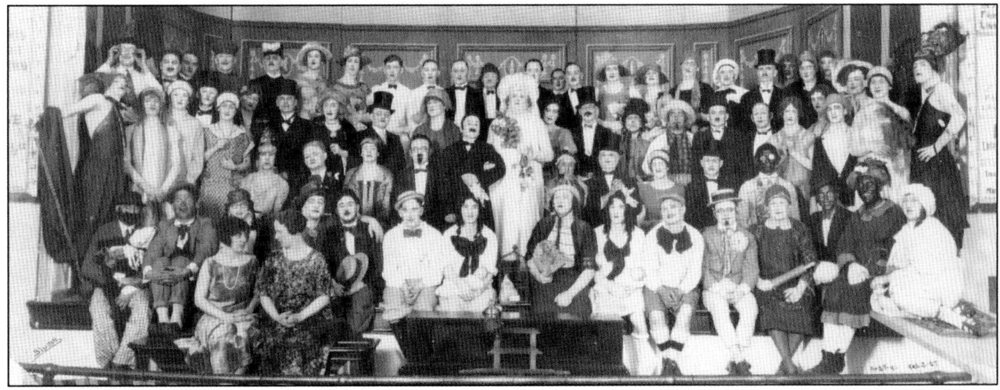

On February 3, 1927, Worthington's Stoddard Corps No. 1 of the Women's Relief Corps sponsored a play, possibly as a fundraising project. The incredibly large cast of 70 Worthington-area men put on the play *A Womanless Wedding*. According to the *Nobles County Times*' account, "the show was unanimously acclaimed by those present as the best home talent production ever given in Worthington."

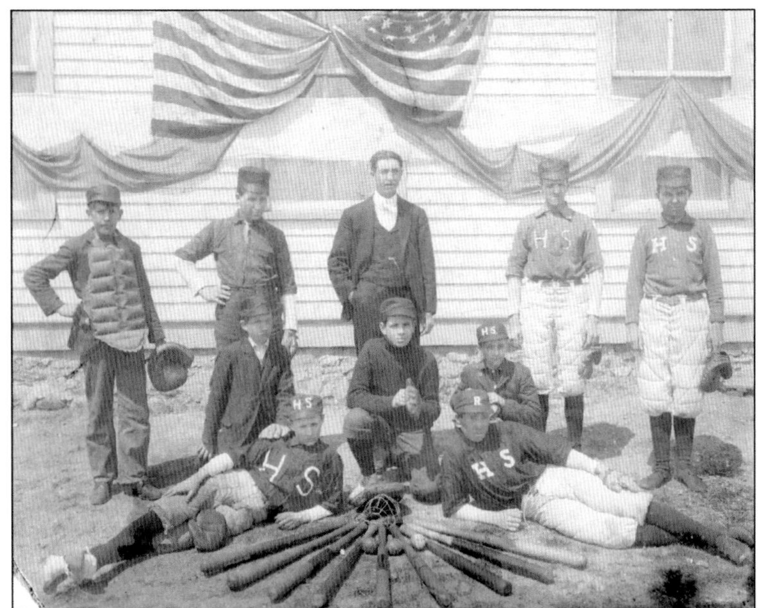

Baseball was one of the more popular team sports in the late 1800s and early 1900s. Pictured is the 1909 Rushmore High School team. Squad members are, from left to right, (first row) Harry Whipkey and Tone Malmquist; (second row) unidentified, Ernest Gillis, and Will Whipkey; (third row) two unidentified, Prof. Clyde Jones, Wilbur Renshaw, and Andy Malmquist.

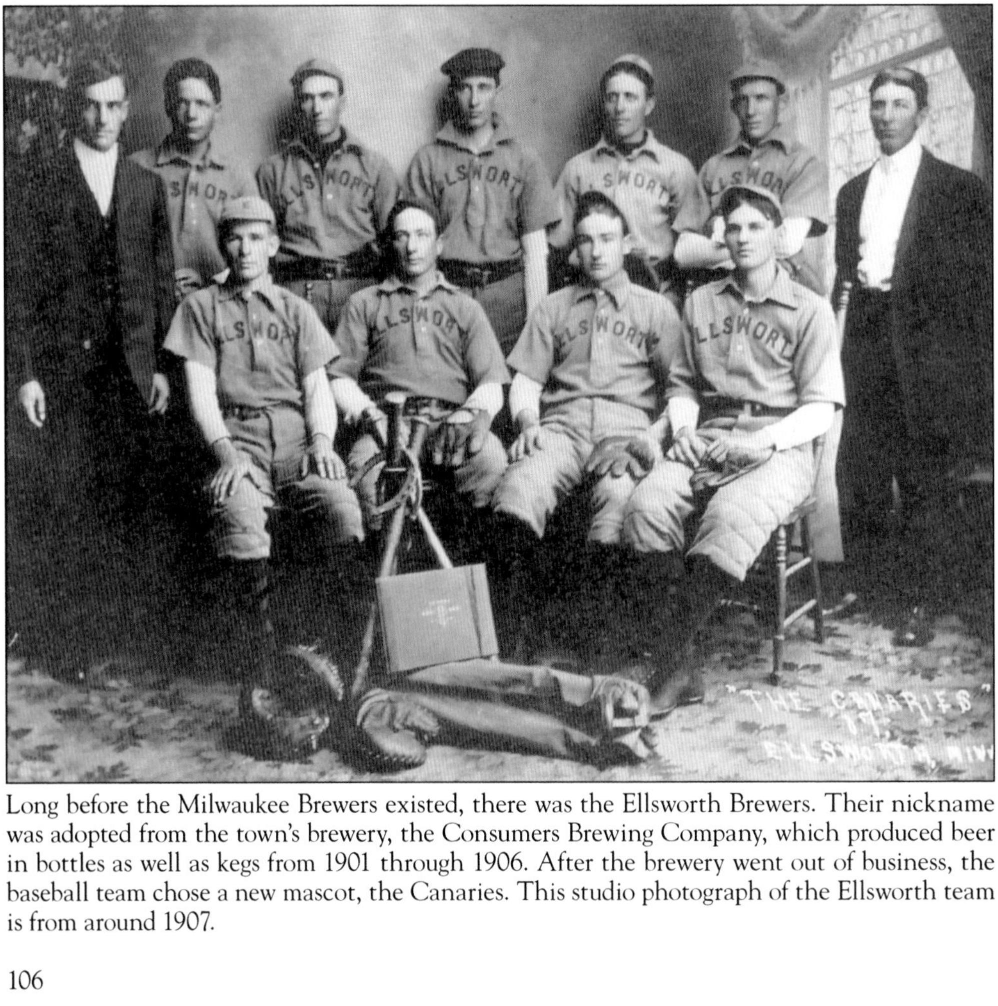

Long before the Milwaukee Brewers existed, there was the Ellsworth Brewers. Their nickname was adopted from the town's brewery, the Consumers Brewing Company, which produced beer in bottles as well as kegs from 1901 through 1906. After the brewery went out of business, the baseball team chose a new mascot, the Canaries. This studio photograph of the Ellsworth team is from around 1907.

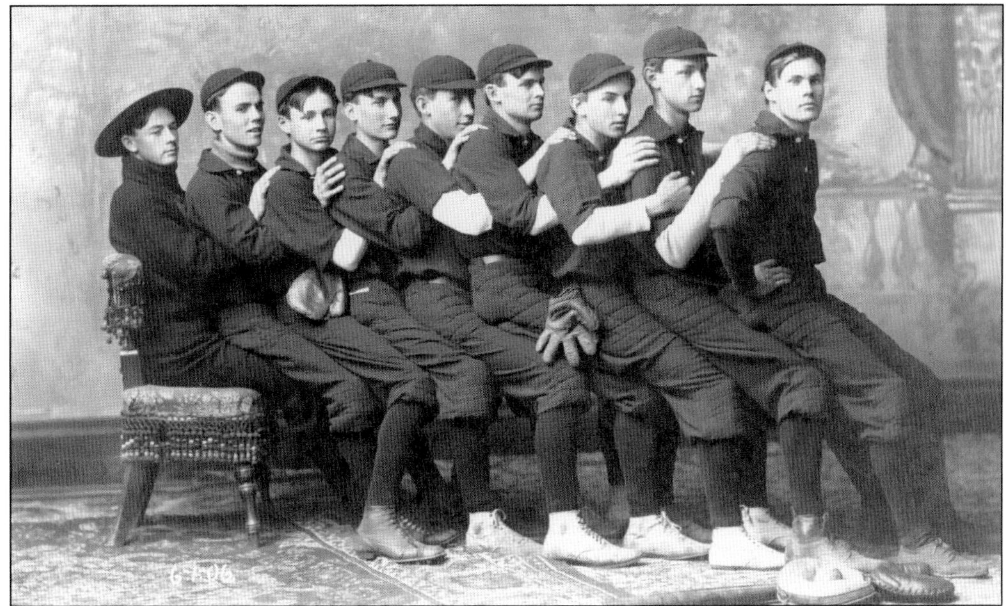

This nontraditional pose of the Worthington High School baseball team was taken in a local photographer's studio. Dated June 1, 1906, the picture may have been intended for inclusion in the school's yearbook as the team photograph. Some of the ballplayers have their gloves hanging by their waists; there are two catcher's mitts and a baseball bat lying on the floor in the right foreground.

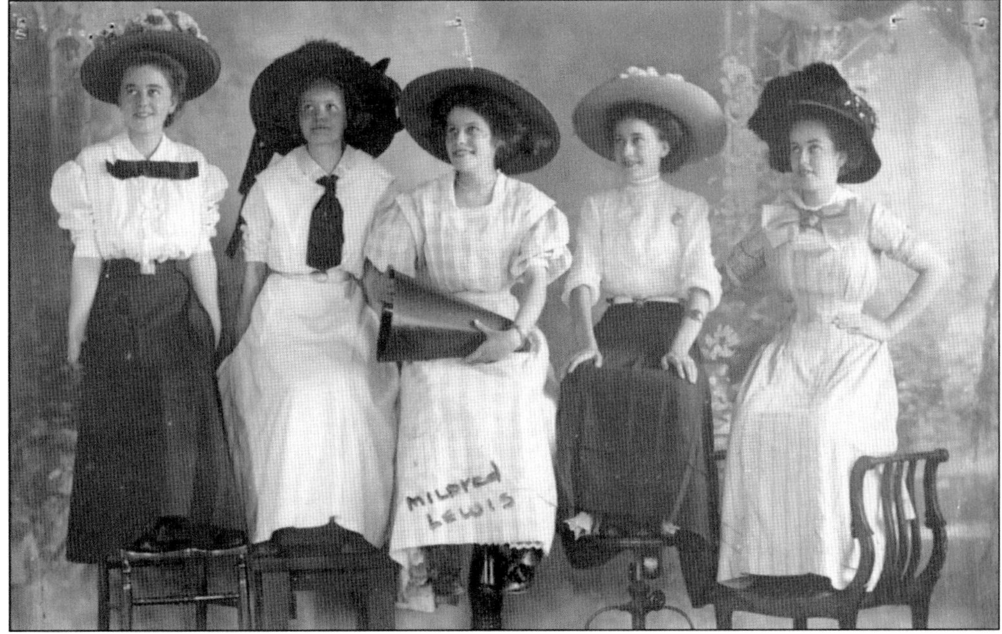

From the presence of the megaphone in the center girl's lap, it has been speculated that these five young ladies could be a Worthington High School cheerleading squad. The middle student is the only one who has been identified; her name, Mildred Lewis, has been written on the photograph itself. If they are indeed cheerleaders, this may indicate that they did not dress in uniforms at the time.

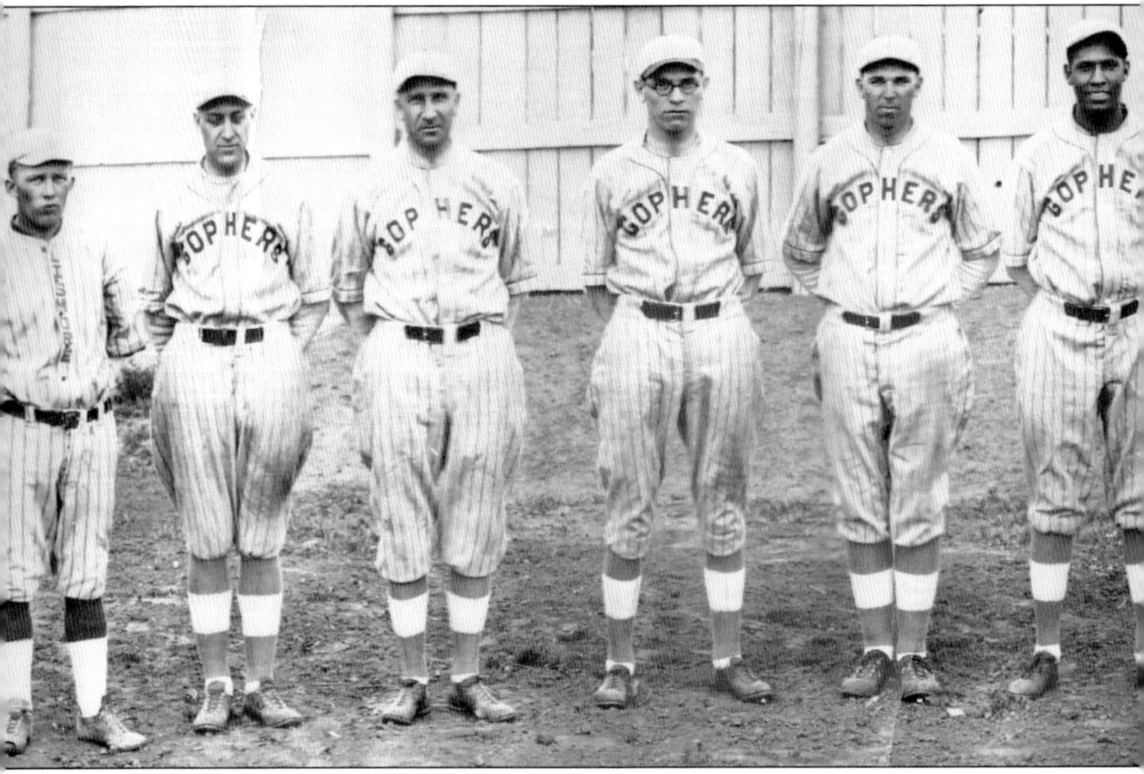

From the 1920s to the 1950s, some town teams played semiprofessional baseball. A few of their most valuable players were salaried. Perhaps the greatest team to ever play baseball in Nobles County was the 1926 Lismore Gophers. Their "hired gun" was John Donaldson, a black hurler who was paid $450 per month to pitch for the team. During the 1926 season, he pitched 25 complete games. Donaldson and his wife and son resided in Lismore for the entire summer. By

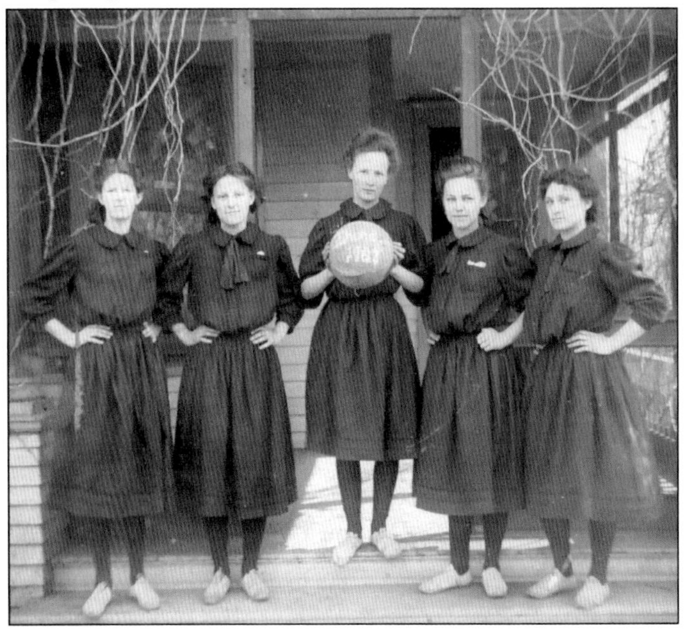

This photograph of the 1908 Dundee High School girls' basketball team was taken by Ernest Cords of Dundee. From left to right are Edith Deutschman, Mayme Deutschman, Mrs. Jones, Elizabeth Schmidt, and Kitty Chaney. Even though girls' basketball was discontinued some years later, it appeared to be quite popular at the time. The photographer was a popular and colorful character. During the summer months he did farm work, but taking pictures was his passion.

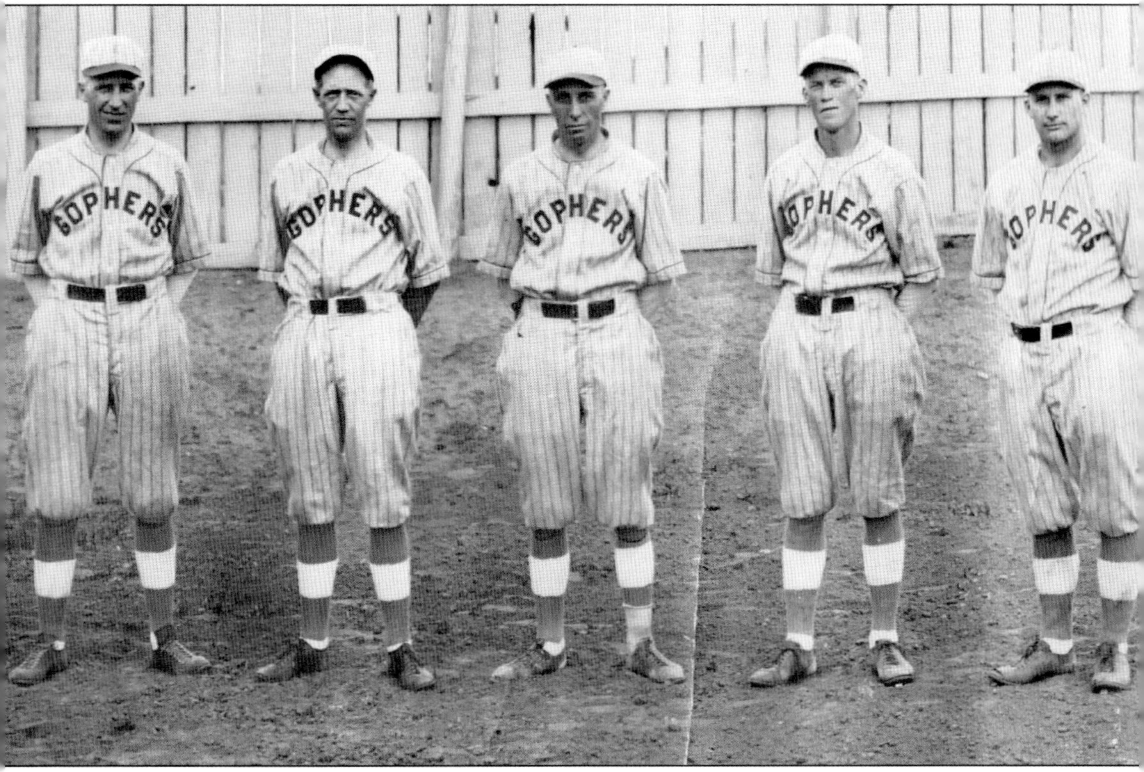

some accounts, Donaldson has been rated the fourth best Negro Leagues pitcher of all time. Team members are, from left to right, Matt Baltes, Ed Tentler, L. Corwin, Ike Lowe, Shorty Krogman, Donaldson, Jack Thompson, Fred Kerner, Charlie Lopshire, Rob Knips, and Leo Baltes. Manager Herman Olberding is not pictured. (DL.)

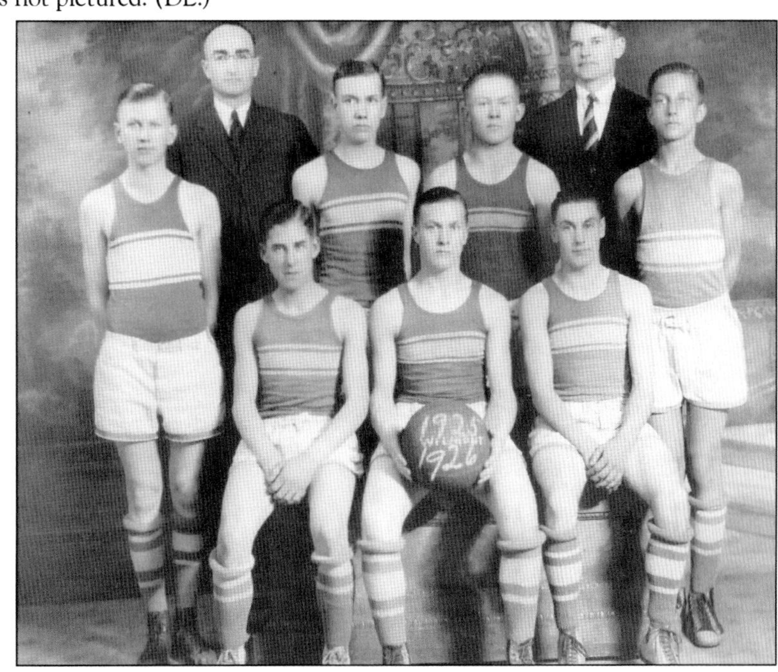

The Wilmont Public School boys' basketball team was crowned Nobles County champions for the 1925–1926 season, compiling a record of 22 wins and no losses. Members of the team are, from left to right, (first row) Peter Gerber, Vic Lebens, and Lloyd Densmore; (second row) Louis Spartz, Professor Schmidt, Leo Spartz, Edmund Sievers, Ed Olson, and Fritz Lebens.

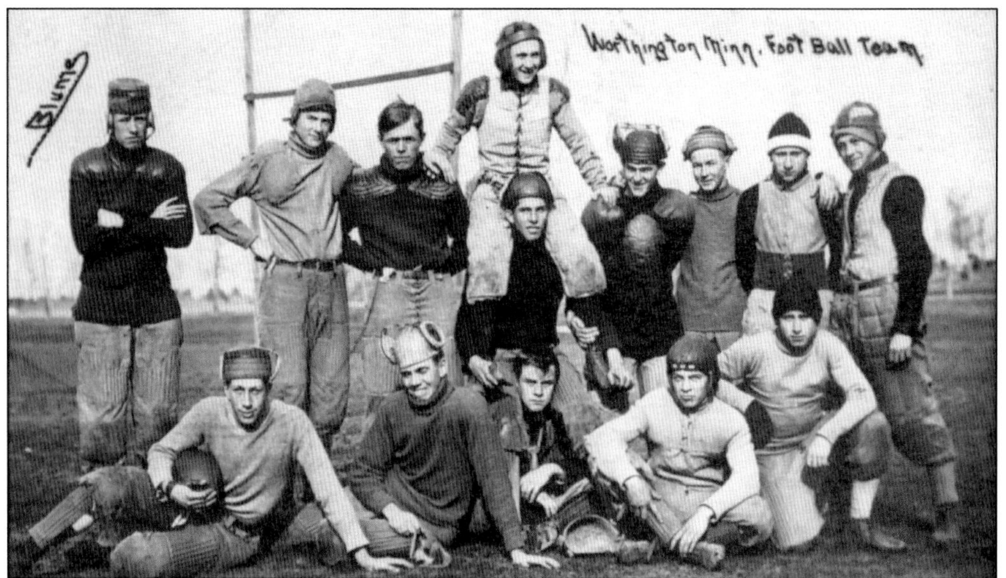

Despite the motley appearance of the 1910 Worthington High School football team, it apparently knew how to play the game. On the bottom of this photo postcard, someone has written the score of the game between Worthington and the Pipestone Indians, 6-0 in favor of Worthington. Given the players' attire, this picture was probably taken after a practice scrimmage.

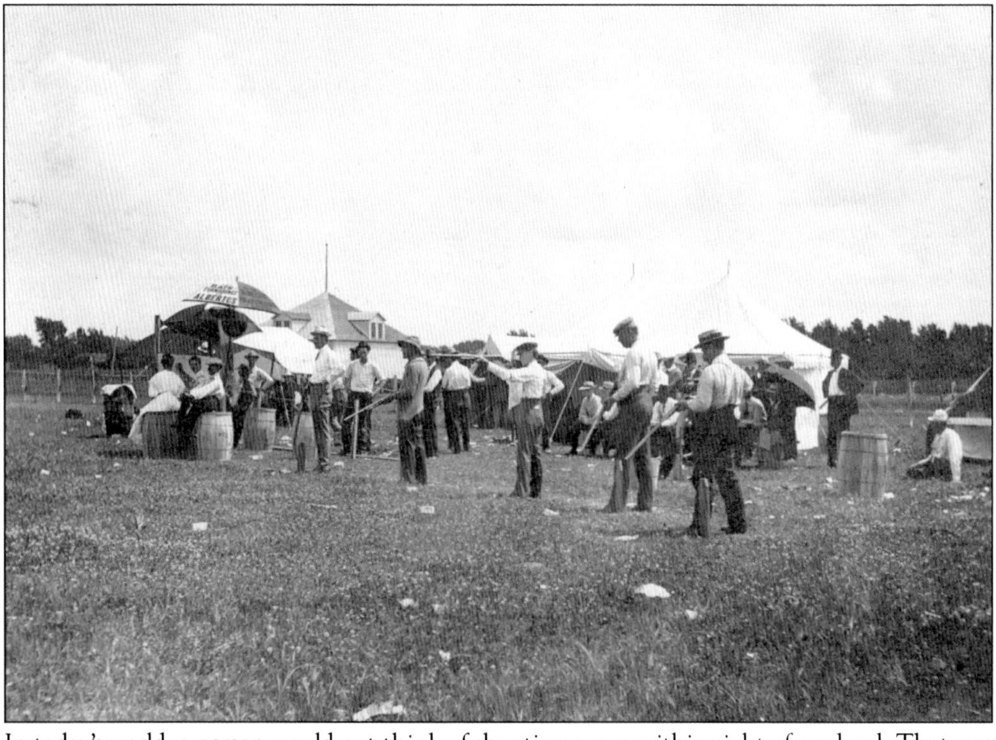

In today's world, a person would not think of shooting a gun within sight of a school. That was not the case in the early 20th century. In the background of this trapshooting contest is a building that appears to be a country schoolhouse. It looks like it was in the immediate Worthington area, as one of the umbrellas advertises a Worthington retailer, the Albertus Clothing Store.

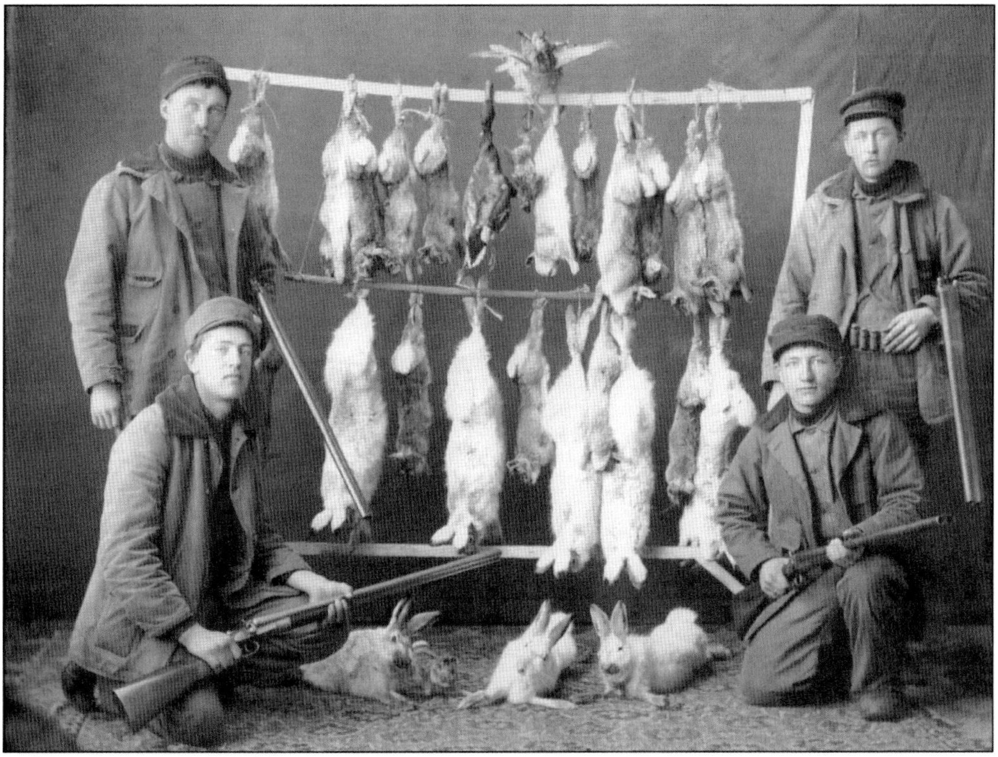

Though these four hunters are unidentified, it is believed they were in the Bigelow area when they shot their prey. Whoever they were, their skill in hunting rabbits cannot be questioned. They bagged several jackrabbits, cottontails, a few other smaller varmints, and a strange looking bird that is perched on the top rack. Given today's scarcity of jackrabbits, one would have to wait quite a while to ever see this many at one time. (HP.)

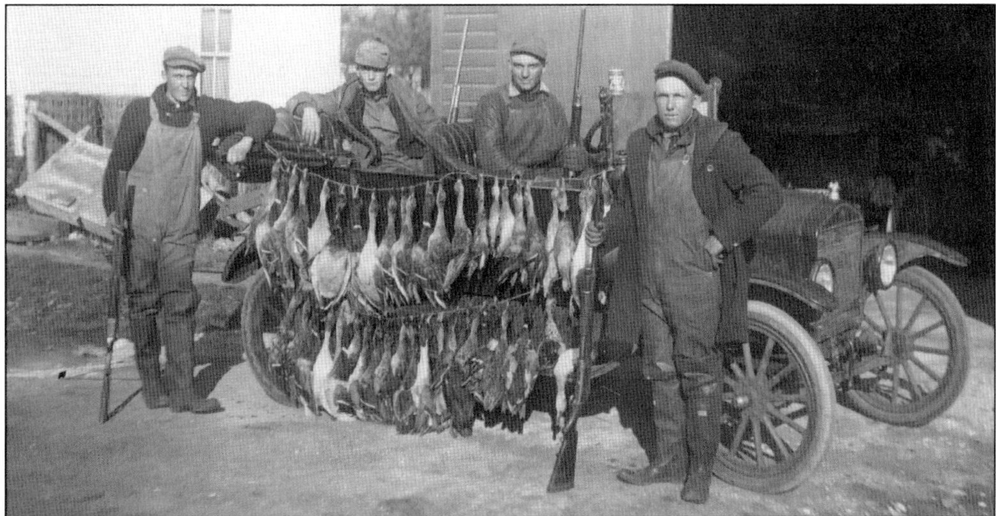

This c. 1925 hunting trip yielded these four hunters more than 40 ducks—the bag limits then were more lenient than today. Though the hunters are unidentified, they are believed to have been hunting in the Graham Lakes area. Without a roof on the car, the men could have fired their shotguns while sitting in it. (JD.)

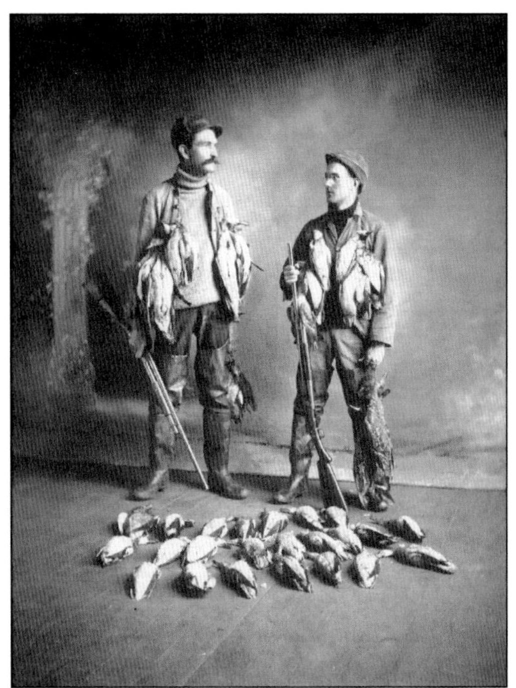

Hunting and fishing have been popular as far back as people can remember. This interest continues today, though it would be hard to imagine hunters hauling their dead quarry to a studio to have their pictures taken. Nevertheless, that is what was done here. J.M. Messer (left), a Worthington abstractor, and banker George Dayton's son, Draper, pose with their day's bounty in the studio of Lilian Yates, Worthington's first professional female photographer. (LFi.)

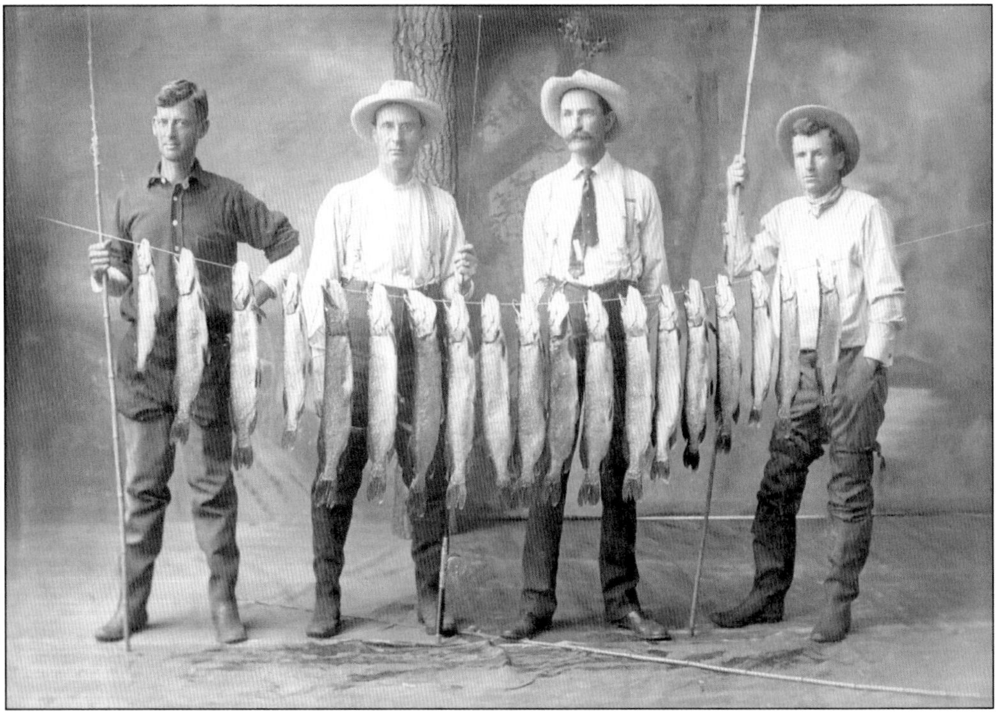

Messer also appears in this c. 1910 picture, second from the right, but this time he and his partners took their trophies to a different photographer's studio, E.F. Buchan. Notice the two cane poles held by two of the fishermen. Apparently, this was the equipment they used to catch the fish. Buchan had this image commercially printed as a souvenir postcard that was popular in Worthington retail shops. (LFi.)

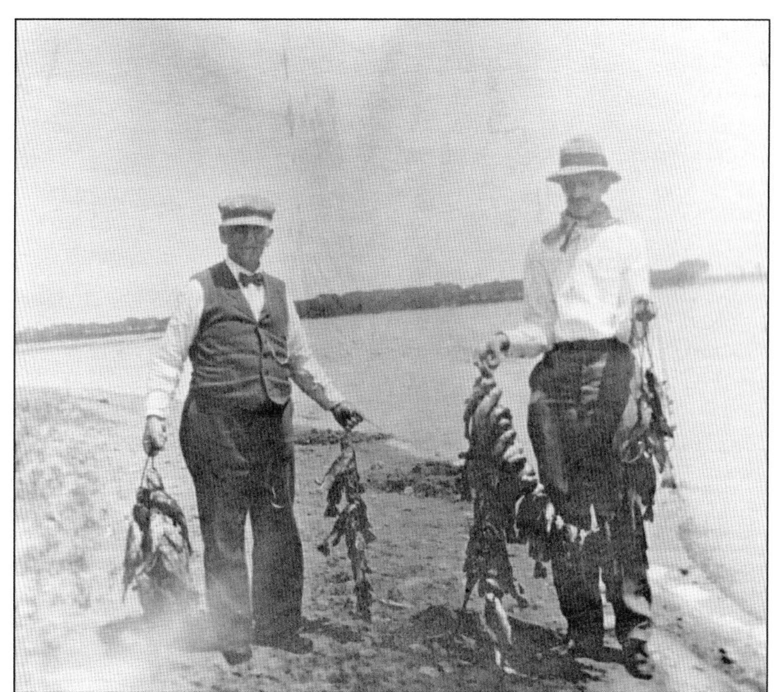

Henry Read arrived in Worthington in 1873, but three years later resettled in rural Summit Lake Township. Since living there, he was active both as a township officer and a school district official. When the village of Reading was formed in 1899, the locals named the townsite in honor of Read. He is pictured on the left with a friend holding the stringers of fish they caught on Summit Lake.

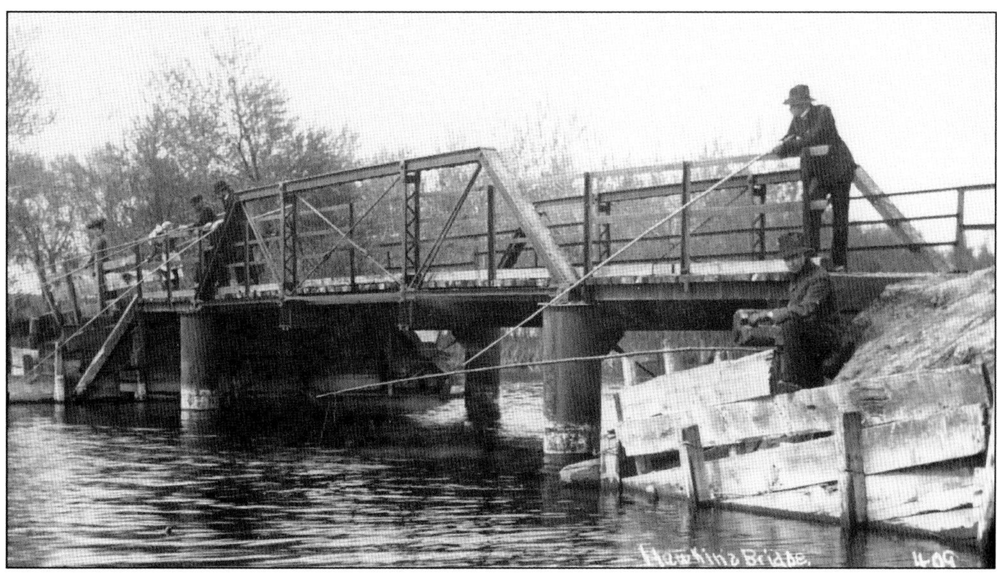

For as long as anyone can remember, this bridge over Lake Ocheda has been known as Hawkinson's Bridge. It was given this name because of its proximity to the land of Peter and Emma Hawkinson, who immigrated here in the 1880s. Their farmland in Bigelow Township surrounded the bridge and lake on the western side. Over the years, the bridge has been a popular fishing spot.

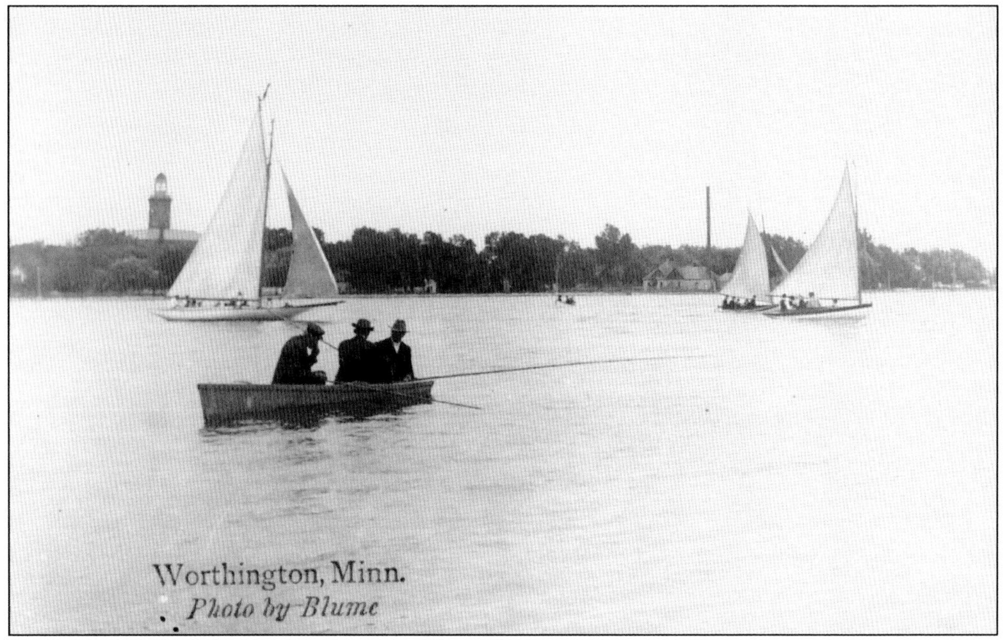

This c. 1910 image of Worthington's Lake Okabena offers evidence of the popularity of water recreation activities in the early 20th century. Three men are fishing from the rowboat in the foreground. As in an earlier photograph, they appear to be using cane poles. Three sailboats are skimming across the lake's surface. Visible in the background are the courthouse steeple and the power plant's tall smokestack.

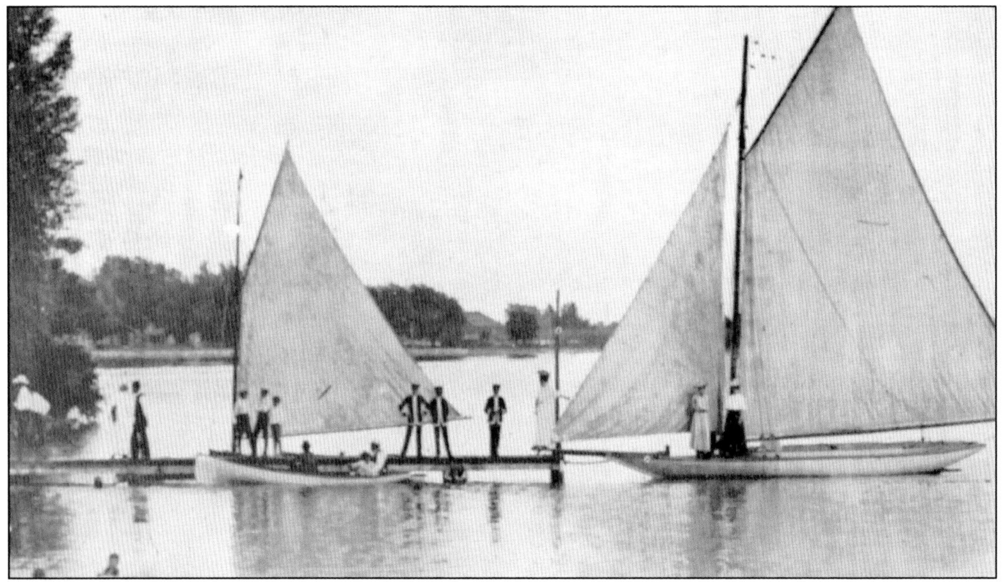

With the prairie's ever present wind, it is easy to understand the popularity of sailboats, some shown here on Worthington's Lake Okabena. These boats are docked close to shore by the lake's Tourist Park, which has since been renamed Chautauqua Park. The women on the large sailboat are dressed in formal-looking clothes. It was probably not stylish or appropriate for women of the time to go casual.

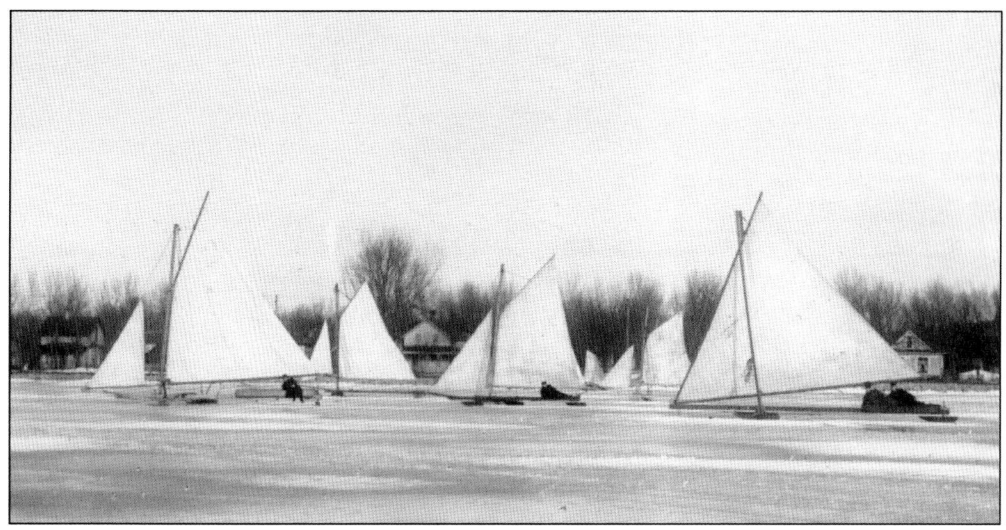

During the winter months, people enjoyed a different set of recreational activities made possible by the cold weather. They were known to ice skate and play hockey on Lake Okabena's frozen surface, slide down hills or the toboggan slide on wooden sleds, and use fishing poles or spears to catch fish through holes in the ice. More adventurous individuals sped across the lake on ice boats that harnessed the raw energy of the winter winds.

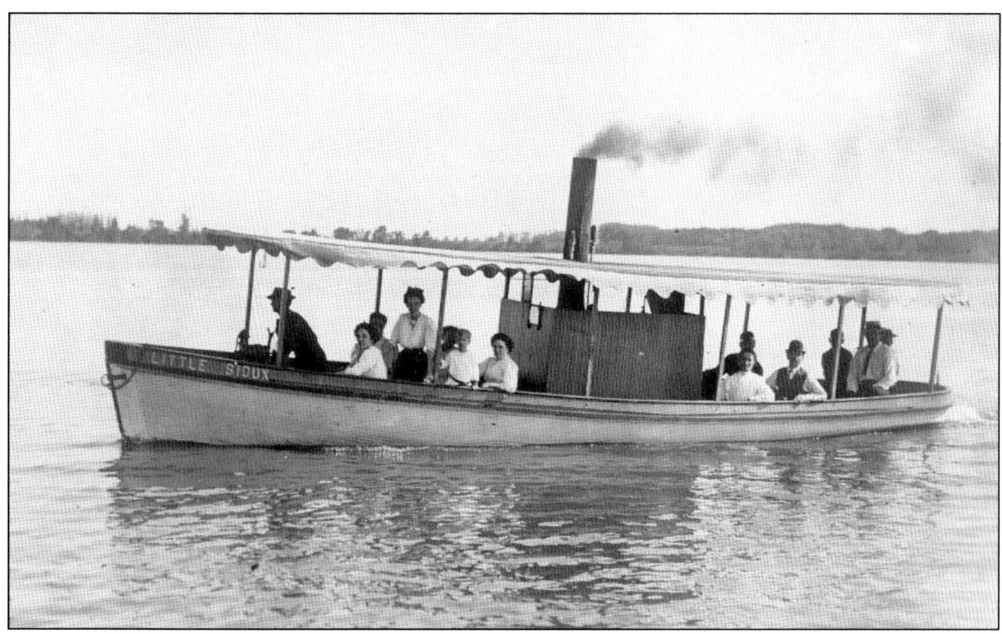

A popular summer activity in Worthington, especially on weekends, was taking a leisurely boat ride on Lake Okabena's steamboats, the *Little Sioux* and the *Philathea*. During the Chautauqua event, the *Little Sioux*, shown here, ferried visitors from the bathhouse to the festival grounds and back. It made these runs every 10 minutes before and after the afternoon and evening sessions. In between, riders could get a scenic seven-mile trip around the lake's shoreline for 25¢. The *Little Sioux* could also be rented for picnic and moonlight excursions.

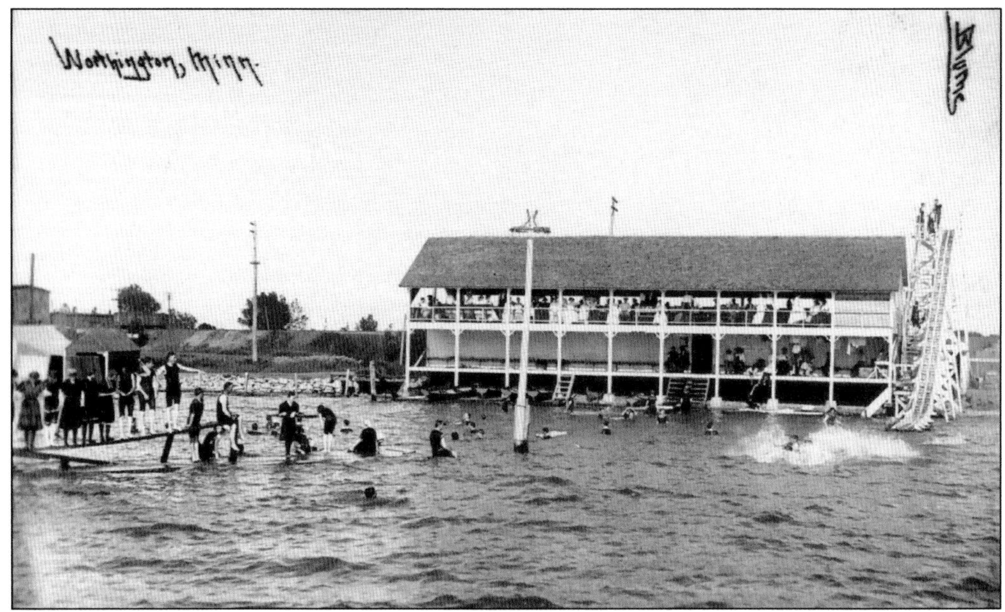

Over the years, Worthington's Lake Okabena has been a focal point for many of the town's recreational and social activities. Just down the shore from the first fairground site, the Worthington Bath House Association erected this bathhouse and water slide, which became a popular recreation destination during the summer months. People came from miles around to enjoy these unique lakeshore amenities.

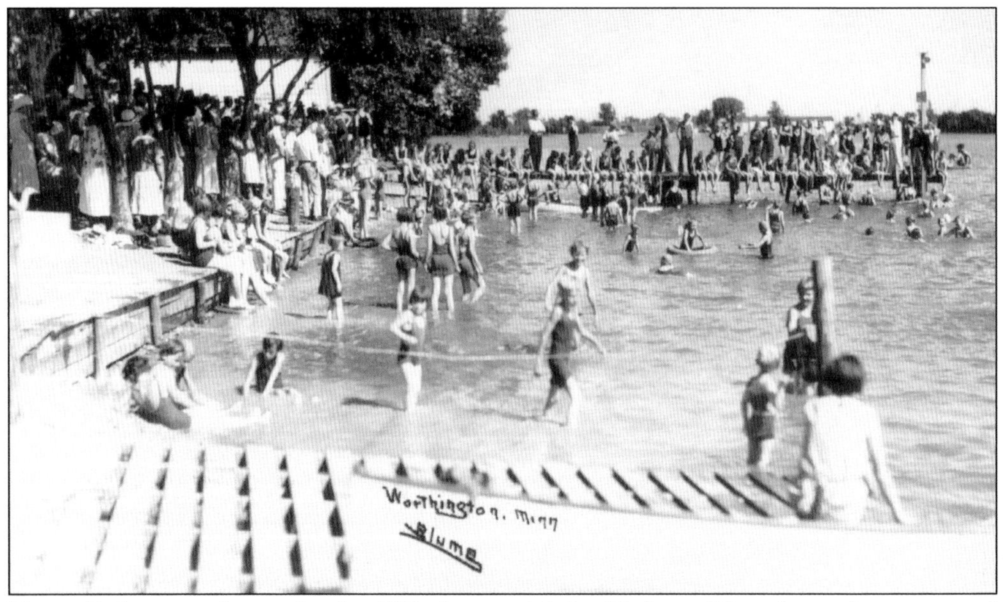

Tourist Park was on the north side of Worthington's Lake Okabena. Though people participated in various activities at this location, including swimming, boating, and fishing, it eventually became the town's most popular swimming hole. For years, Red Cross swimming lessons were offered at the park. In 1950, the park was renamed Chautauqua in recognition of this site's role as the grounds for the historic Chautauqua festival.

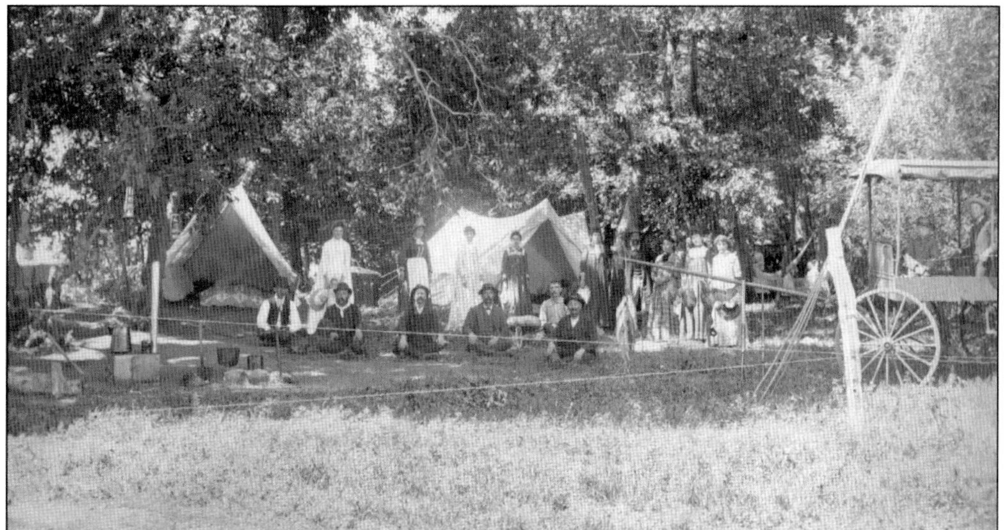

There is more to this picture than meets the eye. On the surface, it seems to show people camping in a pastoral setting. Their tents are pitched, a cooking fire pit has been built, and, if one looks carefully enough, the game they have caught can be seen hanging. However, camouflaged in the underbrush is a row of people who appear to be quietly observing the scene. Were they interested passersby or did the photographer stage the entire scene?

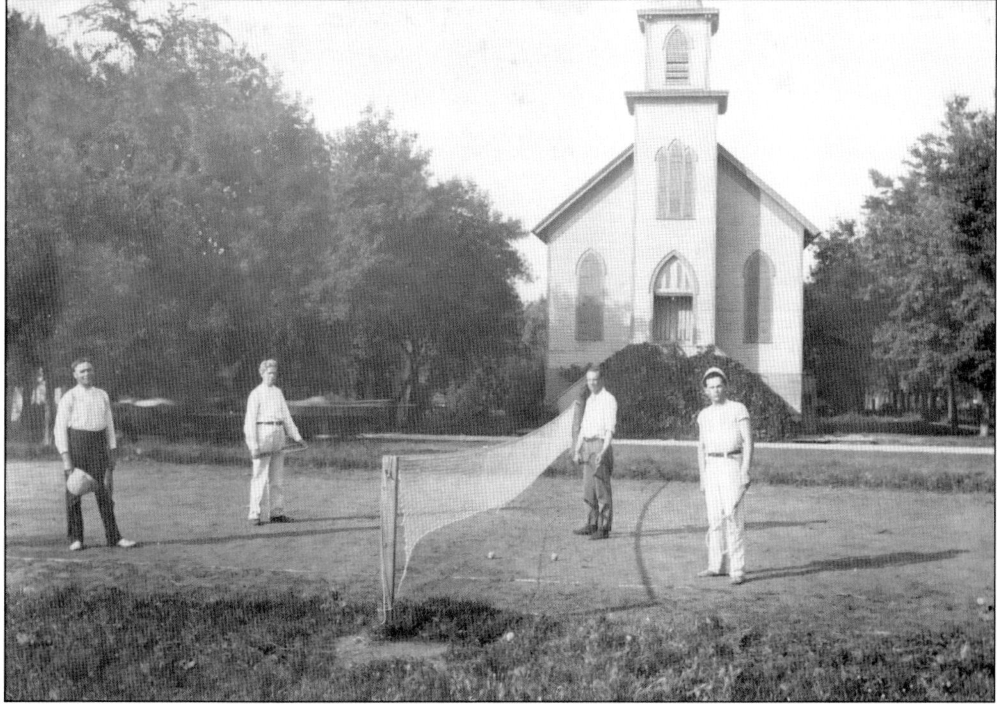

In Worthington's early days, many of the community's recreational activities centered around the lake. However, there were also other sporting activities like baseball and trap shooting. This picture indicates that there were tennis enthusiasts as well. Though it is unknown if there were actually any tennis courts, these individuals have improvised their own court by stringing a net across the street in front of the Union Congregational Church.

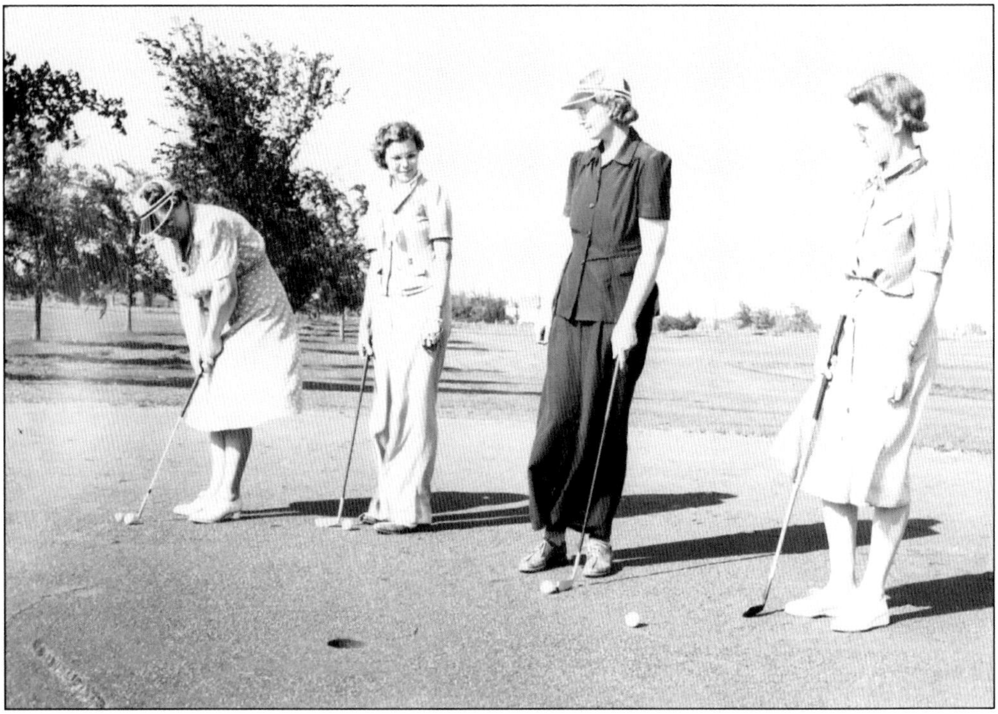

In Worthington, the concept of a golf course took hold in the 1920s. A group of local men banded together to form the Worthington Playground Association. They acquired a parcel of land on which Worthington's golf course is presently located. It was known as Harmon Field. In 1930, the first clubhouse was built, and by the end of the decade, golf memberships were being sold. These four women are seen standing on one of the course greens.

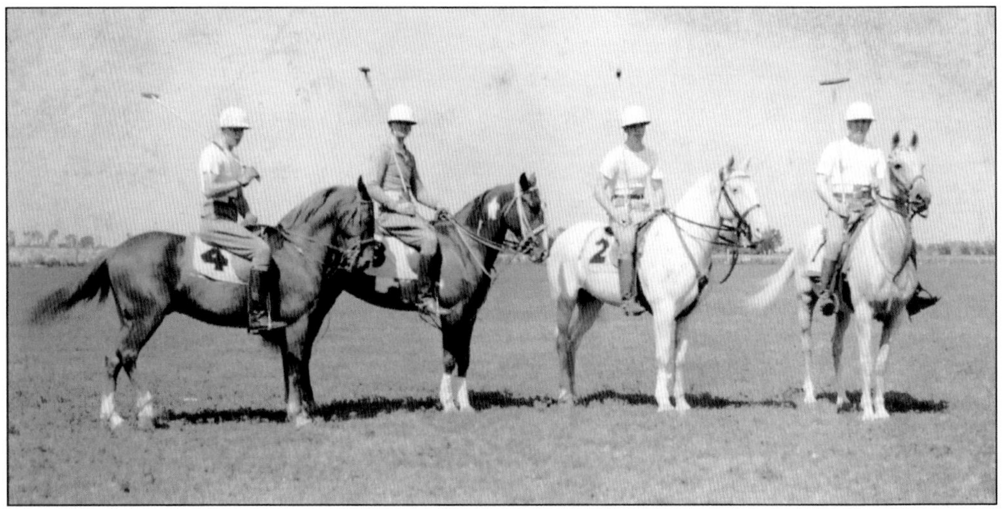

In contrast to golf, polo is a sport few county residents have played or even seen. Dr. A.L. Burch, a Worthington veterinarian, established a local polo squad in the 1930s. He recruited a team of horsemen, including the Albinson brothers, Alfred, Lloyd, and Bob, as well as Graydon Habicht. The Albinson boys stabled their horses at the Albinson Lumber Yard, which is now Lamperts. Worthington's original polo field was at the site of today's airport but was later moved to a field where Centennial Park is currently situated.

Eight

Potpourri

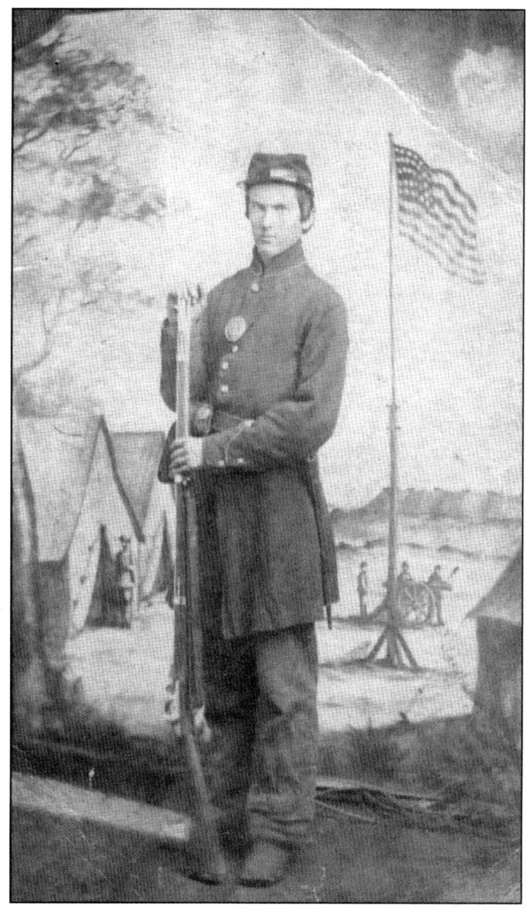

A significant factor in the settlement of Nobles County was the in-migration of many Civil War veterans. This young soldier, Reuben S. Hurd, joined Company A of the 10th Vermont Volunteer Infantry when he was 18 years old. He came to Worthington in 1885, when he was 40. Eventually, he and a partner started a livestock-buying firm, becoming the first people from Worthington to ship cattle and horses by the carload. He was the last surviving Civil War veteran in the county and for years was a fixture in the town's Memorial Day parades. He was 101 when he died.

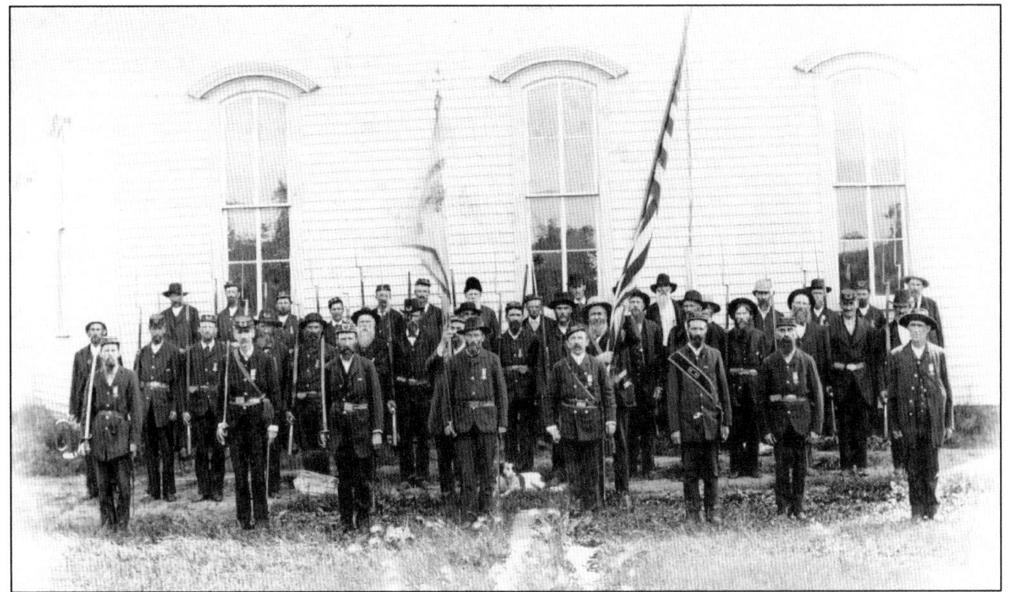

Many of Worthington's early settlers had fought in the Civil War, qualifying them for membership in the Grand Army of the Republic (GAR), a national fraternal organization for Union soldiers. Worthington's GAR lodge was chartered in 1872. It was named the Stoddard Post No. 34 after the first Civil War veteran to die in Worthington. This photograph, taken in the 1880s, shows the GAR members standing in formation by the town's school.

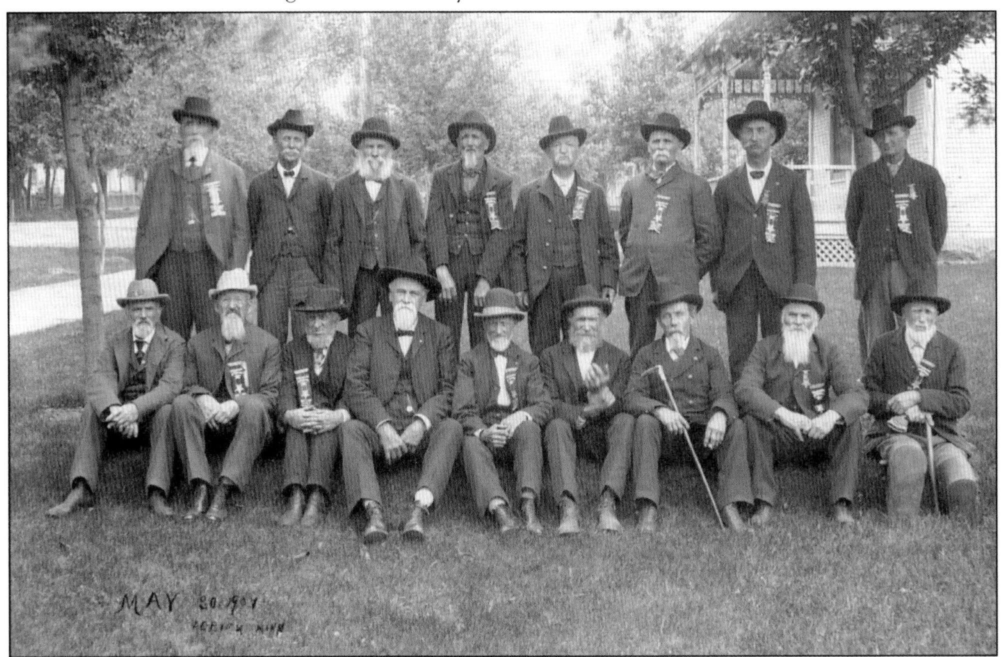

The western half of Nobles County also had several Civil War veterans among its early residents. Consequently, a GAR lodge was established in Adrian on September 25, 1883. It was registered as the Nathaniel Lyon Post No. 46 with 30 original members. By 1901, its active members had dwindled to only seven, so the post opted to surrender its charter. This is a reunion of the membership some three years later on Memorial Day.

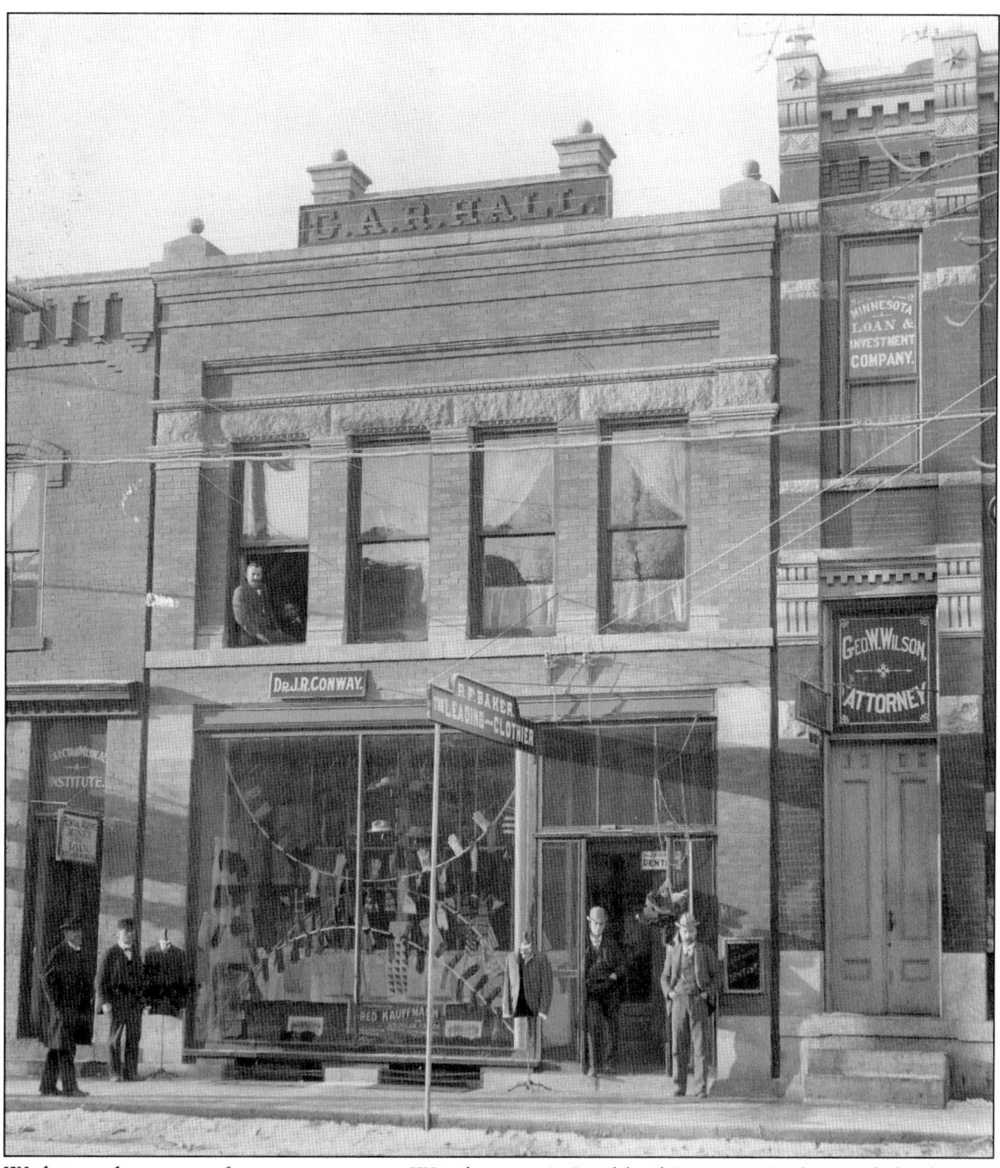

Within only a year of its organization, Worthington's Stoddard Post No. 34 boasted the largest GAR membership in the entire state of Minnesota—125. Soon, however, the region's grasshopper plagues forced many settlers from their land, including these former soldiers. The lost membership resulted in Post No. 34 being disbanded. Some 10 years later, the local economy had recovered, and settlers began migrating back to this corner of the state. In 1883, the local GAR lodge was re-established under the same charter and name as before. The new membership decided to relocate the lodge rooms to the Masonic hall. They remained there until some years later, when the post was moved to its third site, the second floor of the Chaney and Mackay store building. Around 1900, the GAR Stoddard Post moved to its fourth location, the R.F. Baker Block, which was located on the west side of Tenth Street, a few stores south of the Third Avenue corner. In those days, a single building was often referred to as a block. The GAR hall was on the second floor, as indicated by the stone sign on top of the building.

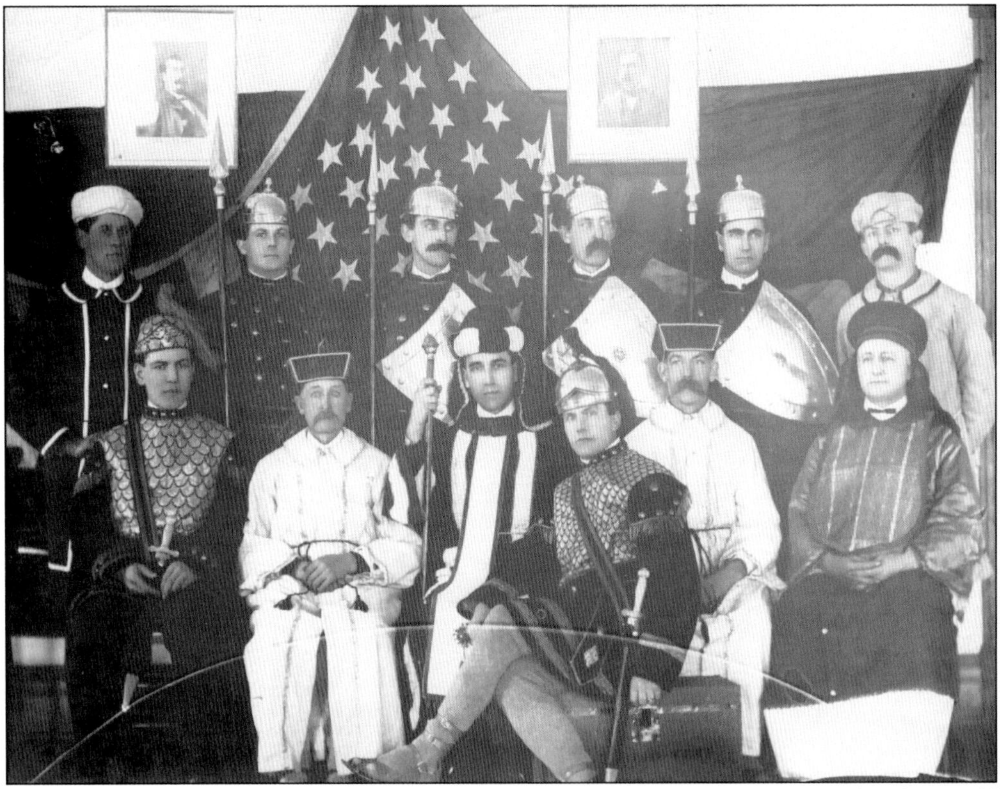

By 1908, there was a host of fraternal and secret societies active in Worthington. Today, few would be familiar with any of these organizations: Brotherhood of American Yeomen, Knights of the Maccabees, Modern Woodmen of America, Independent Order of Odd Fellows, Ancient Order of United Workmen, and Royal Neighbors of America. Pictured here around 1903 are members of yet another fraternal group, the Knights of Pythias, dressed in their official garb.

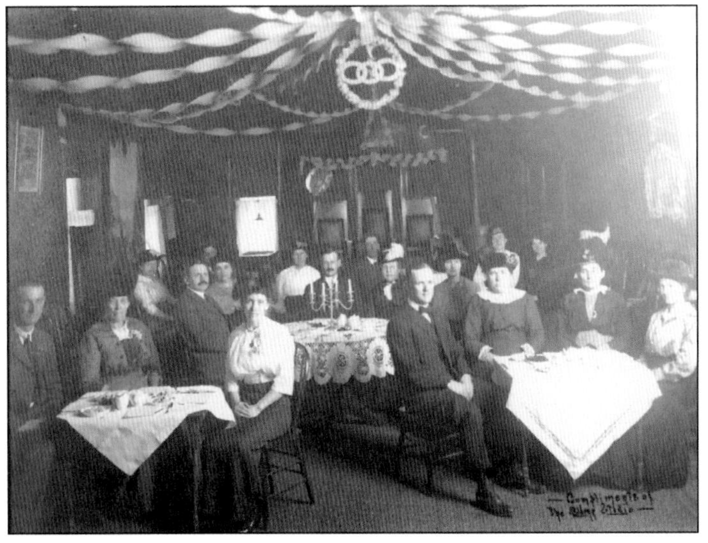

Some of these fraternal groups also had lodges in other county towns. The Wilmont chapter of the Odd Fellows was first organized in 1903, just a few years after the community was established. Though many of the societies were exclusively for men, the Odd Fellows, with their Rebeccahs affiliate, included both genders and youth ages 16 to 18. This c. 1904 Wilmont lodge gathering appears to be a special celebration.

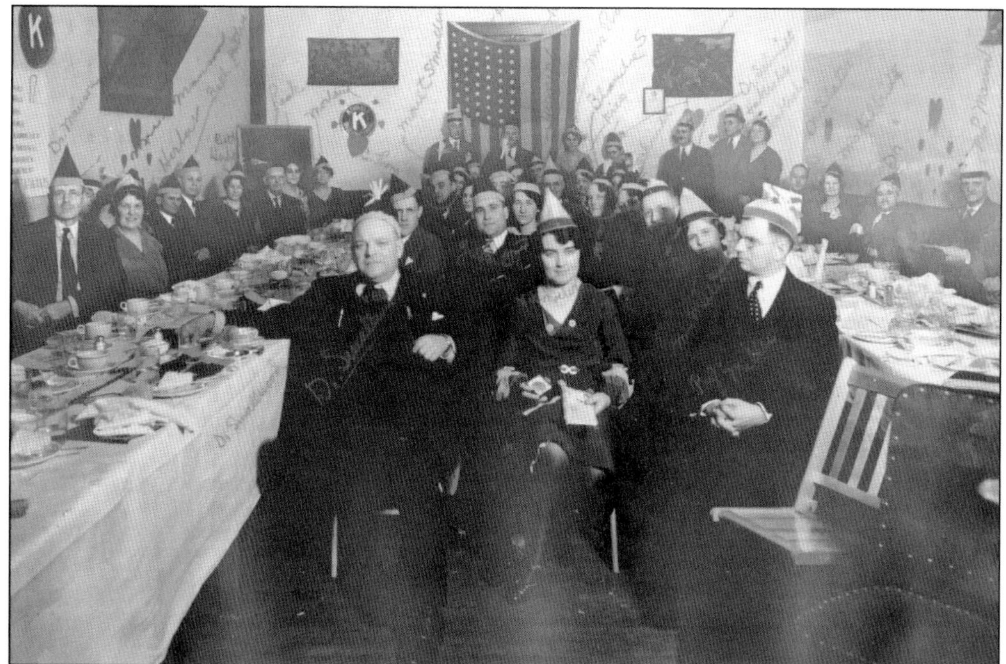

With the passing of time, some of these older groups disbanded in favor of new and different organizations. One of those got its start in 1922 when the Worthington Kiwanis Club was formed. The Kiwanians were particularly committed to supporting youth activities such as Boy Scouts, baseball leagues, high school proms, and holiday parties. This is a c. 1929 Valentine's party hosted by the club members for the "queens," presumably their wives.

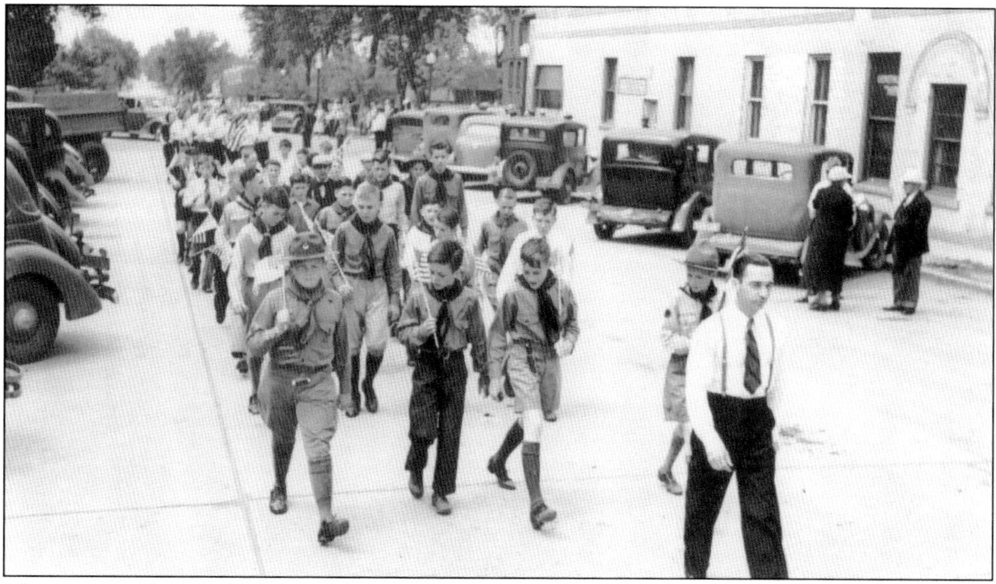

There were also clubs for youth—Scouts, 4-H, YMCA, church groups, and school-based organizations. Around 1940, a Worthington Boy Scout troop takes part in a street parade. The occasion is unknown, but the Scouts are marching south down Ninth Street in front of the National Guard armory. The man leading them is their troop leader, H. Marvell Tripp, a longtime Scout promoter.

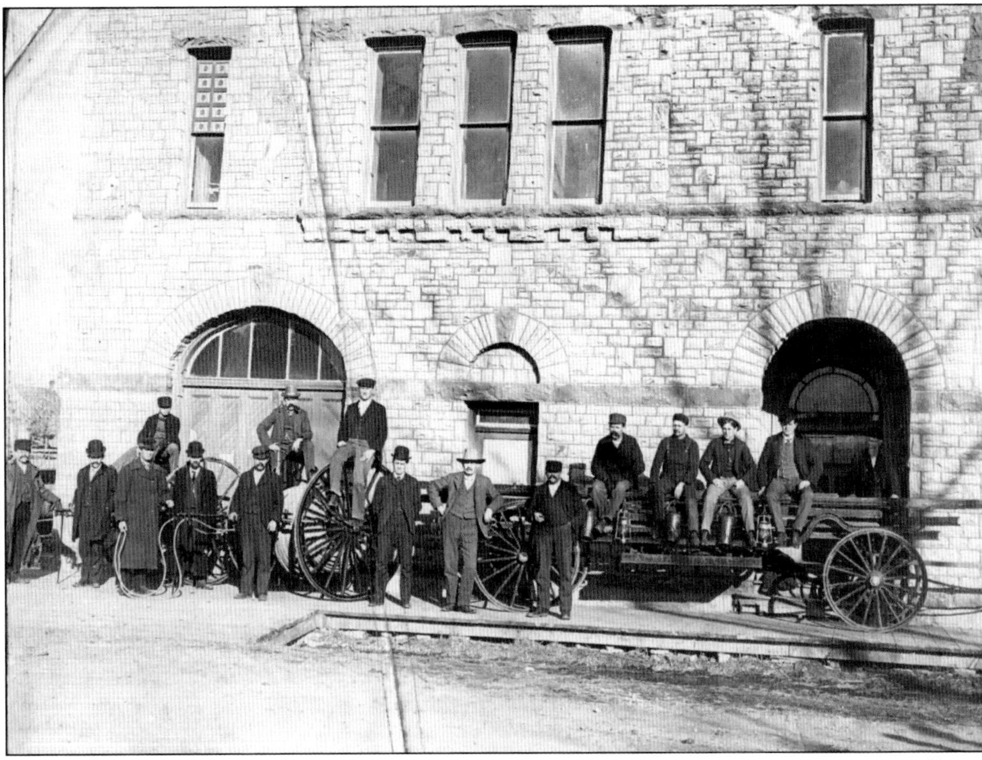

As seen in chapter six, pioneer town fires could be extremely destructive if they were allowed to burn out of control. To combat this danger, many towns organized their own volunteer fire fighting forces. Adrian's brigade was formed in 1894. Its initial equipment included two hose carts with 1,000 feet of hose and an early hook-and-ladder truck, as seen here.

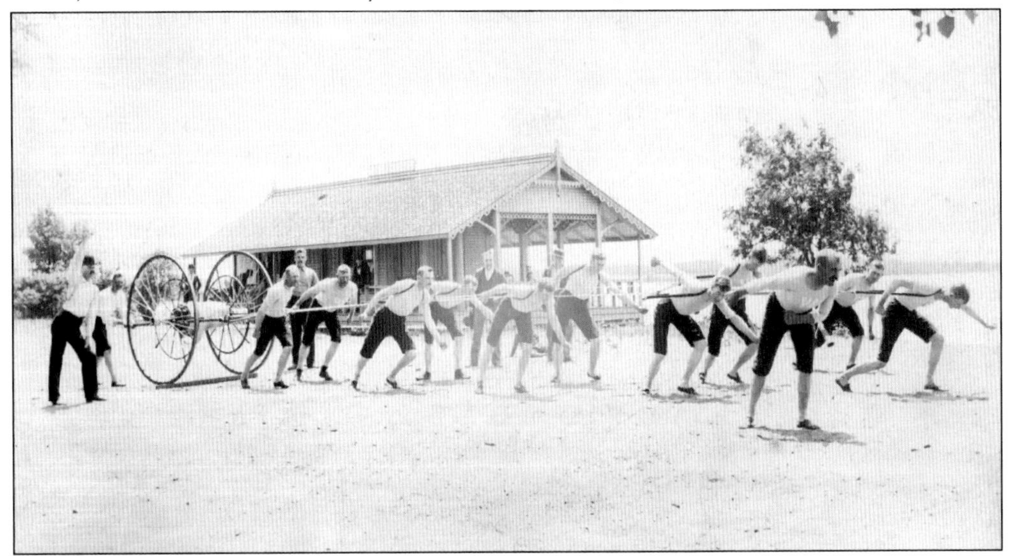

Worthington's volunteer firemen appear to be completing a drill honing their skills in pulling and maneuvering the hose-reel cart. It is unknown if this training session was focused on real-life scenarios or in preparation for an upcoming fire-fighting competition; these were sometimes held in area towns. The firemen staged this practice lakeside in front of the Idlewild Pavilion.

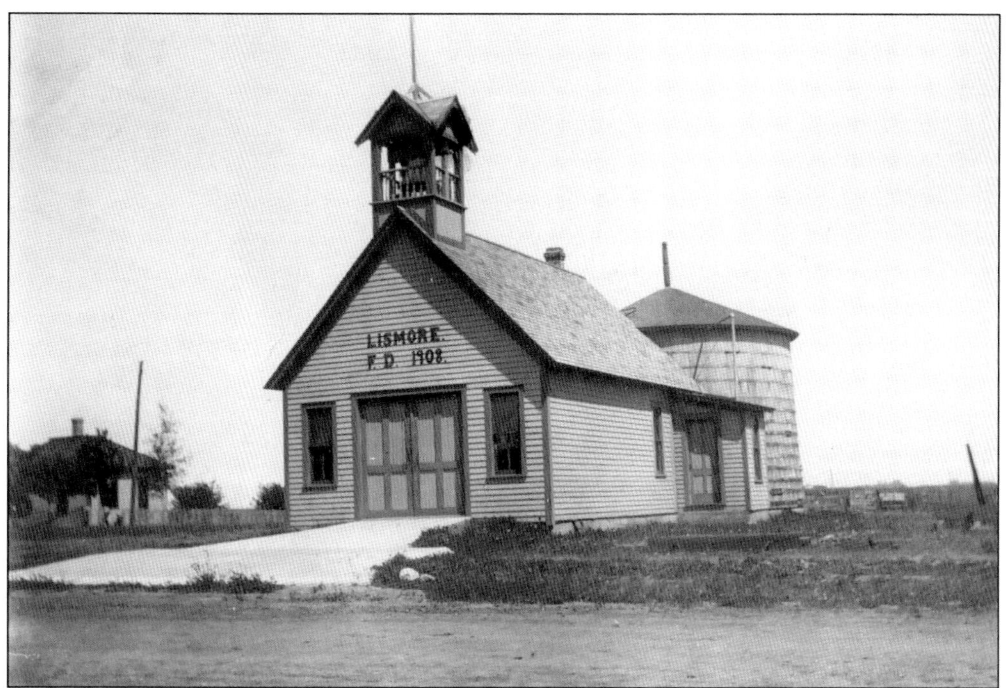

Before Lismore established a volunteer fire department in 1908, its protection from spreading fires relied on the use of 36 buckets manned by willing residents. They would access water from any town well close to the fire. When the department built this fire hall, its equipment consisted of two hose carts, a chemical cart, a gasoline pump, and a water storage tank.

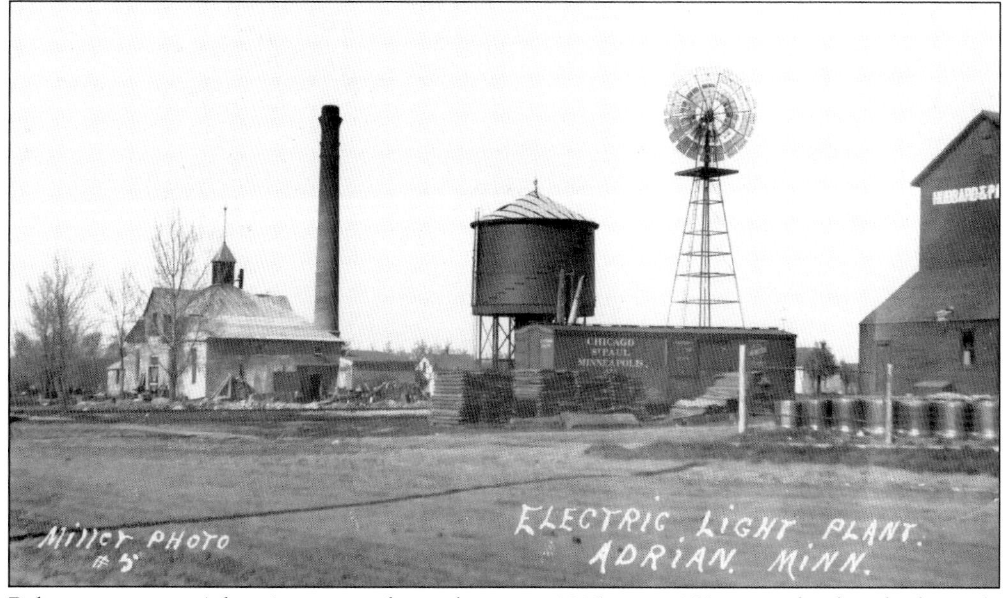

Believe it or not, Adrian's estimated population in 1895 was 1,072, just a few hundred people less than today's count. To accommodate the community's growing needs, the city decided to develop its infrastructure by building a new electricity plant and waterworks. These facilities were constructed over a six-month period from June through December 1894. They were located on North Main Street. The water tank had a capacity of 35,000 gallons. (PD.)

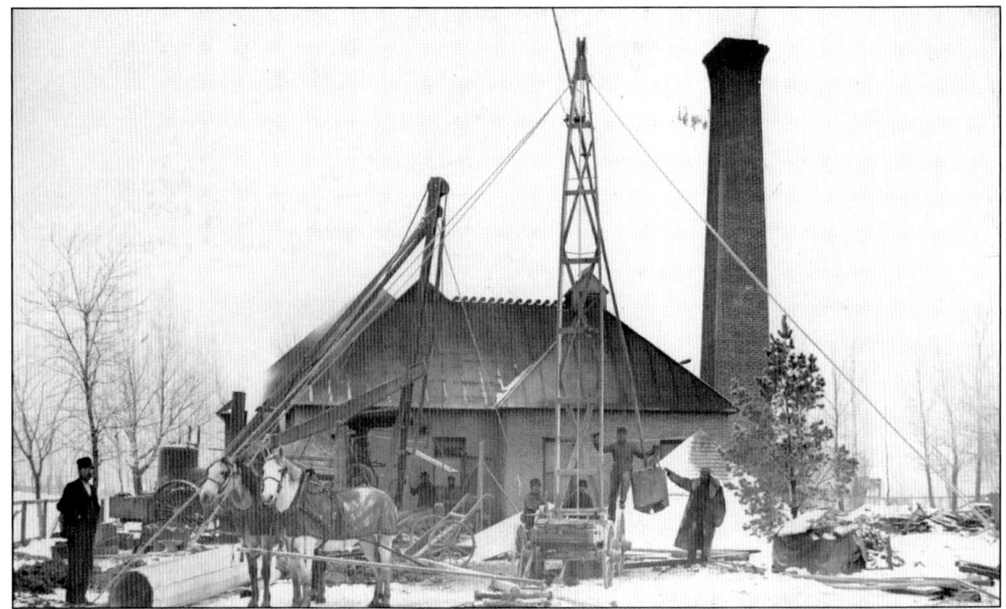

Worthington likewise experienced considerable growth and needed to address its demand for improved utilities. In 1891–1892, the town constructed a new waterworks facility, as seen here. The photograph shows workers drilling a water well on the site. A new electric plant was erected in 1895, and the town's first lights were turned on the night of December 10. There were originally 300 electricity subscribers.

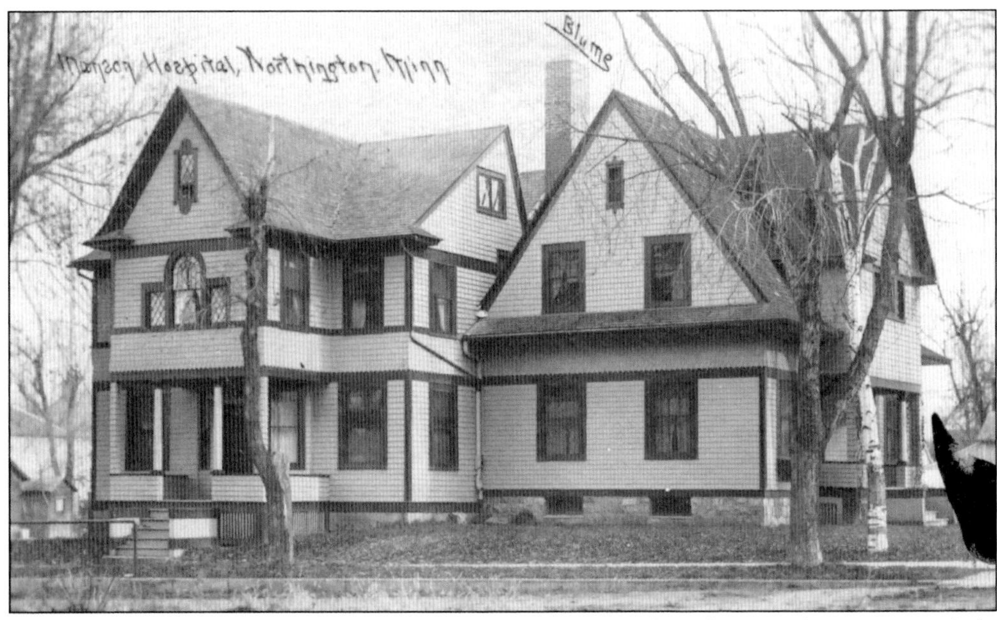

As a young doctor, Dr. F.M. Manson came to Worthington for a few months in 1899 to help fight a smallpox epidemic. He never left. In 1906, he built an addition onto his home, thereby establishing the town's first hospital, seen here, which could accommodate nine to 10 patients. In 1917, Dr. Manson made history a second time: He was the first Worthington resident to volunteer for service in World War I.

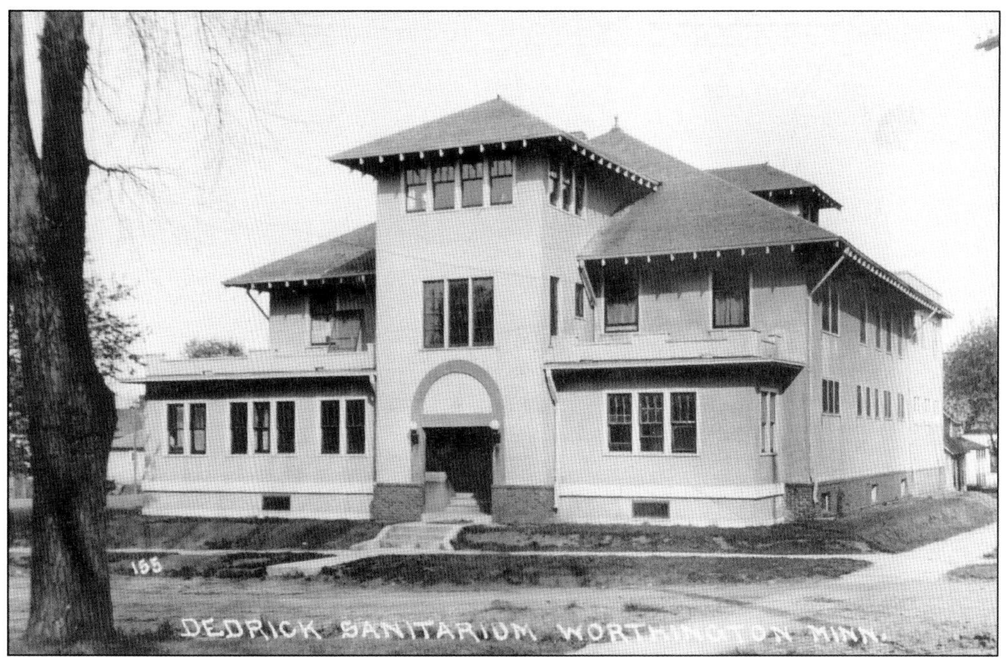

This place was for sufferers from catarrh, la grippe, constipation, nervousness, or any one of several ailments. Dr. S.C. Dedrick, a chiropractor, opened a sanitarium in 1903 on the corner of Ninth Street and Fourth Avenue in Worthington. He promoted Dedrick Sanitarium as "the only institution of its kind in the United States." His cure-all consisted of chiropractic adjustments supplemented with sulfur baths. In 1920, the Shore family converted the building into an apartment complex.

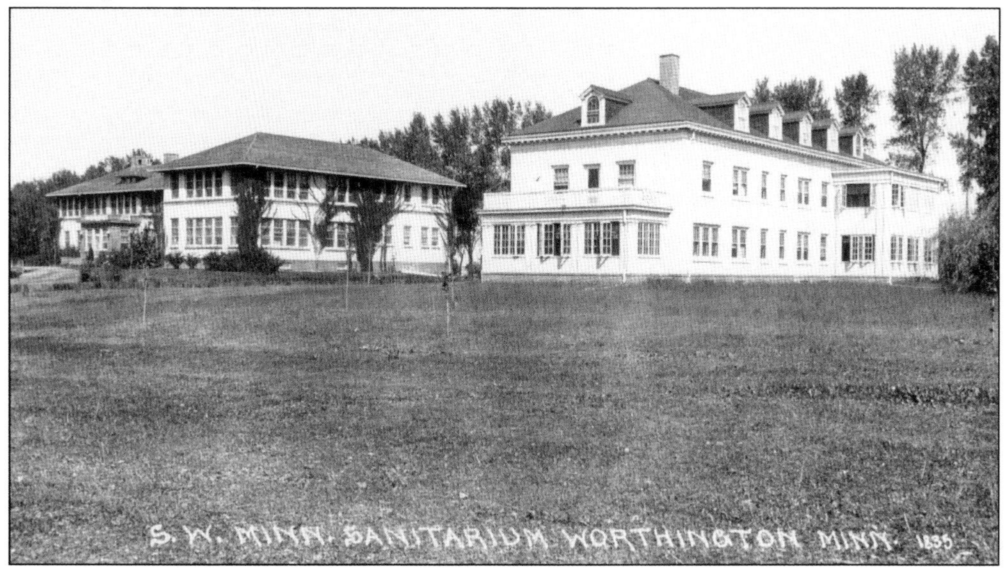

This is Worthington's more famous sanitarium, the Southwestern Minnesota Sanitarium, which was constructed as part of a larger service system designed to treat people afflicted with tuberculosis. As the result of an association that included eight southwestern Minnesota counties, this facility was built in 1917 on the south side of Lake Okabena. It remained open until 1957, when the buildings were sold to the Southwestern Minnesota Crippled Children's School.

Consistent with our mission to preserve history on a local level, this book was printed in South Carolina on American-made paper and manufactured entirely in the United States. Products carrying the accredited Forest Stewardship Council (FSC) label are printed on 100 percent FSC-certified paper.

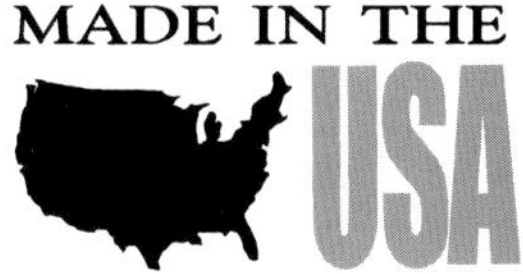